Combating Racism and Xenophobia:

Transatlantic and International Perspectives

Report of the Transatlantic Commission on Race, Ethnicity, Immigration, and Citizenship 2000-2010

***

To Christopher, Kiara, Ashley, and Justin

***

Combating Racism and Xenophobia:

Transatlantic and International Perspectives

Cedric Herring
Editor

Institute of Government and Public Affairs
University of Illinois

2011

Institute of Government and Public Affairs
University of Illinois

I N S T I T U T E   O F
GOVERNMENT & PUBLIC AFFAIRS
UNIVERSITY OF ILLINOIS
URBANA-CHAMPAIGN • CHICAGO • SPRINGFIELD

Printed in the United States of America.
ISBN   9780615525778

Contents

Preface

The Transatlantic Commission on Race, Ethnicity, Immigration, and Citizenship is composed of European and American representatives. The purpose of the Commission is to analyze, review, and clarify what can be done in to ameliorate the problems associated with racism and immigration issues in order to respond effectively to their pernicious effects on society. It also seeks to understand how to create a harmonious society in which we all benefit from the richness of experience and perspectives that comes from a multiracial, multiethnic, and multicultural society. At the same time, the Commission formulates strategies and recommendations to advance parity among races and ethnic groups. The Commission is designed to promote international dialogue focused on what can be learned from successes and failures on both sides of the Atlantic.

The genesis of the Commission was a 2002 Transatlantic conference on race that was developed by the PEOPLE Programme and co-sponsored by the European Union, the University of Illinois, Howard University, and the PEOPLE Programme. The Commission was charged with addressing sensitive and extraordinarily important legal and policy issues and making recommendations.

This book represents an important part of the work of the Commission. It provides background information and analysis that should serve as the basis for deliberations. It consists of two parts: (1) a series of background papers and analyses by world leaders, scholars, and policymakers who have written on themes related to the work of the Commission; and (2) charts that display the key differences between racial and ethic groups on the Human Development Index for United States cities. The Human Development Index is also explained in chapter 8 of this book. This latter set of figures represents an important product of the Commission's work.

Robert Rich and Edward "Buzz" Palmer
Co-Executive Directors of the Transatlantic Commission on Race, Ethnicity, Immigration and Citizenship
January, 2011

Introduction

Combating Racism and Xenophobia
on Both Sides of the Atlantic

Cedric Herring
University of Illinois at Chicago

Throughout history, race and ethnicity have played critical roles in shaping politics, international policies, and the everyday experiences of a vast majority of individuals around the globe. Most nations around the world are now having to face up to culture clashes and the challenges that accompany globalization and the increased movement of people across national borders. Such conflicts include increased competition among racial and ethnic groups for jobs, housing, education, and other scarce resources. Other challenges include international migration and immigration that often change the complexions, racial and ethnic mixes, and cultural compositions of nations. Such transformations are not easy. They often lead to racial tensions, racial discrimination, xenophobia, and at times, even deadly confrontations and warfare.

As Doudou Diène, Special Rapporteur to the United Nations reports, racism and racial discrimination are on the upswing and becoming widespread throughout the world. While racial discrimination in the West used to be the province of extremist, far-right political parties, it is now becoming a regular part of democratic systems, being blended in, for example, with the fight against terrorism. Racism and xenophobia are coming out of the closet, in a sense, and gradually creeping into the policies of mainstream political actors.

Behind the recent upswing in xenophobia is growing anti-immigration activism. Some of the anti-immigrant activists have clear ties to openly racist organizations, and even some of those activists who do not still espouse thinly-disguised bigotry. In the eyes of most of these groups, immigrants (typically immigrants of color) are responsible for nearly all their country's ills, from poverty and urban decay to crime, urban sprawl, and environmental degradation. In the United States and Europe, the growing xenophobia also includes the "crusade" against terrorism that often pits the West against Islamic peoples, especially peoples from the Middle East.

Societies in Europe, the United States, and other parts of the world are in rapid transition. This transition is characterized by changing demographic, economic, and political patterns that, in turn, raise critical issues with respect to governance, fair and just public policy, and the meaning of citizenship. In this context, questions related to ethnicity, race, religion, and citizenship as well as immigration and migration are critical on both sides of the Atlantic.

By the year 2010 in the United States, immigrants, people of color, and women comprised the majority of new entrants into the labor force. In Europe, there were growing tensions directly related to waves of in-migration of Muslims and people from Pakistan and India, who are obtaining growing political influence. Some of these tensions have to do with educational and employment opportunities. Jacques Delors, the former Chairman of the European Union, noted that if a solution was not found for the problems of immigration, the European Union could implode.

In the United States, race has been a critical issue that has had a significant effect in many areas of national policy. The historic rise in international migration over the past thirty years has brought a tide of new immigrants to the United States from Asia, South America, and other parts of the globe. The American dream of opportunity and upward mobility is still appealing to the more than one million immigrants who arrive in the United States each year. The job market prior to the Great Recession of 2007 was expanding sufficiently to absorb them without driving down wages significantly or preventing the native-born population from finding jobs. Immigration has not led to welfare dependency among

2

immigrants, nor is there any compelling evidence that welfare is a magnet for immigrants. With the exception of undocumented Mexican and Central-American immigrants, studies show that most other immigrant groups have attained sufficient earnings and job mobility to move into the economic mainstream.

Overall, immigration has been beneficial for the United States. Immigrant success stories represent the fulfillment of the American dream. In contrast, the persistent inequality suffered by native-born African Americans demonstrates the limits of that dream. While recent immigrants have unquestionably brought economic and cultural benefits to U.S. society, the costs of increased immigration may fall particularly heavily upon those native-born groups who are already disadvantaged. While the experiences of blacks and immigrants in the United States are not directly comparable, their fates are connected. The arrival of large numbers of immigrants of color in recent decades has transformed relations between minority populations in the United States. In many instances, it has created new kinds of competition between native-born people of color and immigrants of color. In particular, recent immigrants have secured many of the occupational niches once dominated by blacks. In many instances, these immigrants now pass these jobs on through ethnic hiring networks that exclude African Americans. These patterns demand that we pay renewed attention to the entrenched problems of racial disadvantage that still beset native-born African Americans who have struggled to overcome the legacies of racism, ethnic intolerance, and destructive policies.

Immigration is one of the driving forces behind social change in the United States. It continues to restructure the way Americans think about race and ethnicity. The complex politics of immigration have become intertwined with economic perceptions and realities, racial and ethnic divisions, and international relations. With recent immigration at a near record high, there is speculation that the increased presence of immigrants will intensify the competition for housing and educational opportunities among minority groups. Within predominantly African-American neighborhoods themselves, the establishment of small immigrant businesses has raised concerns that these may hinder local residents from starting up similar ventures.

In much of Europe, countries are also struggling with racial and ethnic diversity to an unprecedented degree. In some instances, these struggles with issues of diversity are driven by immigration from former colonies. In others, they are driven by the demand for cheap labor. In some cases, these factors are mutually reinforcing. Irrespective of the underlying cause, this new diversity in Europe often generates new problems such as racial discrimination in housing, education, and employment; political disenfranchisement; and racial strife and violence. Unfortunately, to Americans, these are the ordinary problems of a nation that has been divided by race since its inception. To Europeans, however, the difficulty of handling racial diversity is fairly new. Although several European countries ruled colonial subjects for centuries, it is only since the disintegration of those empires since World War II that these European nations have confronted significant problems of racial diversity within their own borders (Curtin 1992).

Although the racial and ethnic problems facing European nations may be similar to American racial problems, the responses of European states to racial diversity and its associated troubles has not been uniform. Countries often conceive of the challenges of diversity in very different ways. Ultimately, this leads them to seek vastly different solutions for similar policy problems. But even those nations that have similar conceptions of race relations and diversity pursue different tactics to attend to race and ethnicity policy problems that are similarly framed. For example, the United States has been a constant and familiar point of reference for the discussion of racial politics in Great Britain. British policymakers and scholars have often seen their own evolving problems of racial conflict as being similar to those in the United States. They have sought to imitate American successes and keep away from American mistakes in making racial policy. As a consequence, these two nations share an approach to race as a political category. They both emphasize the equal treatment of individuals, and they

4

both see legitimacy in racial groups as social and political units. But despite these political similarities and their likeminded approaches to race as a political category, the United States and Great Britain have opted for different approaches to racial policy. In particular, they have responded differently to the important policy challenges of job discrimination. As Lieberman (1999:3–4) suggests,

> American and British employment discrimination policy differ both in the explicit policies they enacted—the kind of discrimination that is proscribed, the structure of the institutions established to fight discrimination, and the powers available to those institutions—and in the ways in which those policies have been implemented. Briefly, British law as enacted by Parliament in the Race Relations Act of 1976 takes a much broader view of discrimination and gives greater potential power to the state than American law as enacted by Congress in the Civil Rights Act of 1964. Ironically, however, American antidiscrimination practice has been much more potent than in Britain. Despite apparently weaker legislation, the United States has developed producing a welter of policies and practices known collectively as affirmative action, while Britain, whose law explicitly authorizes "positive action," has shied away from such practices.

So, despite common concerns about racial and ethnic diversity, these nations turn to different solutions. In part, this is due to different conceptualizations of what is at the root of the problem. In the United States, the focus is squarely on race, racism, and racial discrimination. In Great Britain and other European nations, the focus tends to be on xenophobia and other forms of intolerance that lead to discrimination. Racism, racial discrimination, and xenophobia are distinct phenomena. Nevertheless, as an international report on international migration, racism, discrimination, and xenophobia puts it, "While racism generally implies distinction based on difference in physical characteristics, such as skin coloration, hair type, facial features, etc., xenophobia denotes behavior specifically based on the perception that the other is foreign to or originates from outside the community or nation" (International Labor Office, the International Organization for Migration, and the Office of the United Nations High Commissioner for Human Rights, 2001).

Racism is a structural relationship of domination, subordination, and social control in which a racial group gains and maintains advantage over others on the basis of resource allocation decisions that are linked to race and biased assumption about the genetic or cultural inferiority of certain racial groups. It is one of the most prominent and pervasive evils around the globe. It legitimates the subordination and exclusion of people and deprives them of their full humanity because of their racial-ethnic identity. In many societies, it so fully permeates customs and institutions that no one can fully escape the consequences of it. No member of a dominant group can fully avoid benefiting from it, and no member of subordinate groups can avoid the consequences of oppression. Racism is, finally, about power—the abuses of power by a dominant group intent upon preserving its economic, social, political, or religious privileges and the resulting deprivations of opportunity imposed on a subordinate group.

Racism's evil twin, xenophobia, is the intense dislike or fear of strangers or people from other countries. It describes attitudes, prejudices, and behaviors that reject, exclude, and often vilify people based on the perception that they are outsiders or foreigners to the community, society, or national identity.

Racial discrimination is defined in international law as being "any distinction, exclusion, restriction, or preference based on race, color, descent, or national or ethnic origin which has the purpose or effect of nullifying or impairing the recognition, enjoyment or exercise, on an equal footing, of human rights and fundamental freedoms in the political, economic, social, cultural, or any other field of public life."

Combating Racism and Xenophobia: Transatlantic and International Perspectives provides an analysis of racism, racial discrimination, and xenophobia in the United States, Europe, and other parts of the world. This book provides a non-technical summary of some of the best thinking on racism and xenophobia from internationally-known world leaders, diplomats, and scholars who focus on the international dimensions of intolerance and what can be done to eliminate such problems. Using Transatlantic institutions as examples, it also provides insights and tangible recommendations that, when implemented, go a long way toward resolving problems that stem from racism and xenophobia.

How did the book come about, and who is its target audience? This volume is the outgrowth of a series of international conferences and meetings dealing with the twin issues of racism and xenophobia. The Transatlantic Conference on Race and Xenophobia was held in Chicago in October 2002. That conference was the first of three meetings designed to bring together United States and European elected officials, policymakers, academics, nongovernmental organization representatives, business leaders, and journalists to analyze, critique and compare what we had learned during the latter decades of the twentieth century about addressing racism and xenophobia politically and economically, in theory and in practice, on both sides of the Atlantic. The second conference was held at Howard University, and the third at the European Parliament in Brussels, Belgium. In addition, leaders from various sectors were convened at the United Nations in order to meet with then-Secretary General of the United Nations, Kofi Annan. Since then, there have been subsequent meetings in London (where the Transatlantic Commission was launched). Doudou Diène, Special Rapporteur to the United Nations, carried out special missions to various European nations as well as the United States to observe race relations in these nations. In addition, the Transatlantic Commission has commissioned reports from scholars who were asked to draft reports based on their observations, analyses, and insights.

The target audience for *Combating Racism and Xenophobia: Transatlantic and International Perspectives* is those informed people in the United States and Europe who are concerned about ameliorating the problems associated with racism, xenophobia, and anti-immigrant efforts. The book also seeks to engage those entities and change agents that can help in these efforts. Such entities include but are not limited to governments, NGOs, and civil society organizations. In essence, this volume represents an effort to facilitate dialogue and exchange among leaders from Europe and North America around such issues. It seeks to help North American and European leaders understand similarities and differences in their policymaking processes and institutions. It offers the chance for readers to become better informed by various vantage points. Perhaps most importantly, it provides a vehicle for leaders from various backgrounds and domains to look beyond their own national borders to improve the quality of policymaking and to advance the quality of life for residents in their nations, especially in those areas that are related to racial equity and diversity.

But how do we confront racism and xenophobia? *Combating Racism and Xenophobia: Transatlantic and International Perspectives* provides answers to this question. In doing so, it addresses issues such the role of the media in generating and perpetuating unhelpful images and distortions. It also examines specific policy issues that have special relevance to the lives of people of color on both sides of the Atlantic. It also explores the importance of racially-charged politics in both America and Europe and the impact that these racialized contexts have on our inability to make as much progress as we would like.

In the first chapter, then-United Nations Secretary-General Kofi Annan makes a "Call for Action against Racism." His chapter is composed of three addresses that provide a framework for understanding and combating racism, anti-Semitism, and Islamophobia. In this chapter, he discusses how discrimination and other injustices trap people in poverty and how poverty becomes the pretext for injustice—and so new wrongs are piled on the old.

"Children learn racism as they grow up, from the society around them—and too often the stereotypes are reinforced, deliberately or inadvertently, by the mass media." No one who is true to the principles and values such as truth, decency, and justice can be neutral in the fight against intolerance. There is a need to unlearn the stereotypes that have become so entrenched in so many minds and so much of the media. There is also a need to unlearn the habit of xenophobia. He suggests that the "pressures of living together with people of different cultures and different beliefs from one's own are real, especially in a world of intense economic competition and in which there have been sudden influxes of immigrants, as has happened in Europe over the last generation or two. But that cannot justify demonization, or the deliberate use of fear for political purposes."

In chapter 2, Special Rapporteur to the United Nations Doudou Diène reports on the rise in racism and xenophobia in many European countries and the United States. In particular, he calls attention to three alarming trends that are clearly visible: (1) the resurgence of racist violence, (2) the political instrumental-ization of racism and xenophobia, and (3) the intellectual legitimization of racism. He suggests that there is an unmistakable resurgence of racist violence, conducted primarily but not exclusively by neo-Nazi groups. Physical violence represents a shift from words to action, seen in the growing number of attacks—including murders—that target members of ethnic, cultural, or religious communities. He also says that a number of political parties have been trying to give political clout and legitimacy to openly racist and xenophobic ideas, thus embarking on populist and demagogic rhetoric that eventually wins votes. Alarmingly, these once-extremist political parties are gradually becoming a conventional feature of politics in various countries, at times integrating government coalitions, occupying cabinet positions, and being able to implement their platforms through concrete policies. Furthermore, their racist ideas gradually impregnate otherwise more moderate parties and societies, helping discriminatory proposals become mainstream. He writes that "This

9

phenomenon amounts to a democratization of racism, representing one of the gravest threats faced by democratic societies." Finally, he shows that these two trends cannot be dissociated from a third development that ultimately reinforces racist discourse. In many circles, there are attempts by leading scholars and intellectuals to provide a justification, and ultimately a legitimization, of racist and xenophobic policies. These so-called academic statements can occur under the clout of legitimacy conferred by science.

In the following chapter, Mary Robinson, former President of Ireland and United Nations High Commissioner for Human Rights and Secretary-General to the World Conference against Racism, writes about "All Different, All Equal: From Principle to Practice." She writes that racist attitudes in communities and incidents of institutionalized racism in police, immigration, and prison officers are on the rise throughout Europe. She indicates that in some ways, the problem is the same as it ever was: hatred based on fear—fear of economic competition, fear of loss of identity. In other ways, the patterns of modern racism are worryingly different. She calls particular attention to gender and racism and recognizes the double discrimination that can occur. In response to the question of who has the power and the responsibility to effect change, she suggests that a heavy duty rests on the shoulders of national governments and politicians.

Chapter 4 by Christopher Wambu, Professor of Africana Studies at Hunter College, is entitled "African-American Civil Society and International Politics: Mechanics of Leverage at the Domestic and International Level." In this chapter, Professor Wambu asks, "What can African-Americans bring to the table of international affairs?" He suggests that in a fragmented world, black Americans, if audacious enough, could be a voice of reason, balance, and advancement in a public arena that has become vulgarized and polarized across the board by right-wing ideologues who have captured center stage. Many overarching African-American values wrought from their historical experiences confronting disparities in the United States often connect more with the rest of the world than do the values and concerns of conservative white Americans. Undoubtedly, African-Americans are not monolithic, but the contradictions in American life are profound, and African-Americans continue to be disproportionately affected by the disparities.

The next chapter by James S. Jackson, Daniel Katz Distinguished University Professor of Psychology and Director of the Institute for Social Research at the University of Michigan, and Toni Antonucci, the Elizabeth M. Douvan Collegiate Professor of Psychology, is entitled "European Public Opinions about Immigration and Migrants." That chapter provides an overview of the attitudes and beliefs of majority native populations from European Union nations concerning minority immigrant populations. This paper utilizes data from the Eurobarometer surveys of the European Union (EU) to examine the attitudes and beliefs of national majority respondents toward immigrants in their respective countries. A heuristic framework outlines how macro contextual, social, cognitive, and affective factors, as well as sources of social and political civility, may all influence sentiments and behaviors of native populations toward immigrant groups. The results reveal that while some attitudes and beliefs indicate broad tolerance and acceptance of immigrants, a great many more reflect intolerance and rejection. Increased life expectancy and reduced numbers of children among native members of advanced industrial countries will result in the need for increased migrant labor over the next few decades. Although the data are drawn from the European Union, they are reflective of native populations in most advanced industrial nations. The chapter calls for additional research on the intersection of immigration, public opinion, and the experiences of migrants in order to maximize the positive and minimize the negative experiences of both immigrants and native members of their host countries.

Chapter 6 by Moshe Semyonov, the Bernard and Audre Rapoport Chair Professor of the Sociology of Labor at Tel Aviv University and Professor of Sociology at the University of Illinois at Chicago, and Anastasia Gorodziesky, Postdoctoral Research Fellow in Sociology in the Center for Advanced Studies in the

Social Sciences (CEACS) at Juan March Institute in Madrid, Spain, complements the Jackson and Antonucci chapter. It is entitled "The Ways Europeans View Foreigners' Impact on Society: A Cross-National Comparison." As its title suggests, this chapter provides much needed information about the ways Europeans view foreigners' impact on their societies. The data presented in this chapter clearly reveal that negative views toward foreigners dramatically increased at the end of the twentieth century. Currently, antiforeigner sentiments are widely spread across European countries, even in countries with relatively low presence of foreign populations. Foreigners and immigrants are not viewed by the majority of the native population in positive terms. Rather, they are believed to exert negative impact on society. The native populations tend to suggest that foreigners are exploiting the welfare and health systems, taking jobs away from the local populations, and causing crime and delinquency in society. Indeed, foreigners are viewed as a source of competitive threat. The chapter also points out that negative views toward out-group populations tend to be more pronounced in places with high proportions of the out-group population and in places with depressed economic conditions. Thus, in an era when the foreign population is consistently rising and becoming a source of tension and even violence, the issues discussed in the chapter should become a major focus of study and inquiry.

In chapter 7, Shashi Tharoor, then-Under Secretary-General of the United Nations, presents "Unlearning Intolerance" He identifies eight things that must have a place in any strategy to combat Islamophobia. He discusses laws and norms, education, limiting the power and influence of hate media, leadership, two-way integration of cultures and peoples, dialogue (particularly interfaith dialogue), understanding the policy context, and combating terrorism and violence carried out in the name of Islam or any religion. He says that terrorism and bigotry both emerge from blind hatred of an Other—with a capital O—and that in turn is the product of three factors: fear, rage, and incomprehension: fear of what the Other might do to you, rage at what you believe the Other has done to you, and incomprehension about who or what the Other really is. These three elements fuse together to ignite the deadly combustion that assaults and even destroys people whose only sin sometimes is that they feel none of these things themselves. The ends to both terrorism and to Islamophobia are to be found in the same place. If they are to be tackled and ended, we will have to deal with each of these factors by attacking the ignorance that sustains them. We will have to know each other better, learn to see ourselves as others see us, learn to recognize hatred and deal with its causes, learn to dispel fear, and above all, just learn about each other.

In the final chapter, Alice Palmer and I present findings from our research in "America's Human Development Report on Race." We generated statistics for over two hundred American cities on things such as mean years of educational attainment, percent with bachelor's degrees, percent below the poverty line, mean household income, per capita income, mortality rates, infant mortality rates, and neo-natal mortality rates by race/ethnicity for each of these cities. We used this information to point out racial and ethnic disparities in the quality of life experienced by residents in various American cities.

In short, we believe that *Combating Racism and Xenophobia: Transatlantic and International Perspectives* is an important work on a timely subject. We believe that we have assembled the works of leading scholars and experts in the area who have written the definitive yet accessible book about how such issues continue to affect the lives of people on both sides of the Atlantic and throughout the world.

Chapter 1

A Statement against Racism, Anti-Semitism, and Islamophobia

Kofi Annan,
United Nations Secretary-General Emeritus

We must share experiences, perspectives and assessments of how far we have come, and how much further we must go, if racism is to be defeated.

One thing we can celebrate is the fact that racism is now universally condemned. Few people in the world today openly deny that human beings are born with equal rights.

But far too many people are still victimized because they belong to a particular group—whether national, ethnic, religious, or defined by gender or by descent.

Often this discrimination veils itself behind spurious pretexts. People are denied jobs ostensibly because they lack educational qualifications; or they are refused housing because there is a high crime rate in their community.

Yet these very facts, even when true, are often the result of discrimination. Injustice traps people in poverty, poverty becomes the pretext for injustice—and so new wrongs are piled on the old.

In many places people are maltreated and denied protection on the grounds that they are not citizens but unwanted immigrants. Yet often they have come to a new country to do work that is badly needed or are present not by choice but as refugees from persecution in their own country. Such people have a special need for protection and are entitled to it.

In other cases, indigenous peoples and national minorities are oppressed because their cultures and self-expressions are seen as threats to national unity, and when they protest, this is taken as proof of their guilt.

In extreme cases—which alas are all too common—people belonging to such groups are forced from their homes or even massacred because it is claimed that their very presence threatens another people's security.

Sometimes, these problems are in part the legacy of terrible wrongs in the past such as the exploitation and extermination of indigenous peoples by colonial powers or the treatment of millions of human beings as mere merchandise to be transported and disposed of by other human beings for commercial gain.

The further those events recede into the past, the harder it becomes to trace lines of accountability. Yet the effects remain. The pain and anger are still felt. The dead, through their descendants, cry out for justice.

Tracing a connection with past crimes may not always be the most constructive way to redress present inequalities in material terms. But man does not live by bread alone. The sense of continuity with the past is an integral part of each man's or each woman's identity.

Some historical wrongs are traceable to individuals who are still alive or corporations that are still in business. They must expect to be held to account. The society they have wronged may forgive them as part of the process of reconciliation, but they cannot demand forgiveness, as of right.

Far more difficult are the cases where individual profit and loss have been obscured by a myriad of other, more recent transactions—yet there is still continuity between the societies and states of today and those that committed the original crimes.

Each of us has an obligation to consider where he or she belongs in this complex historical chain. It is always easier to think of the wrongs one's own society has suffered. It is less comfortable to think in what ways our own good fortune might relate to the sufferings of others in the past or present. But if we are sincere in our desire to overcome the conflicts of the past, all of us should make that mental effort.

A special responsibility falls on political leaders, who have accepted the task of representing a whole society. They are accountable to their fellow-citizens, but also—in a sense—accountable for them and for the actions of their predecessors. We have seen, in recent decades, some striking examples of national leaders assuming this responsibility, acknowledging past wrongs, and asking pardon from—or offering an apology to—the victims and their heirs.

Such gestures cannot right the wrongs of the past. They can sometimes help to free the present—and the future—from the shackles of the past.

But in any case, past wrongs must not distract us from present evils. Our aim must be to banish from this new century the hatred and prejudice that have disfigured previous centuries.

The struggle to do that is at the very heart of our work at the United Nations. This year especially, at such events as the Conference on the Least Developed Countries, the Special Session on HIV/AIDS, or next month's Special Session on Children, we have often found racism and discrimination among the biggest obstacles to overcome.

And in our peacekeeping and peace-building work, we often find ourselves wrestling—again and again—with the effects of xenophobia and intolerance.

Only if we tackle these evils at their source can we hope to prevent conflicts before they break out. And that means taking firm action to root them out in every society, for alas, no society is immune.

The leaders of our Member States resolved, in their Millennium Declaration, "to take measures to ensure respect for and protection of the human rights of migrants, migrant workers and their families, to eliminate the increasing acts of racism and xenophobia in many societies, and to promote greater harmony and tolerance in all societies."

With those words, Mr. President, they gave this conference its true agenda. We must not leave this city without agreeing on practical measures which all states should take to fulfill that pledge. It must be reflected in our budgets and development plans, in our laws and institutions—and, above all, in our school curricula.

Let us remember that no one is born a racist. Children learn racism as they grow up from the society around them, and too often the stereotypes are reinforced, deliberately or inadvertently, by the mass media. We must not sacrifice freedom of the press, but we must actively refute pseudo-scientific arguments and oppose negative images with positive ones, teaching our children and our fellow citizens not to fear diversity, but to cherish it.

This conference has been exceptionally difficult to prepare because the issues are not ones where consensus is easily found.

Yes, we can all agree to condemn racism. But that very fact makes the accusation of racism against any particular individual or group particularly hurtful. It is hurtful to one's pride because few of us see ourselves as racists. And it arouses fear because once a group is accused of racism, it becomes a potential target for retaliation, perhaps for persecution in its turn.

Nowhere is that truer today than in the Middle East. The Jewish people have been victims of anti-Semitism in many parts of the world, and in Europe they were the target of the Holocaust, the ultimate abomination. This fact must never be forgotten or diminished. It is understandable, therefore, that many Jews deeply resent any accusation of racism directed against the State of Israel—and all the more so when it coincides with indiscriminate and totally unacceptable attacks on innocent civilians.

Yet we cannot expect Palestinians to accept this as a reason why the wrongs done to them—displacement, occupation, blockade, and now extra-judicial killings—should be ignored, whatever label one uses to describe them.

But, my friends, mutual accusations are not the purpose of this conference. Our main objective must be to improve the lot of the victims.

Let us admit that all countries have issues of racism and discrimination to address. Rather than pick on any one country or region, let us aim to leave here with a commitment from every country to draw up and implement its own national plan to combat racism in accordance with general principles that we will have agreed.

For weeks and months our representatives have labored to reach agreement on those principles. And they have made great progress. Large parts of the Declaration and Programme of Action have been agreed, including texts on such difficult issues as indigenous peoples, migrants, refugees, and "people of African descent."

Friends, this conference is a test of our international community—of its will to unite on a topic of central importance in people's lives. Let us not fail this test. The buildup to this conference has prompted an extraordinary mobilization of civil society in many different countries. It has raised expectations which we must not disappoint.

If we leave here without agreement, we shall give comfort to the worst elements in every society. But if, after all the difficulties, we can leave with a call to action supported by all, we shall send a signal of hope to brave people struggling against racism all over the world.

Let us rise above our disagreements. The wrangling has gone on for too long. Let us echo the slogan that resounded throughout this country during the elections of 1994, at the end of the long struggle against apartheid: SEKUNJALO. The time has come.

On Anti-Semitism

The United Nations is true to one of the most sacred purposes of the world's peoples in whose name the Organization was founded:

"to practice tolerance and live together in peace with one another as good neighbors." No Muslim, no Jew, no Christian, no Hindu, no Buddhist—no one who is true to the principles of any of the world's faiths, no one who claims a cultural, national, or religious identity based on values such as truth, decency, and justice—can be neutral in the fight against intolerance.

Clearly, our success in this struggle depends on the effort we make to educate ourselves and our children. Intolerance has to be unlearned. Tolerance and mutual respect have to be learned.

Future seminars will deal with other specific groups against whom intolerance is directed in many parts of the world, notably Muslims and migrants—groups which overlap, but each of which, sadly, encounters prejudice in its own right.

Yet anti-Semitism is certainly a good place to start because throughout history, it has been a unique manifestation of hatred, intolerance, and persecution. Anti-Semitism has flourished even in communities where Jews have never lived, and it has been a harbinger of discrimination against others. The rise of anti-Semitism anywhere is a threat to people everywhere. Thus, in fighting anti-Semitism we fight for the future of all humanity.

The Shoah, or Holocaust, was the epitome of this evil. Germany in the 1930s was a modern society, at the cutting edge of human technical advancement and cultural achievement. Yet the Nazi regime that took power set out to exterminate Jews from the face of the earth.

We know—and yet we still cannot really comprehend—that six million innocent Jewish men, women, and children were murdered just because they were Jews. That is a crime against humanity which defies imagination. The name *United Nations* was coined to describe the alliance fighting to end that barbarous regime, and our organization came into being when the world had just learned of the full horror of the concentration and extermination camps. It is therefore rightly said that the United Nations emerged from the ashes of the Holocaust. And a human rights agenda that fails to address anti-Semitism denies its own history.

Worldwide revulsion at this terrible genocide was the driving force behind the Universal Declaration of Human Rights. As the Preamble to the Declaration says, "disregard and contempt for human rights have resulted in barbarous acts which have outraged the conscience of mankind." And it was no coincidence that, on the day before it adopted the Declaration in 1948, the General Assembly had adopted the Convention on the Prevention and Punishment of the Crime of Genocide.

It is hard to believe that sixty years after the tragedy of the Holocaust, anti-Semitism is once again rearing its head. But it is clear that we are witnessing an alarming resurgence of this phenomenon in new forms and manifestations. This time, the world must not, cannot be silent.

We owe it to ourselves as well as to our Jewish brothers and sisters to stand firmly against the particular tide of hatred that anti-Semitism represents. And that means we must be prepared to examine the nature of today's manifestations of anti-Semitism more closely, which is the purpose of your seminar.

Let us acknowledge that the United Nations' record on anti-Semitism has at times fallen short of our ideals. The General Assembly resolution of 1975, equating Zionism with racism, was an especially unfortunate decision. I am glad that it has since been rescinded.

But there remains a need for constant vigilance. So let us actively and uncompromisingly refute those who seek to deny the fact of the Holocaust or its uniqueness, or who continue to spread lies and vile stereotypes about Jews and Judaism. When we seek justice for the Palestinians—as we must—let us firmly disavow anyone who tries to use that cause to incite hatred against Jews, in Israel or elsewhere.

The human rights machinery of the United Nations has been mobilized in the battle against anti-Semitism, and this must continue. I urge the special rapporteurs on religious freedom and on contemporary racism, working with the Office of the High Commissioner for Human Rights (which has recently strengthened its anti-discrimination unit), to actively explore ways of combating anti-Semitism more effectively in the future. All parts of the Secretariat should be vigilant. And of course—as always—we look to our friends in civil society to keep us up to the mark. It is very good to see so many non-governmental organizations represented here today.

My friends, next January it will be sixty years since the first of the death camps were liberated by advancing Soviet forces. There could be no more fitting time for Member States to take action on the necessity of combating anti-Semitism in all its forms—action comparable, perhaps, to the resolutions they adopted on apartheid in the past, or the admirable recent resolution of the Commission on Human Rights, which asked the Special Rapporteur on contemporary forms of racism to examine the situation of Muslim and Arab peoples in various parts of the world, with special reference to physical assaults and attacks against their places of worship, cultural centers, businesses and properties. Are not Jews entitled to the same degree of concern and protection?

Member states could follow the excellent lead of the Berlin Declaration, recently issued by the Chairman of the Organization for Security and Cooperation in Europe. Let me remind you that the Declaration condemned without reserve all manifestations of anti-Semitism, and all other acts of intolerance, incitement, harassment, or violence against persons or communities based on ethnic origin or religious belief, wherever they occur.

The Declaration also condemned all attacks motivated by anti-Semitism or by any other forms of religious or racial hatred or intolerance, including attacks against synagogues and other religious places, sites, and shrines. And it declared unambiguously that international developments or political issues, including those in Israel or elsewhere in the Middle East, never justify anti-Semitism.

The Berlin Declaration proclaimed those principles, which I hope the broader membership of the United Nations will adopt. Even more important, it must make sure these principles are put into practice and carefully monitor its own progress in doing so. The fight against anti-Semitism must be our fight. And Jews everywhere must feel that the United Nations is their home too.

We must make this vision a reality while we still have survivors of the holocaust among us—people like my dear friend Elie Wiesel, with whom I have the great honor of sharing this platform. We owe them no less.

Let me quote something Elie once wrote, which could make a wonderful mission statement for this whole series on "Unlearning Intolerance:"

"There is divine beauty in learning, just as there is human beauty in tolerance. To learn means to accept the postulate that life did not begin at my birth. Others have been here before me, and I walk in their footsteps. The books I have read were composed by generations of fathers and sons, mothers and daughters, teachers and disciples. I am the sum total of their experiences, their quests. And so are you."

Confronting Islamophobia:
Education for Tolerance and Understanding

When a new word enters the language, it is often the result of a scientific advance or a diverting fad. But when the world is compelled to coin a new term to take account of increasingly widespread bigotry, that is a sad and troubling development. Such is the case with Islamophobia.

The word seems to have emerged in the late 1980s and early 1990s. But the phenomenon dates back centuries. Today, the weight of history and the fallout of recent developments have left many Muslims around the world feeling aggrieved and misunderstood, concerned about the erosion of their rights and even fearing for their physical safety. So the title of this series is very appropriate: there is much to unlearn.

There is a need to unlearn the stereotypes that have become so entrenched in so many minds and so much of the media.

Islam is often seen as a monolith when it is as diverse as any other tradition, with followers running the gamut from modernizers to traditionalists. Some commentators talk as if the world of Islam was more or less identical with the Arab world—whereas in fact a majority of Muslims are not native Arabic speakers. The most populous Muslim countries are to be found in non-Arab Asia—from Indonesia through southeast and south Asia to central Asia, Iran, and Turkey, which of course is both in Asia and Europe. There are many predominantly Muslim countries in sub-Saharan Africa, and large minorities of Muslims are to be found on every continent.

Islam's tenets are frequently distorted and taken out of context, with particular acts or practices being taken to represent or to symbolize a rich and complex faith. Some claim that Islam is incompatible with democracy, or irrevocably hostile to modernity and the rights of women. And in too many circles, disparaging remarks about Muslims are allowed to pass without censure, with the result that prejudice acquires a veneer of acceptability.

Stereotypes also depict Muslims as opposed to the West, despite a history not only of conflict but also of commerce and cooperation and of influencing and enriching each other's art and science. European civilization would not have advanced to the extent it did had Christian scholars not benefited from the learning and literature of Islam in the Middle Ages and later.

There is also a need to unlearn the habit of xenophobia.

Fear of the "other" is so widespread and ferocious that we may be tempted to think of it as an immutable attribute of the human animal. But people are not hardwired for prejudice. In some cases they are taught to hate. In others, they are manipulated into it by leaders who exploit fear, ignorance, or feelings of weakness.

The pressures of living together with people of different cultures and different beliefs from one's own are real, especially in a world of intense economic competition and in which there have been sudden influxes of immigrants, as has happened in Europe over the last generation or two. But that cannot justify demonization, or the deliberate use of fear for political purposes. That only deepens the spiral of suspicion and alienation.

Unlearning intolerance is in part a matter of legal protection. The right to freedom of religion—and to be free from discrimination based on religion—is long enshrined in international law, from the UN Charter to the Universal Declaration of Human Rights, the International Covenant on Civil and Political Rights, and other instruments. Such standards have been incorporated into the laws of many countries. United Nations special rapporteurs continue to monitor the exercise and infringements of this right and to recommend ways to combat Islamophobia and other forms of racism and intolerance.

But laws and norms are just a starting point.

Any strategy to combat Islamophobia must depend heavily on education—not just about Islam, but about all religions and traditions, so that myths and lies can be seen for what they are.

We must prevent the media and Internet from being used to spread hatred while of course safeguarding freedom of opinion and expression.

There is a crucial need for leadership. Public authorities should not only condemn Islamophobia, but ensure that law enforcement and other practices follow through on pledges of nondiscrimination.

In many countries of Christian tradition, large Muslim communities are a relatively new phenomenon. Integration is a two-way street. Immigrants must adjust to their new societies, and societies must adjust, too. Hosts and immigrants alike need to understand each other's expectations and responsibilities. And they need to be able, where necessary, to act against common threats such as extremism.

24

Interfaith dialogue can be useful. But problems are not caused by the similarities among religions that are typically celebrated in such dialogue. They are caused by other similarities—the propensity of human beings to favor their own groups, beliefs, and cultures at the expense of others. Interfaith activities could take a more practical direction, building on the examples of those communities in which different peoples come together regularly in professional associations, or on the sporting field, or in other social settings. Such day-to-day contacts carry less of the artificiality of established dialogue and can be especially useful in demystifying the other.

An honest look at Islamophobia must also acknowledge the policy context. The historical experience of Muslims includes colonialism and domination by the West, either direct or indirect. Resentment is fed by the unresolved conflicts in the Middle East, by the situation in Chechnya and by atrocities committed against Muslims in the former Yugoslavia. The reaction to such events can be visceral, bringing an almost personal sense of affront. But we should remember that these are political reactions—disagreements with specific policies. All too often, they are mistaken for an Islamic reaction against Western values, sparking an anti-Islamic backlash.

Efforts to combat Islamophobia must also contend with the question of terrorism and violence carried out in the name of Islam. Islam should not be judged by the acts of extremists who deliberately target and kill civilians. The few give a bad name to the many, and this is unfair. All of us must condemn those who carry out such morally reprehensible acts, which no cause can justify. Muslims themselves, especially, should speak out, as so many did following the September 11 attacks on the United States, and show a commitment to isolate those who preach or practice violence and to make it clear that these are unacceptable distortions of Islam. Indeed, it is essential that solutions come from within Islam itself—perhaps in the Muslim tradition of "ijtihad," or free interpretation. Such open inquiry, such openness to what is good and bad in their cultures and others, may well offer a very useful path on this question and others.

Islamophobia is at once a deeply personal issue for Muslims—a matter of great importance to anyone concerned about upholding universal values—and a question with implications for international harmony and peace. We should not underestimate the resentment and sense of injustice felt by members of one of the world's great religions, cultures, and civilizations. And we must make the reestablishment of trust among people of different faiths and cultures our highest priority. Otherwise, discrimination will continue to taint many innocent lives, and distrust might make it impossible to move ahead with our ambitious international agenda of peace, security, and development.

We live in one world. We need to understand and respect each other, live peacefully together, and live up to the best of our respective traditions. That is not as easy as we might like it to be. But that is all the more reason to try harder, with all our tools and all our will.

Chapter 2

Observations Concerning Racism and Xenophobia Worldwide

Doudou Diène, Special Rapporteur—United Nations

I. Main Observations Concerning Racism and Xenophobia Worldwide

Over the past years, I have given a large amount of attention to the rise in racism and xenophobia in many European countries. In particular, I have expressed my concerns regarding three alarming trends that are clearly visible in the region as well as in the rest of the world.

(i) Resurgence of Racist Violence

There is an unmistakable resurgence of racist violence, conducted primarily but not exclusively by neo-Nazi groups. Physical violence represents a shift from words to action, seen in the growing number of attacks—including murders—that target members of ethnic, cultural or religious communities.

(ii) Political Instrumentalization of Racism and Xenophobia

A number of political parties have been trying to give political clout and legitimacy to openly racist and xenophobic ideas, thus embarking on populist and demagogic rhetoric that eventually wins votes. Alarmingly, these once extremist political parties are gradually becoming a conventional feature of politics in various countries, at times integrating government coalitions, occupying cabinet positions and being able to implement their platforms through concrete policies. Furthermore, their racist ideas gradually impregnate otherwise more moderate parties and societies, helping discriminatory proposals become mainstream. This phenomenon amounts to a democratization of racism, representing one of the gravest threats faced by democratic societies.

(iii) Intellectual Legitimization of Racism

These two trends cannot be dissociated from a third development that ultimately reinforces racist discourse. In many circles, there are attempts by leading scholars and intellectuals to provide a justification, and ultimately a legitimization, of racist and xenophobic policies. These so-called academic statements can occur under the clout of legitimacy conferred by science, as the ideas put forward recently by the Nobel laureate James Watson make evident. His statements concerning people of African descent, in particular his wrongful claims to scientific status and his implicit attempt to establish hierarchies among races are a major drawback in the fight to promote the rights of Afro-descendents worldwide and to correct the historical legacy of racism and discrimination that they faced.

The need to fight racism against Afro-descendents is nowhere more evident than in the American continent. The long-term impact of slavery and segregation are still seen in most of the region. As I noted in my official mission to Brazil in 2005, the founding of the system of slavery on racist intellectual and ideological pillars—describing the enslaved Africans as culturally and mentally inferior in order to legitimize their status as an economic good and the legal organization of slavery by the European powers—has profoundly impacted the mentalities and societal structures of all the countries in the hemisphere. Concrete action needs to be taken by governments in the region, starting from a firm declaration of political willingness to address this legacy.

However, in recent years many countries in the region started to review, and sometimes eliminate, important policies such as affirmative action. In 1994, after visiting the United States, my predecessor as Special Rapporteur expressed the view that thirty years of intense struggle against racism and racial discrimination have not yet made it possible to eliminate the consequences of over three hundred years of slavery and racial discrimination, calling for the revitalization of affirmative action programs. The argument is still relevant today, as I defended following my mission to Brazil.

**

In my recent reports, I have highlighted the threat posed by defamation of religions and religious intolerance. Bearing in mind the need not to establish hierarchies among different forms of discrimination, I would like to underline two particular forms of intolerance that require attention: (i) the resurgence of anti-Semitism and (ii) the intensification of Islamophobia in the aftermath of 9/11.

Anti-Semitism is historically the oldest form of discrimination, but unfortunately remains profoundly impregnated in many societies, particularly in the new Europe, and is advancing in the rest of the world. Hence, it requires constant vigilance and the strongest political will in order to be eradicated.

Islamophobia has also become an acute form of religious intolerance, being openly expressed by influential personalities in political and intellectual circles and promoted in electoral campaigns. Islamophobia displays a mix of ingredients that leads to a wrongful view of a conflict of religions and civilizations: the association of Islam to violence and terrorism, the suspicion concerning Islamic religious teachings, the prohibition to display visual signs like veils, headscarves, and minarets. These contemporary developments imply that the fight against racism today also needs to take place in the context of the fight against religious intolerance.

**

Ultimately, racist and xenophobic discourse is characterized by its affirmation of the immutable nature of cultural, ethnic, or religious identities. It thus reflects a certain isolationism that stems from the conflict between old national identities and the profound multiculturalization of societies. This gives rise to identity crises that are key to the increasingly dominant idea of "integration by assimilation," which denies the very existence of values and memories specific to national minorities and immigrants, and thus their contribution to the national identity of their host countries.

In this context, while anchoring efforts to combat racism and xenophobia in the legal framework of human rights is a fundamental way of achieving progress and expressing the universality of those rights, it is not sufficient on its own to eliminate the root causes of discriminatory culture and mentalities. The new battlegrounds in the struggle against discrimination—identity constructs, value systems, images, and perceptions—require that legal strategies to combat racism be accompanied by an ethical and cultural strategy that promotes the link between efforts to combat racism and xenophobia and the construction over the long term of an egalitarian, democratic, and interactive multiculturalism.

II. COUNTRY VISITS TO OSCE MEMBER STATES
Canada

I visited Canada from September 15–26, 2003. The purpose of the visit, pursuant to the implementation of the Programme of Action of the Durban Conference, was to assess the present situation in Canada, with regard to the question of racism, racial discrimination and xenophobia, and hence the state of relations between the various communities, against the country's characteristically multi-ethnic and multicultural background.

In the course of the visit, I found that Canada as a country is proud of its ethnic, racial, cultural, and religious diversity, which is supported by a multifaceted, multicultural policy; democratic institutions; and a protection of human rights, as well as by many programs and projects run by a number of federal and provincial departments. I also found a readiness in the country to innovate, especially with regard to the implementation and elaboration of treaties with aboriginal communities. The Canadian Government considers that these innovations have achieved significant results.

Nevertheless, my contacts with representatives of the various ethnic, racial, cultural and religious groups, particularly the representatives of aboriginal communities, indicated that Canadian society is not free of racial discrimination. The members of these groups whom I interviewed consider that they suffer discrimination in the areas of education, health, employment, and housing. As far as the representatives of these aboriginal communities are concerned, the historical disregard for their land rights, despite the many treaties signed with the Canadian Government, reflects persistent discrimination against them.

In my concluding recommendations, I noted the need for an intellectual and ethical strategy, which could both respond adequately to the deep emotional and psychological experience of discrimination and encourage attitudes to evolve toward a form of multiculturalism, which would not be limited to the mere equalitarian and democratic superimposition of communities, but which is likely to facilitate interactions, mutual, interpersonal and intercommunity awareness and respect for cultural differences. The Canadian Government has made it clear, however, that in recent years programs and measures have been introduced by the federal Government and by the provincial authorities to facilitate civil participation and the exercise of sovereignty based on harmonious intercommunal relations respectful of cultural differences.

Switzerland

I visited Switzerland from January 9–13, 2006, with the principal objective of assessing the situation of racism, racial discrimination, and xenophobia, as well as policies and measures adopted by the government to combat these phenomena.

In my concluding observations, I emphasized the growing role in political platforms and in the media, of rhetoric based on the "defense of national identity" and "the threat of foreign presence." This rhetoric reflects the existence in Swiss society of a current of political opinion that is favorable to a defense of identity against immigration and hence prone to xenophobic tendencies. In this regard, Switzerland illustrates one of the profound causes of

31

the increase of racism and xenophobia in Europe: the important role of the political exploitation of racism in electoral debate.

In particular, while recognizing some positive steps taken by the country, I noted the weakness in the current political and legal strategy to combat racism and xenophobia, in particular in two marked tendencies: the tendency to approach immigration and asylum issues purely from a security point of view and to criminalize foreigners, immigrants, and asylum-seekers; and the considerable number of acts of police violence with racist and xenophobic overtones against these groups as well as the judicial and administrative impunity enjoyed, according to the victims, by the perpetrators.

In this visit, I also tried to analyze the central role played by the process of the multiculturalization of Swiss society in the increase of manifestations of racism and xenophobia. In this process, the challenge to national identity arising from the cultural, ethnic, and religious diversity of society is the source of identity-related tensions, and the political, legal, and cultural awareness, recognition, and treatment of these tensions are the factors which will determine the construction of multicultural togetherness.

Russian Federation

I visited the Russian Federation from June 11–17, 2006, with the principal objective of analyzing the situation of racism, racial discrimination, and xenophobia in the country, in particular in light of the multiple incidents of racial and xenophobic violence reported by human rights organizations and by the national and international press. Another objective of this visit was to monitor and analyze one of the deep-rooted causes of the renewed upsurge in racism and xenophobia in many countries: the change from the multiculturalism of Soviet society, marked by the ideological multiculturalism of the "friendship amongst peoples," and current society.

In my general conclusions, I pointed out that there was no official racist policy in the Russian Federation, but underlined the existence of a marked tendency of racism and xenophobia in Russian society, which centers around the following factors: the upsurge in racist incidents, in which the degree of violence leads to murder in some cases; the activism of neo-Nazi groups; the extension of this violence to members of human rights organizations; the inaction of certain police services and legal agencies and, as a result, the existence of a certain measure of impunity enjoyed by the perpetrators of these acts; and the existence of racist, xenophobic, and anti-Semitic political platforms.

I also noted that, among the deep-rooted causes of this rise in racist and xenophobic ideology and violence lies the ideological context of a political nationalism that is the subject of an ethnic interpretation by extreme right groups and trends.

As main conclusions, I highlighted the importance of the official recognition of the increase of racism and xenophobia and of the expression of a strong political will on the part of the government to combat it; the implementation of a national program of action against racism and xenophobia, with the democratic participation of all national communities and human rights organizations; the strengthening of the legal and judiciary systems for punishing the perpetrators of the manifestations and acts of racist violence; and the link between efforts to combat racism and xenophobia and the building of an interactive egalitarian and democratic multiculturalism. In that regard, a cultural and intellectual strategy is needed in order to eradicate the profound roots of racism.

Italy

I conducted an official visit to Italy from October 9–13, 2006, in order to assess the situation of racism, racial discrimination, and xenophobia, particularly in the light of the current strong migratory pressure and the legislative and political legacy of xenophobia inherited from the racist and xenophobic political platforms that marked the previous government coalition.

In my report to the Human Rights Council on this visit, I noted the Italian Government's firm commitment to combating racism and xenophobia as illustrated by the implemented or planned legislative reforms on immigration and citizenship, the efforts to improve the situation of Roma and Sinti communities and for the recognition of those communities, and, finally, a greater sensitivity to multiculturalism.

Although racism is not a deeply rooted feature of Italian society, there is a disturbing trend toward xenophobia and an increase in manifestations of racism. These in part stem from the legacy and impact of the policies and programs of the previous government coalition, which contained parties that promoted overtly racist and xenophobic platforms. This dynamic is currently being fostered by the persistence of these platforms in certain extreme right-wing parties, particularly at regional and local levels, and it is being strengthened by certain media and political parties that exploit the fears that have arisen both from the current migratory pressure and from the identity crisis facing Italian society as a result of the process of ethnic and religious multiculturalization. These racist manifestations and processes mainly affect the Sinti and Roma communities, immigrants and asylum-seekers—primarily those of African origin but also those from Eastern Europe—and the Muslim community.

In my recommendations, I underlined the need to address the socio-economic inequalities faced by communities discriminated against vis-à-vis the rest of Italian society, and the importance of continuing to express, at the highest national level, a firm political will to combat racial discrimination. I also emphasized the importance of adopting a legal strategy for the implementation of existing legislation to combat discrimination; redefining the National Plan of Action put in place following the World Conference against Racism, Racial Discrimination, Xenophobia and Related Intolerance held in Durban in 2001; reforming the law governing immigration; adopting comprehensive legislation and an overall policy on asylum; and recognizing the Roma and Sinti communities as national minorities. Finally, he recommends the elaboration of a cultural strategy which links the combat against racism with the long-term construction of a democratic, egalitarian and interactive multiculturalism through the promotion of mutual knowledge and interaction between the different communities.

In elaborating a cultural and ethical strategy not only against the pervasiveness of racist and xenophobic platforms but also for the comprehensive eradication of one of the sources of these platforms, particularly in European countries—the identity crisis arising from the contradiction between old national identities and the multiculturalism of societies—the authorities should, in my view, invite the Italian people to recall their history of immigration as well as their geographical and cultural proximity to and long history of interaction with the peoples, cultures, and religions of the Mediterranean.

Lithuania, Latvia, and Estonia

I have recently concluded an official mission to the three Baltic countries from September 16–28, 2007. My visit to the Baltic region was motivated by two main factors. First, I wanted to assess how these countries are dealing with their complex historical heritage, which placed different communities and ethnic groups in close contact with each other under difficult and sometimes violent circumstances, particularly in the twentieth century. Second, I tried to examine how the three countries, which have been so far isolated from large-scale migratory pressures, are preparing their societies for the likely arrival of a larger number of non-European migrants, refugees, and asylum-seekers following their accession to the European Union and ever-increasing integration in the world economy.

In Lithuania, I highlighted the existence of a comprehensive and progressive legal framework that addresses racism and discrimination, calling for further vigilance to combat racism and full implementation of the existing legal instruments. A number of State institutions are developing actions to promote a multicultural integration of minority groups. However, there are important problems faced by the Roma community, and even though the government has taken steps to solve them, further progress is still needed. Multiculturalism should be a permanent response to racism and discrimination that complements the existing legal strategy, in particular through the promotion of interaction among communities, which creates mutual understanding and tolerance.

In Latvia, I highlighted the historical multicultural tradition of the Latvian society, which provides an important societal basis for efforts to eradicate racism and discrimination. Important laws and mechanisms addressing discrimination are in place, but a more holistic and comprehensive national legislation to combat all forms of racism and discrimination would be another step forward in the fight against racism. I also recommended that Latvia establish an independent institution to investigate allegations of racism and discrimination, whilst reinforcing the office of the Ombudsman. One of the issues of concern I examined was the question of citizenship, which is seen as problematic and discriminatory by some communities, and illustrated by the high number of stateless persons in the country. Latvia's legal strategy in the fight against discrimination should be complemented with a cultural strategy that promotes interaction among communities, tolerance, and a view of multicultural integration.

In Estonia, I praised the political will demonstrated by the government to tackle racism and discrimination, highlighting the existence of legal mechanisms that address racism and discrimination. As in Latvia, I also called for the adoption of comprehensive and holistic legislation focusing on all forms of discrimination, and for the establishment of an independent institution empowered to investigate allegations of racism and discrimination. In particular, I highlighted the importance of community initiatives such as that developed in the city of Jõhvi, which fosters interactions between different minorities supporting the concept of multiculturalism. However, the issue of citizenship and language still represents the most important obstacle faced by the Estonian society. The high number of Russian-speaking stateless people is sizeable and seen by some communities as evidence of discrimination. Furthermore, linguistic requirements for the acquisition of citizenship have also been seen as problematic by minorities. I recommended to the Latvian Government that it should consider moving toward a multilingual policy, where the role of minority languages is recognized and preserved.

III. CONCLUSIONS

In view of the information I collected throughout the exercise of my mandate, including fact-finding missions, allegations of human rights violations that I systematically receive, conferences and seminars that I attend, and discussions within the United Nations system, I have recently put forward a number of concrete recommendations for the international community:

(i) Strong political will is needed to fight racism, in particular to fight the political and electoral instrumentalization of racist and xenophobic discourse and the trivialization of racist ideas;

(ii) Countries should engage in the implementation of the Durban Declaration and Programme of Action;

(iii) The treatment of issues relating to migration, asylum, and the situation of foreigners and national minorities should give priority to the respect of their rights, in accordance with international law, in particular instruments like the International Covenant on Civil and Political Rights, the International Convention on the Elimination of All Forms of Racial Discrimination and the Durban Declaration;

(iv) To fight racism and xenophobia, countries should promote the construction of plural identities, pointing toward a "democratic multiculturalism" centered around two key concepts: the promotion of reciprocal knowledge between communities and of interaction among them;

(v) To eradicate racism, the fight against religious intolerance, including anti-Semitism, Christianophobia, and Islamophobia is essential;

(vi) The international community should systematically oppose incitement to racial and religious hatred, aiming to strike a thin but vigilant balance between freedom of expression and freedom of religion, thus recognizing the holistic character of all rights enunciated in the International Covenant on Civil and Political Rights;

(vii) Finally, the international community needs to be vigilant concerning manifestations of racism in sports, supporting measures taking locally and internationally, through international sporting bodies like the International Olympic Committee and FIFA.

Addendum
MISSION TO THE UNITED STATES OF AMERICA
Introduction

At the invitation of the Government, the Special Rapporteur visited the United States of America from May 19–June 6, 2008 (Washington, DC; New York; Chicago; Omaha; Los Angeles; New Orleans and the Louisiana and Mississippi Gulf Coast; Miami; and San Juan, Puerto Rico). He held extensive meetings with federal authorities at the executive, legislative, and judicial branches as well as with local authorities (see appendix).

Apart from the agenda with state institutions, including the Supreme Court, the Special Rapporteur also had extensive meetings with civil society organizations active in the area of racism and xenophobia, minority communities, as well as victims of racism and racial discrimination.

The Special Rapporteur wishes to express his gratitude to the Government of the United States for its full cooperation and openness throughout the visit as well as a particular appreciation to Justice Stephen Breyer at the Supreme Court. He also wishes to express his sincere thanks to all civil society organizations that actively participated and contributed to the success of his mission.

In particular, he wishes to thank Global Rights for its support throughout the mission.

I. GENERAL BACKGROUND
A. Historical and political context

The first inhabitants of North America are believed to have arrived crossing from the Bering Strait toward the end of the last Ice Age. Before the advent of European explorers in the late 15th century, a population of one to two million people is believed to have populated North America. Epidemic diseases brought by the Europeans and violence obliterated many Native American peoples.

The United States of America became an independent State after the American Revolutionary War (1775–1783). The three documents that emerged from independence—the Declaration of Independence (1776), the United States Constitution (1787) and the Bill of Rights (1791)—are among the first formal legally-binding documents recognizing inalienable individual rights such as freedom of religion, freedom of expression, and freedom of assembly.

The contradictions between the agrarian and slave-based South and the manufacturing, liberalizing, and generally anti-slavery North exploded when the Republican candidate, Abraham Lincoln, won the 1860 presidential election. By that time, 4 million slaves and eighty-eight thousand free blacks lived in the United States alongside twenty-seven million whites. While the American Civil War (1861–1865) brought about the legal end of slavery and the adoption of the fourteenth amendment to the Constitution, including the equal protection clause, differential treatment to blacks living in the South would continue well into the twentieth century. Jim Crow laws were enacted in many States, legitimated by the "separate but equal" doctrine legitimated by the Supreme Court in *Plessy v Ferguson*.

The "separate but equal" doctrine remained until the emergence of the civil rights movement in the mid-twentieth century. Though the starting point of the movement is difficult to trace, the landmark decision by the Supreme Court on *Brown v Board of Education* in 1954, striking down racial segregation in schools, certainly had a fundamental impact in unleashing the changes that took place in subsequent years. The movement culminated in the adoption of the Civil Rights Act of 1964, a milestone document that set the institutional framework for the protection of human rights in contemporary United States of America.

B. Demographic, ethnic and religious composition

According to the U.S. Census Bureau, in 2006 the United States had a population of around 299 million, composed as follows: 73.9 percent white, 12.4 percent black or African American, 4.4 percent Asian, 0.8 percent American Indian and Alaska Native, 0.1 percent Native Hawaiian and other Pacific Islander, 6.3 percent of other races, and 2 percent of people with two or more races.[1] The U.S. Census Bureau correctly does not define Hispanic or Latinos as a race, as individuals of South and Central American origin may be of any race. In 2006 Hispanics or Latinos composed 14.8 percent of the population.[2]

In 2007, the foreign-born population in the United States (those not U.S. citizens or U.S. nationals at birth) amounted to approximately 38 million people, or 12.6 percent of the total population.[3] Forty-two-and-a-half percent of those foreign-born residents were naturalized citizens. Out of the foreign-born population, 47.5 percent are Hispanics, 23.4 percent are Asians, 20.3 percent are non-Hispanic whites, and 7.8 percent are blacks.

C. International human rights instruments

The United States is party to the International Covenant on Civil and Political Rights (ICCPR),[4] the International Convention on the Elimination of All Forms of Racial Discrimination (ICERD), and other international human rights instruments. With respect to both the ICCPR and the ICERD, the United States has adopted a number of formal reservations, understandings, and declarations. In the case of ICERD, with respect to Articles 4 and 7, and in the case of ICCPR, with respect to Article 20, the United States has taken treaty reservations to these provisions, explaining that their scope is at odds with the extensive protections contained in the U.S. Constitution and U.S. laws in the areas of individual freedom of speech, expression, and association.

D. Methodology
The Special Rapporteur carried out extensive meetings with authorities at the executive, legislative, and judiciary branches to collect their views and opinions as well as information concerning government programs, legislation, and judicial decisions. Additionally, an agenda with civil society organizations, communities, and associations representing minority groups, victims of discrimination, journalists, and student leaders was organized.

The Special Rapporteur structured his meetings around three questions: (i) Is there still racism, racial discrimination, xenophobia, and related intolerance in the United States? (ii) If so, who are their main victims, and what are their main manifestations and expressions? (iii) What are or should be the governmental policies and programs to fight these phenomena at the political, legal, and cultural levels?

II. LEGAL FRAMEWORK
The fourteenth amendment of the Constitution, adopted on the aftermath of the Civil War, contains an Equal Protection Clause that formally recognizes the principle of equality before the law. It provides that "[No State shall] deny to any person within its jurisdiction the equal protection of the laws." The fifteenth amendment, ratified on February 3, 1870, further extends the right to vote to all races.

The civil rights movement of the 1960s led to the signature by President Lyndon B. Johnson of the Civil Rights Act in 1964.

The Act constituted a historic landmark in the elimination of *de jure* racial discrimination in the country and in setting up the institutional and legal structure to combat discrimination. The Act also set up the Commission on Civil Rights, which was mandated to inter alia investigate denials of the right to vote, study and collect information concerning legal developments constituting a denial of equal protection of the laws under the Constitution, and appraise the laws and policies of the Federal Government in this regard.[5] The Act was further complemented by the Civil Rights Act of 1968, which prohibited discrimination in the sale, rental, and financing of housing.

The enforcement of nondiscrimination provisions of the Constitution and federal legislation is primarily carried out by the Civil Rights Division at the Department of Justice, which is composed of over seven hundred staff. The Civil Rights Division carries out enforcement actions in areas that include criminal cases, disability rights, education, employment, housing, and voting. Other Federal agencies are also involved in the enforcement of equal protection legislation, such as the Equal Employment Opportunity Commission and the Office of Fair Housing and Equal Opportunity at the Department of Housing and Urban Development.

III. PUBLIC POLICIES AND MEASURES TO FIGHT RACISM, RACIAL DISCRIMINATION, XENOPHOBIA AND RELATED INTOLERANCE

A. Law enforcement

Law enforcement in the United States involves agencies at the federal, state, and local levels. While the Special Rapporteur met with several officials at the local level, his analysis is based primarily on agencies, and policies developed, at the Federal level.

Racial discrimination by law enforcement agencies is prohibited by the Constitution and federal statutes.[6] These include the Violent Crime Control and Law Enforcement Act of 1994 and the Omnibus Crime Control and Safe Streets Act of 1968. Officials at the Civil Rights Division of the Department of Justice underscored the fundamental importance that it attaches to combating police misconduct, including racial discrimination by police officers, which amounts to approximately half of its Criminal Section's caseload.

Officials at the Civil Rights Division as well as at the Department of Homeland Security highlighted the importance of training of law enforcement officials. The Federal Law Enforcement Training Center has existed since 1970 and currently provides law enforcement training to Federal agencies. Particular trainings focusing on cultural awareness and relations with minority communities have also been developed.

In what concerns overrepresentation of minorities in the criminal justice system, it was recognized that disparities in incarceration rates exist between minorities—particularly African Americans—and whites. However, as the United States affirmed in its latest periodic report to the Committee on the Elimination of Racial Discrimination (CERD), the reasons for such disparities are complex and do not necessarily indicate differential treatment of persons in the criminal justice system.[7]

Racial profiling
The Supreme Court has produced solid jurisprudence prohibiting racial profiling. For example, in *Wren v. United States* (1996), the Court stated that "the Constitution prohibits selective enforcement of the law based on considerations such as race," making explicit reference to the Equal Protection Clause. In *United States v. Armstrong* (1996), repeating *Oyler v. Boles* (1962), the Court further affirmed that "the decision whether to prosecute may not be based on 'an unjustifiable standard such as race, religion, or other arbitrary classification.'" The ruling in *United States v. Montero-Camargo* (1996) further cautioned against the use of factors that are facially race-neutral but in effect can be discriminatorily used against minorities (e.g., searches against individuals living in high-crime areas that are also predominantly inhabited by minorities).

43

In June 2003, responding to a call made by President Bush in his State of the Union address in 2001, the Department of Justice issued a *Guidance Regarding the Use of Race by Federal Law Enforcement Agencies* prohibiting the use of race or ethnicity in law enforcement practices, the first time such guidelines had been issued. The guidance was formally adopted by the Department of Homeland Security in June 2004. Officials at the Civil Rights Division highlighted that the guidelines were also incorporated in the training modules that all law enforcement officials have to undergo. While officials recognized that the guidelines do not create rights that can be affirmed in court, they highlighted that racial profiling violates the equal protection clause of the Constitution, which therefore offers overarching protection against this practice.

B. Hate crimes

According to the U.S. Criminal Code, crimes motivated by race, color, religion, or national origin can be investigated and prosecuted by federal authorities only when the crime occurs because of the victim's participation in a federally protected activity (e.g., public education, employment, etc).[8] In cases that do not meet the latter requirement, the jurisdiction lies at the state level. Apart from federal regulations, forty-seven states have laws on hate crimes.

The number of hate crimes reported in the United States has decreased from 8,063 reported incidents in 2000 to 7,624 reported incidents in 2007, a fact that was highlighted by officials at the Civil Rights Division. The trend in the past two years is however the opposite, with an increase from 2005 to 2007. In 2001, a peak of 9,730 such incidents was reached (a 20 percent increase in comparison to 2000), which the FBI Hate Crimes Statistics relates to the aftermath of 9/11. The number of yearly reported incidents fell back to its normal trend from 2002.

In 2007, 3,642 incidents (48.8 percent of total) were moti-vated by race (68 percent of which were anti-black); 1,426

44

incidents (19.1 percent of total) were motivated by religion (65.2 percent of which were anti-Jewish and 10.8 percent anti-Islamic); and 1,102 incidents (14.7 percent of total) were related to ethnicity or national origin (43.5 percent of which were anti-Hispanic).[9]

Officials highlighted the prompt and decisive action of the Civil Rights Division in the aftermath of 9/11 by quickly bringing a number of cases against perpetrators of hate crimes. In particular, thirty-two "9/11 backlash" cases were brought, involving forty-two offenders, thirty-five of whom were convicted. This response, which involved cooperation with state and local officials, is considered as a key factor in explaining the rapid drop in the number of hate crimes after the peak reached in the aftermath of 9/11.

C. Education
Educational policy at the federal level is carried out by the Department of Education. An Office for Civil Rights within the department is mandated "to ensure equal access to education and to promote educational excellence throughout the nation through vigorous enforcement of civil rights." This office enforces several federal laws that prohibit discrimination, including Title VI of the Civil Rights Act of 1964 (discrimination on the basis of race, color and national origin). The Office for Civil Rights enforces this law in all institutions, including elementary and secondary schools and colleges and universities that receive funds from the Department of Education.

An important piece of federal legislation in the domain of education is the No Child Left Behind Act, which was enacted by Congress in 2002. One of its key objectives is to promote more accountability in public schools and to improve the performance of students. In this regard, it also explicitly addresses the need to close the achievement gap between white and minority students.[10] Recent data indicates that although the achievement gap is still large, it has narrowed in recent years.[11]

D. Housing

Extensive legislation to prevent discrimination on housing and lending has been set up over the past decades. This includes the Fair Housing Act (Title VIII of the Civil Rights Act of 1968), which prohibits discrimination in the sale, rental, or financing of housing on the basis of race, color, religion, sex, familial status, or national origin. The Act expanded the protections offered by the Civil Rights Act of 1964 (Title VI), which prohibited discrimination in programs and activities receiving federal financial assistance but refrained from regulating private conduct in the domain of housing.

Federal laws on fair housing are administered and enforced by the Office of Fair Housing and Equal Opportunity (FHEO) at the Department of Housing and Urban Development (HUD). The number of complaints filed with HUD and the Fair Housing Assistance Program (which provides grants to State and local fair housing enforcement agencies) has increased substantially in the last ten years, from 5,818 complaints in 1998 to 10,154 in 2007. However, it is not evident whether this reflects an increase in housing discrimination or better knowledge of fair housing laws and willingness to report cases of discrimination. In 2007, 43 percent of complaints were based on disability, 37 percent on race, 14 percent on family status, and 14 percent on national origin.[12]

The Special Rapporteur was informed of a number of programs carried out by HUD to promote equal housing opportunity, including financial assistance to public and private institutions carrying out monitoring and enforcement activities of fair housing laws. HUD also has a constant output of relevant research and advocacy materials, which are used not only to raise awareness regarding existing legislation, but also to monitor and inform relevant stakeholders regarding emerging trends and challenges.

The Civil Rights Division at the Department of Justice also carries out enforcement of fair housing laws. As an example of the role played by the Division, the Special Rapporteur was informed of two initiatives. The Fair Housing Testing Program uses paired testing techniques to detect cases of discrimination in the housing market. In addition, by launching Operation: Home Sweet Home in 2006, the Department of Justice committed to conduct a record number of tests to expose and combat discriminatory practices in housing.

E. Employment
Discrimination related to employment on the basis of race, color, religion, sex, or national origin is prohibited under the Civil Rights Act of 1964 (Title VII). The enforcement of these provisions, along with other legislation prohibiting employment discrimination is conducted by the Equal Employment Opportunity Commission (EEOC). The EEOC has a total staff of some twenty-two hundred employees in fifty-two offices throughout the country and a budget of around US\$ 330 million, which allows it to file around eighty thousand charges per year. In 2007, charges related to employment discrimination based on race were 37 percent of the total whereas national origin represented 11.4 percent of all charges.

In his meeting with the Vice-Chair of EEOC, the Special Rapporteur was informed about the E-RACE Initiative (Eradicating Racism and Colorism from Employment). The Initiative has some clearly defined goals, including to improve data collection in order to better identify, investigate, and prosecute allegations of discrimination; improve the quality of EEOC's litigation; develop strategies to tackle emerging issues of race and color discrimination; and promote voluntary compliance to eradicate race and color discrimination.

The EEOC also shared with the Special Rapporteur some of the issues of concern for the Commission. Particular emphasis was placed on the emergence of subtle forms of discrimination, which are harder to identify and to act upon. Reference was also made to the persistence of discrimination and the consistency in the number of racial discrimination charges filed every year since 1964.

The Special Rapporteur also met, at the Department of Labor, with the Assistant Secretary for Employment Standards and the Civil Rights Enforcement Division. The Department enforces compliance of federal contractors to laws that prohibit discrimination. The Special Rapporteur was informed that the Department plays an active role in investigating federal contractors rather than simply responding to complaints. It also develops partnerships with the EEOC and other bodies to improve enforcement actions.

F. Measures to prevent discrimination in the aftermath of the events of 11 September 2001

Many officials have noted symbolic and concrete actions taken to prevent discrimination against people of Arab and Muslim descent in the aftermath of 9/11, starting with the remarks made by President Bush during a visit to the Islamic Center on September 17, 2001.[13] These community outreach efforts were described as a best practice in the fight against terrorism by the Special Rapporteur on the promotion and protection of human rights and fundamental freedoms while countering terrorism in his report on the United States.[14]

The Special Rapporteur was briefed on the *Initiative to Combat Post 9/11 Discriminatory Backlash*, designed by the Department of Justice to combat violations of civil rights against Arab, Muslim, Sikh, and South-Asian Americans.[15] Key strategies within this program include measures to ensure that cases of discrimination are reported and handled promptly, identifying policies that might involve bias crimes and discrimination, and reaching out to affected communities to inform them of existing mechanisms. Two special positions were created at the Civil Rights Division: a Special Counsel for Post 9/11 National Origin Discrimination and a Special Counsel for Religious Discrimination.

Experts from the Department of Homeland Security also highlighted some initiatives developed after 9/11 to prevent dis-

48

crimination against people of Arab and Muslim descent. Reference was made to the *Guidance Regarding the Use of Race by Federal Law Enforcement Agencies*, in particular its provision that "in investigating or preventing threats to national security or other catastrophic events [...] Federal law enforcement officers may not consider race or ethnicity except to the extent permitted by the Constitution and laws of the United States." The Special Rapporteur was also informed of the Traveler Redress Inquiry Program, which allows the public to clarify problems of misidentifications with individuals placed on watch lists.[16]

G. Measures taken in the aftermath of Hurricane Katrina

Since the Special Rapporteur received allegations concerning possible racial bias in reconstruction efforts in the aftermath of Hurricane Katrina, he raised the issue with several Government authorities in order to collect additional information from some of the federal agencies and visited affected areas.

The Civil Rights Division of the Department of Justice highlighted its proactive role in the aftermath of Katrina, reflected in the launching of Operation: Home Sweet Home in February 2006. While the initiative had a nationwide focus, it initially concentrated on the areas where Katrina victims were relocated, increasing the reach of its testing program to identify cases of housing discrimination. Emphasis was also place in areas where a surge of hate crimes had occurred, as these crimes are often correlated with housing discrimination.[17]

The Department of Housing and Urban Development noted actions developed to provide adequate housing to those displaced by Katrina. These include additional disaster-relief funding for the affected areas; limited extensions of a foreclosure moratorium; grants for home-owners whose houses were damaged or destroyed; and funding to local public housing projects. The Office of Fair Housing and Equal Opportunity at HUD also developed proactive actions to raise awareness in the Gulf Coast region about fair housing obligations, in cooperation with the Federal Emergency Management Agency (FEMA), which leads relief efforts.

The Special Rapporteur also makes reference to the United States latest periodic report to CERD, which analyzed concerns about the disparate effects of Katrina on racial or ethnic minorities. In the report, the United States stated that "recognizing the overlap between race and poverty in the United States, many commentators conclude nonetheless that the post-Katrina issues were the result of poverty (i.e., the inability of many of the poor to evacuate) rather than racial discrimination *per se*."[18]

H. Immigration

The Special Rapporteur met with the Office of Citizenship at the U.S. Citizenship and Immigration Service (CIS) and was briefed concerning CIS's policy to reinvigorate assimilation efforts, particularly in what concerns English proficiency of migrants. Officials pointed out that they viewed assimilation of migrants into the United States as a key element for integration into the labor market, the educational system, and social life more broadly, but this did not imply the abandonment of cultural or religious diversity, upon which the United States was founded. The Special Rapporteur was informed that CIS had intensified its efforts to diminish the backlog in citizenship applications and thus respond more rapidly to applicants.[19]

CIS officials referred to the naturalization exam, which has been recently reformed in order to become more uniform nationwide. The naturalization test contains an English reading and writing section as well as questions on U.S. history and government. CIS produces and distributes study materials to help immigrants prepare for the test. Information guides are also available to new immigrants with information on rights and responsibilities as well as practical help on issues such as employment education and taxes.[20]

Immigrants are entitled to some constitutionally-protected rights regardless of their immigration status. In *Plyler v. Doe*, the

Supreme Court established that denying free public education to children on the basis of immigration status is unlawful. Furthermore, although the Immigration and Nationality Act protects only documented migrants from employment discrimi-nation, unfair documentary practices and retaliation, EEOC noted several judicial decisions that prevent courts from disclosing the immigration status of plaintiffs in employment discrimination cases.

IV. VIEWS OF CIVIL SOCIETY AND THE COMMUNITIES CONCERNED

A. Law enforcement
One of the key issues mentioned by civil society was the weak record of civil rights enforcement by the Federal Government. In particular, reference was made to the limited number of cases filed by the Civil Rights Division of the Department of Justice, especially when compared to previous administrations. This has led to a growing perception of discredit by civil society organizations in the Division's commitment to enforce civil rights laws.

Racial disparities in the criminal justice system

The most critical issue of concern raised by civil society organizations, minority communities, and victims themselves was related to racial disparities in the criminal justice system. Interlocutors pointed to an overrepresentation of individuals belonging to racial and ethnic minorities in the criminal justice system. While in mid-2007 black males constituted around 12.5 percent of the population, they comprised 38.9 percent of the number of people in U.S. prisons and jails.[21] Black males are therefore 6.5 times more likely to be incarcerated than white, non-Hispanic males. While many civil society organizations agreed that part of the explanation to these disparities is related to social factors, particularly the overlap of poverty and race, it was pointed

51

out that racial discrimination also plays a key role in explaining this phenomenon.

Studies have identified racial disparities at several stages of law enforcement activities. A key example is traffic stops. A report by the Department of Justice recently found that whereas white, black, and Hispanic drivers were stopped by the police at similar rates, black and Hispanic drivers were approximately 2.5 times more likely to be searched; the rate of arrests was two times higher for blacks and 50 percent higher for Hispanics; blacks were 3.5 times more likely and Hispanics were almost 2 times more likely to experience use of police force.[22] Another example concerns sentencing outcomes. A majority of studies show evidence of racially discriminatory sentencing; in particular, that individuals belonging to minorities tend to be disadvantaged in terms of the decision to incarcerate or not and in receiving harsher sentences than white individuals with comparable social and economic status.[23]

Mandatory minimum penalties have been pointed out as an important factor that promotes racial bias. A striking example refers to mandatory minimum sentences for possession of crack and powder cocaine. These sentences establish more severe penalties for persons arrested for possessing or selling crack cocaine, 81 percent of whom are African American, than for those in possession of or selling powder cocaine, 71.8 percent of whom are white or Hispanic.[24]

Civil society also pointed to evidences of racial bias in the application of the death penalty. In 2005, African Americans comprised nearly 42 percent of the number of death row inmates but only around 12 percent of the general population.[25] The key factor that shows evidence of racial bias in the death penalty, according to many organizations, is the race of the victim. Nationwide, even though the absolute number of murders of blacks and whites is similar, some 80 percent of people on death row have been convicted of crimes against white victims.[26] Interlocutors pointed to the critical situation in some states. In Alabama, for example, whereas 65 percent of all murders involve black victims, 80 percent of people currently awaiting execution in the state were convicted of crimes in which the victims were white.

Juvenile justice was an issue of concern for civil society organizations, particularly when it represents an entry point into criminal justice (see subsection III.C). The rate of detention of youth in 2003 was five times higher for African Americans and two times higher for Hispanics than for whites.[27] The Special Rapporteur was also presented with data concerning the disproportional representation of African-American youth in several stages of the juvenile justice process, including arrests, detentions, petitions, and prison.[28] Reference was made to the issue of sentencing of youth to life without parole, which is applied in thirty-nine states, as well as on reported racial bias in these practices, particularly in certain states. In the twenty-five states for which data is available, the rate of African Americans serving life without parole sentences is on average ten times higher than whites, relative to the state population. In California, the rate is eighteen times than that of white youth. Even after controlling for differences in murder arrest rates, racial disparities remain.[29]

Racial profiling

Civil society generally refers to two main forms of racial profiling. First, a particular form of the practice targets predominantly African-American or Hispanic minorities, generally but not exclusively in stops and searches by local and state police.[30] Second, in the context of counterterrorism policies, racial profiling practices have reportedly targeted primarily people of Arab, Muslim, South Asian, or Middle-Eastern descent, particularly in air travel and border control.

Some civil society accounts point to widespread existence of racial profiling. It has been suggested that approximately thirty-two million people in the United States report having been victims of this practice.[31] While exact numbers may be difficult to assert, it was a common recognition among virtually all interlocutors that the practice of racial profiling continues to exist. Numerous anecdotal accounts of victims of racial profiling in stop and search operations by the police were heard, including a testimony by an African-American member of Congress who was a victim of such an incident.

Several organizations expressed concern at the National Special Entry-Exit Registration Program (NSEERS) put in place in 2002. The special registration program required male non-citizens over the age of sixteen and from twenty-five countries to register with local immigration authorities. Twenty-four of these countries have a majority Muslim population.[32] While the initial require-ments of re-registration after thirty days and one year of continuous presence in the United States have been suspended,[33] the program continues to be considered by civil society as discriminatory on the basis of national origin and religious background.

Civil society organizations expressed criticisms regarding recent attempts to address the issue. The *Guidance Regarding the Use of Race by Federal Law Enforcement Agencies* issued by the Department of Justice was criticized, particularly because it "does not cover profiling based on religion, religious appearance or national origin; does not apply to local law enforcement agencies; does not include any enforcement mechanism; does not require data collection; does not specify any punishment for federal officers who disregard it; contains a blanket exception for cases of 'threat to national security and other catastrophic events' and 'in enforcing laws and protecting the integrity of the Nations' borders.'"[34]

B. Hate crimes

Interlocutors highlighted that the main weakness of federal hate crimes legislation is the dual requirement that needs to be met for the Federal Government to be able to investigate and prosecute a case: bias-motivated violence and relation to a federally protected activity. In cases that do not meet these requirements, the jurisdiction lies at the state level. However, many states lack the capacity and resources to thoroughly investigate and prosecute such crimes. In this regard, a Local Law Enforcement Hate Crimes Prevention Act designed to strengthen the role of the Federal Government in the investigation and prosecution of such crimes and to expand the grounds for protection was approved in the House of Representatives and the Senate in 2007. However, it was withdrawn after an expression by the White House that the president would veto the bill, which was seen as "unnecessary and constitutionally questionable."[35]

While many interlocutors expressed concern regarding the number of hate crimes in the United States, some NGOs highlighted that the government response has in general been more vigorous than in other countries.[36]

C. Education
De facto school segregation
One of the most important decisions by the U.S. Supreme Court in the fight for racial equality was *Brown v. Board of Education* prohibiting school segregation. However, interlocutors pointed out that despite the end of *de jure* segregation and positive changes, particularly in the 1960–1980 period, the trend has since been reversed. The percentage of black students in predominantly minority schools, which was 77 percent in 1968 and decreased to 63 percent in 1988, had surged to 73 percent in 2005.[37] Civil society organizations expressed concern at recent U.S. Supreme Court decisions—*Parents Involved in Community Schools v. Seattle School District* and *Meredith v. Jefferson County Board of Directors*—that ruled that race-conscious integration measures are unconstitutional. In the view of many NGOs, these race-conscious measures are a necessary measure to ensure racial integration and make an essential contribution to de-segregation of schools, particularly in the South. Some organizations also pointed out that the rise of segregation also has an impact on the quality of education received by students belonging to minorities. Furthermore, a

concern was expressed that the Court may have abandoned the notion that racial diversity can be considered a compelling interest that justifies the use of race-based criteria. This view is present in the dissenting opinion of Justice Breyer in the *Community Schools* case.[38]

Achievement gaps

Civil society representatives highlighted that while the achievement gap between students belonging to minorities and white students has narrowed in the past years, it is still in a similar level to 1990. The introduction of the No Child Left Behind Act placed high emphasis on educational performance; however, interlocutors highlighted the negative incentives created by the Act and its disproportionate effects on minority children. In particular, it was argued that the focus on standardized performance tests that penalize schools that underperform creates an incentive for schools to push out low-performing, at-risk students—a group that is composed disproportionately of minorities—in order to improve the overall school performance.

Schools as an entry point to the criminal justice system

Many NGOs used the metaphor of the "school-to-prison pipeline" to refer to the failure of the school system to educate pupils adequately, serving rather as a conduit to juvenile and criminal justice.[39] Among the chief causes of this phenomenon, interlocutors referred to the widespread application of Zero Tolerance Policies, which call for severe punishment for minor infractions. These measures are considered to have gone beyond reasonable policies to prevent violence in school, leading to what is considered to be an over-reliance on disciplinary methods (e.g., suspensions and expulsions) and the criminalization of school misbehavior (i.e., by referring students with non-violent behavior to juvenile courts). In Texas, for example, "disruptive behavior" corresponded to 17 percent of school arrests and "disorderly conduct" comprised 26 percent of such arrests.[40] In meetings with parents of students that were disciplined, the Special Rapporteur was informed of several practices that exist in some school districts, such as the issuing of fines by the police to students with inappropriate behavior and regular searches and reported cases of excessive use of force by police officers inside schools. Civil society pointed to racial disparities in the application of these disciplinary measures. For example, whereas African-American children represent only 17 percent of public school enrolment, they constitute 32 percent of out-of-school suspensions.[41] Some studies have also indicated that African-American students are more likely than white students to be suspended, expelled, or arrested for the same kind of school conduct.[42]

D. Housing

Concerns about fair housing expressed by civil society generally focus on two major issues: direct discriminatory practices and structural factors that have an impact, even if unintended, on the housing situation of minorities.

According to interlocutors, direct discriminatory practices in housing continue to exist. Data produced in paired testing, which allows for a comparison of treatment between whites and persons of color when they have similar qualifications, identified subtle forms of direct discrimination. This included the practice of "steering" members of racial or ethnic groups toward neighborhoods primarily occupied by those same groups, prohibited under the Fair Housing Act.[43] Steering practices have generally contributed to a persistence of residential segregation. Direct discrimination has also been detected in the rental and sale of houses as well as in mortgage lending, with people of color being more likely to receive higher cost or subprime loans than white borrowers with similar income and other characteristics.[44]

Concerns were expressed that the FHEO, which is the key agency responsible for acting on complaints of housing discrimination, only finds reasonable cause for discrimination in a small number of complaints and that the period of investigation often surpasses the one-hundred-day mark set by Congress.[45] It should be noted, however, that a number of cases are resolved through the conciliation and settlement processes which are encouraged under the Fair Housing Act. At the same time, enforcement actions by the Civil Rights Division at the Department of Justice were also criticized due to the limited number of cases it has initiated. Another problem raised by civil society is the large number of unreported cases of fair housing violations due to lack of knowledge of Fair Housing laws. While the Special Rapporteur was informed by HUD of many awareness-raising initiatives, civil society deemed them insufficient to educate the public.[46]

A particular dimension of the housing problem highlighted by civil society lies in homelessness. The Special Rapporteur visited the Skid Row area in Los Angeles, interacting with a number of homeless persons and civil society support groups. Interlocutors highlighted the disproportionate impact of homelessness among minorities, particular African Americans, as also highlighted by the Human Rights Committee in its 2006 United States periodic report.[47] This problem is often reinforced by the reduction of funds for the construction of public housing. In addition, relations between law enforcement and homeless persons were also highlighted as an important problem, particularly with regard to the enforcement of minor law enforcement violations, which often take a disproportionately high number of African-American homeless persons to the criminal justice system.

The issue of residential segregation was directly observed by the Special Rapporteur, who examined the issue in-depth in his visits outside the capital. Despite some progresses in the 1980–2000 period,[48] they contributed little to change the overall static patterns of residential segregation in the country. Furthermore, civil society noted that residential segregation has a direct impact on school segregation and that the two problems should be tackled together.

E. Employment

Interlocutors stated that ethnic disparities in employment and, more generally, poverty levels have fundamental consequences for the overall situation of racial and ethnic minorities in the United States. Whereas the unemployment rate for non-Hispanic whites in 2007 was 5.2 percent, it was 12.6 percent for American Indians or Alaskan Natives, 12 percent for African-Americans, and 7.3 percent for Hispanics.[49]

While many interlocutors pointed these disparities in unemployment level as an indication of the interplay of race and socio-economic status, concerns over forms of direct and indirect discrimination in employment were also raised. One of the issues that was raised concerns the legal remedies available to undocumented migrants (see subsection III.h). Another issue of concern regards the lack of protection for certain occupations, particularly domestic and agricultural workers, which disproportionately affect African Americans and Hispanics. In some cases, these occupations may be excluded from the legal protections offered by a number of statutes, such as minimum wages, overtime pay, and job safety.

Civil society organizations pointed to inadequate enforcement of Title VII of the Civil Rights Act of 1964, which prohibits employment discrimination based on race, color, religion, sex, and national origin, highlighting the limited number of Title VII cases filed by the Civil Rights Division of the Department of Justice. In particular, reference was made to the low percentage of cases referred to the Civil Rights Division by the EEOC that are actually taken up.

F. Discrimination in the aftermath of the events of September 11

The Special Rapporteur met with several representatives of the Arab, Sikh, Middle Eastern, and South Asian communities in the United States to hear their views concerning the situation after 9/11. Their common view was that their situation had deteriorated quickly in the aftermath of 9/11, particularly due to the extension of national security measures that, in their view, discriminate against these communities. One of the major concerns regards instances of racial profiling, particularly in airports, as well as programs such as NSEERS (see section III.A above).

An increase in cases of discrimination and harassment in the workplace was also reported, not only toward people of Arab or Muslim descent, but also against Sikhs. Serious concern was expressed regarding the long delay in the processing of citizenship applications, which had been disproportionately high for individuals of Arab, Middle Eastern, or South Asian descent.[50]

More broadly, these organizations referred to overall negative perceptions of the American public toward Muslims. Reference was made to a recent USA Today/Gallup poll that showed that 39 percent of Americans felt at least some prejudice against Muslims and that 22 percent would not want Muslims as neighbors.[51] While a number of organizations welcomed outreach initiatives developed by the government in the aftermath of 9/11, they expressed the need for comprehensive actions to address issues of stereotyping and concrete policy changes in areas that have a discriminatory impact on individuals of Arab, Sikh, Middle Eastern, and South Asian descent.

G. Measures taken in the aftermath of Hurricane Katrina

The Special Rapporteur traveled to New Orleans, as well as the Louisiana and Mississippi Gulf Coast, in order to hear local civil society, community leaders, and residents about their concerns in the aftermath of Katrina. In addition, he visited different neighborhoods that were severely affected by the storm, including the 9th Ward of New Orleans. He also met with the Mayor of New Orleans, with whom he discussed the reconstruction efforts and implications for minorities.

Data from the U.S. Census Bureau show the massive impact of Hurricane Katrina in the entire Gulf coast. In the State of Louisiana, 1.3 million people were displaced, with a dramatic depopulation of New Orleans as a whole.[52] However, data indicate the disproportionately high impact of Katrina for African-Americans. For example, whereas the population of whites in New Orleans decreased approximately 39 percent after Katrina, the population of Africa-Americans declined around 69 percent. The ethnic makeup of the city also changed: African Americans formed around 67.3 percent of the population before Katrina and comprised only 58.8 percent after the hurricane.[53]

Interlocutors in the Gulf coast, including displaced families, argued that the Federal Government is not fulfilling its obligation to create adequate conditions for the return of the displaced, particularly in terms of housing. Serious concerns were voiced regarding the demolition of public housing and substitution by private development projects. The demolition of public housing in New Orleans was deemed to have a particularly grave impact for the African-American population, which constitutes the vast majority of public housing residents.[54]

Another issue of concern in the reconstruction phase is employment. According to interlocutors, the combination of the surge in unemployment rates after Katrina and the arrival of a large population of migrant workers, particularly of Hispanic origin, both documented and undocumented, have created a vulnerable environment where workers have been exposed to exploitation and substandard conditions of employment. Ethnic tensions emerged in this context between some African-American and Hispanic individuals, particularly in the context of low wages and stiffened competition for jobs. Attempts to instrumentalize and overstate these tensions were also made, particularly by certain local politicians.[55]

Interlocutors also mentioned cases of excessive use of force by law enforcement officials and military personnel in the early days after Katrina; arbitrary detention of persons who attempted to evacuate the city; inadequate treatment of inmates, particularly in the Orleans Parish Prison; and allegations of racially discriminatory results of decisions by the Army Corp of Engineers to increase the height of the levies in predominantly white neighborhoods.

H. Immigration

The Special Rapporteur held a number of meetings with migrant workers across the country as well as with civil society organizations working with migrant workers. In all of the meetings, migrant workers, particularly those who are undocumented, expressed serious concerns about their vulnerability and dire conditions.

The major issue raised was the disappointment with Congress' failure to approve the comprehensive immigration reform package put forward by the president. Migrant workers expressed the view that the regularization of their status would have represented improved protection and enforcement of their rights. This relates to their serious concern at the lack of legal protection they face, partly a result of the U.S. Supreme Court decision in *Hoffman Plastic Compounds, Inc. v. NLRB*, in which the Court ruled that the National Labor Relations Board did not have the authority to order that employers award back pay for work performed to undocumented workers, victims of unfair labor practices. This decision is allegedly being used by lower courts in cases that restrict the rights of undocumented workers in other domains, including access to justice.[56]

Serious concern was expressed by several civil society organizations regarding worksite immigration enforcement by Immigration and Customs Enforcement (ICE) officials, particularly regarding allegations of the use of an individual's appearance to determine which individuals in a worksite or community should be screened for immigration status. Concerns were also expressed regarding cooperation agreements between ICE and local law enforcement agencies that allow the latter to enforce immigration laws, which could have serious implications in generating distrust among communities and local police.

V. ANALYSIS AND ASSESSMENT

Racism and racial discrimination have profoundly and lastingly marked and structured American society. The United States has made decisive progress in the political and legal combat against racism, through the resistance of communities of victims, the exemplary and powerful struggle of civil rights movements, and the growing political confrontation of racism. However, the historical, cultural, and human depth of racism still permeates all dimensions of life of American society.

The Special Rapporteur noted a strong awareness at all levels of government and society regarding the challenges in the fight against racism. He interprets this finding as a direct legacy of the continuous and determined struggle of the civil rights movement. In particular, he noted the recognition by authorities of the persistence of different manifestations of racism in the country and willingness to tackle this phenomenon. The Special Rapporteur considers awareness and open recognition of manifestations of racism as a precondition of any efforts to adequately tackle the problem. In particular, he commends the United States for the quantity and quality of information on issues related to his mandate, produced both by state institutions and civil society, and including racially- and ethnically-disaggregated data on demographic, social, and cultural indicators. This information is essential for identifying trends and designing effective public policies.

The legacy of the civil rights movement is also reflected in the solid and comprehensive legal framework put in place in the country, particularly after the adoption of the Civil Rights Act of 1964 and extended in a variety of federal and local statutes and institutions. The Special Rapporteur would also like to note the central role played historically by the U.S. Supreme Court in the fight against racial discrimination, starting in *Brown v. Board of Education* and expanded thereafter. The legal and institutional frameworks are in any State the first lines of defense against racism, not only enforcing the obligation to equal treatment, but also giving victims access to remedies and, ultimately, to justice.

63

The vitality of civil society is a third decisive element that contributes to the fight against racism. The Special Rapporteur was impressed with the quality of the work conducted by NGOs across the country, playing a key role in holding governments accountable to their obligation to enforce civil rights laws.

The Special Rapporteur identified a number of challenges in the fight against racism that should be addressed, both at the federal and local levels.

Throughout his mission and in the analysis of documents, the Special Rapporteur was exposed to three broad types of issues: instances of direct racial discrimination; laws and policies that are *prima facie* non-discriminatory, but that have disparate effects for certain racial or ethnic groups; and problems that arise from the overlap of class—specifically poverty—and race or ethnicity.

Instances of direct discrimination and concrete racial bias still exist and are most pronounced with regards to law enforcement agencies. Despite the clear illegality of racial profiling under the fourteenth amendment, recent evidence shows practices that still prevail in law enforcement, such as the disparity in the rate of arrests of minority and white drivers stopped by the police. In the educational system, evidence also shows racial bias in the type of disciplinary action given to white or minority students (see para. 64). In the justice system, evidence of racial bias in conviction rates and length of sentences of both juvenile and criminal courts exist (see paras. 50–55). In addition, programs such as NSEERS have clear ethnic or religious connotations. Direct discrimination was also found in many studies that used paired testing techniques, particularly in the areas of housing and employment. While these cases do not directly involve discrimination by state agents, strong enforcement of human rights is required. The Special Rapporteur notes that the right institutions are already in place to enforce existing laws; however, more robust efforts are required to increase the number of cases taken up every year, creating an important deterrent against future discrimination.

The Special Rapporteur also noted some laws and policies that are *prima facie* non-discriminatory but that have disparate effects for certain racial or ethnic groups. The key example of such practices is mandatory minimum sentences. While the Special Rapporteur welcomes the decision of the U.S. Sentencing Commission to revise the sentencing guidelines for crack cocaine offences, additional work needs to be done to review mandatory minimum sentences for crack cocaine, which disproportionately affect African-Americans.

Socio-economic indicators show that poverty and race or ethnicity continue to overlap in the United States. In 2007, whereas 9 percent of non-Hispanic whites were below the poverty level, 24.7 percent of African Americans, 25.3 percent of American Indians and Alaskan Natives, and 20.7 percent of Hispanics were in that situation.[57] This reality is a direct legacy of the past, in particular slavery, segregation, and the forcible resettlement of Native Americans, which was confronted by the United States during the civil rights movement. However, whereas the country managed to establish equal treatment and non-discrimination in its laws, it has yet to redress the socio-economic consequences of the historical legacy of racism. While noting some progress in this area, particularly in what concerns the representation and participation of racial and ethnic minorities in the high echelons of the political, economic, and cultural arenas and the emergence of a middle class within minority groups, the Special Rapporteur underlines that much still needs to be done in this area.

The overlap between poverty and race in the United States creates structural problems that go far beyond patterns of income. Rather, it interacts with a number of mutually reinforcing factors, such as poor educational attainment, low-paying wages, and inadequate housing, which create a vicious cycle of marginalization and exclusion of minorities. The overrepresentation of minorities in inferior schools, more vulnerable neighborhoods, the juvenile justice system, and the criminal justice system are to a large extent linked to their overall socio-economic situation. At the same time, these trends also contribute to reinforce prejudices and

65

stereotypes, such as an association of minorities to criminality or to poor educational performance.

The consequences of the overlap of poverty and race were clearly seen in the aftermath of Hurricane Katrina. Minorities, as the poorest segments of the population, lived in more vulnerable neighborhoods and were more exposed to the effects of the storm. It is thus not unexpected that these groups suffered from disproportional displacement or loss of their homes. Katrina therefore illustrates the pernicious effects of socio-economic marginalization and shows the need for a robust and targeted governmental response to ensure that racial disparities are addressed.

The Special Rapporteur also noted that the socio-economic marginalization of racial or ethnic minorities has become more acute due to what he perceived as a slow process of *de facto* re-segregation in many areas of the American society. In particular, in his visits to metropolitan areas, he noted the striking pattern of ethnic and racial cleavages that persist and are being reinforced by processes such as gentrification in neighborhoods historically inhabited by minorities. A related aspect is the process of re-segregation in public schools. Several studies have shown that the present level of segregation is similar to that of the late 1960s. These processes not only contribute to keep racial groups physically separated but also affect the marginalization of public services in areas that are predominantly attended by minorities. Ultimately, this creates an obstacle in the most important means of promoting equality of opportunity, which is to offer quality education for all students. In this regard, the Special Rapporteur is particularly concerned about the retraction of affirmative action policies, which make a tangible contribution to enhancing diversity and integration in schools.

The Special Rapporteur would like to make specific reference to the situation of Native Americans, who have been the first people to be historically discriminated in the continent. He was particularly sensitive to the statements made by the Principal

Chief of the Cherokee Nation, Mr. Chad Smith, whom the Special Rapporteur met in Miami, as well as other indigenous leaders met in Omaha and Los Angeles who highlighted the dire socio-economic conditions faced by many Native Americans and the difficulties in preserving their cultural heritage. He recalls the need for constant vigilance for the situation of Native Americans, which should be the subject of particular attention in view of the historical legacy of discrimination against them.

The situation in Puerto Rico also merits particular attention by the government in view of its specificity. A number of particular elements should be borne in mind with regards to Puerto Rico: the ethnic dimension, including the racial makeup of the population and the situation of the black minority in the island; the cultural dimension, including the Hispanic origin of the population; and the political dimension, in particular the specific political status enjoyed by Puerto Rico in the United States. It is therefore essential that specific actions, in line with Puerto Rico's specificities, be undertaken to fight racism in the island.

The Special Rapporteur recalls the idea that he has put forward in many of his reports concerning the need to go beyond a legal strategy that guarantees nondiscrimination. While essential, the legal strategy is only the first stage in the fight against racism. A long-term strategy needs to address the root causes of the phenomenon, particularly in terms of intellectual constructs, prejudices, and perceptions. To fight these manifestations, the only effective solution is to link the fight against racism to the deliberate politically conscious construction of a democratic, egalitarian, and interactive multiculturalism. In his views, this is the most important problem the United States needs to face. A key notion in this regard is the need to promote interaction among different communities as an important means to create tolerance and mutual understanding, strengthening the social networks that hold a society together. Racial or ethnic communities in the United States still experience very little interaction with each other: racially-delimited neighborhoods, schools, and churches prevail. The promotion of more interaction among racial minorities is an

67

essential step that needs to be taken to address the root causes of racism in the United States.

This notion of interactions among communities is also central to understand that the problem of racism in the United States is not solely that between a white majority and minorities, but also occurs among minorities themselves. In particular, many minority groups have been isolated, competing for jobs and social services. Apart from enforcing civil rights laws robustly, promoting more interaction among minorities themselves is an essential step in the fight against racism in the United States.

During the drafting of this report, the United States elected President Barack Obama as its next Head of State. The Special Rapporteur would like to underscore the importance of this event in giving new visibility to minorities in the country. It further corroborates the view expressed in this report that the United States has made fundamental progress in the past decades in giving visibility to members of minorities in the political, economic, and cultural arena. More significantly, this election is the outer reflection of the slow but profound transformation process in the deeper layers of consciousness of every citizen of the United States from all racial and ethnic communities, in the individual confrontation to racism in all dimensions and instances of every-day life.

VI. RECOMMENDATIONS

Congress should establish a bipartisan commission to evaluate the progress and failures in the fight against racism and the ongoing process of re-segregation, particularly in housing and education, and to find responses to check these trends. In this process, broad participation from civil society should be ensured.

The government should reassess existing legislation on racism, racial discrimination, xenophobia, and related intolerance in view of two main guidelines: addressing the overlapping nature of poverty and race or ethnicity and linking the fight against racism to the construction of a democratic, egalitarian, and interactive multiculturalism in order to strengthen inter-community relations.

The federal government—in particular the Civil Rights Division of the Department of Justice, the Equal Employment Opportunities Commission and the Office of Fair Housing and Equal Opportunity of the Department of Housing and Urban Development—should intensify its efforts to enforce federal civil rights laws in its respective domains.

Because the fight against racism needs to take place at the federal, state, and local levels of government, the Special Rapporteur recommends that adequate consultation mechanisms be put in place for a coordinated approach at all levels of government.

As a matter of urgency, the government should clarify to law enforcement officials the obligation of equal treatment and, in particular, the prohibition of racial profiling. This process would benefit from the adoption by Congress of the End Racial Profiling Act. State governments should also adopt comprehensive legislation prohibiting racial profiling.

To monitor trends regarding racial profiling and treatment of minorities by law enforcement, federal, state, and local governments should collect and publicize data about police stops and searches as well as instances of police abuse. Independent oversight bodies should be established within police agencies, with real authority to investigate complaints of human rights violations in general and racism in particular. Adequate resources should also be provided to train police and other law enforcement officials.

Mandatory minimum sentences should be reviewed to assess disproportionate impact on racial or ethnic minorities. In particular, the different minimum sentences for crack and powder cocaine should be reassessed.

In order to diminish the impact of socio-economic marginalization of minorities in what concerns their access to justice, the government should improve, including with adequate funding, the state of public defenders.

The Special Rapporteur recommends that complementary legislation be considered to further clarify the responsibility of law enforcement and criminal justice officials not only to protect human rights, but as key agents in the fight against racism.

In view of the recent recommendations by the Human Rights Committee,[58] the Committee Against Torture,[59] and the Committee on the Elimination of Racial Discrimination,[60] and considering that the use of life imprisonment without parole against young offenders, including children, has had a disproportionate impact for racial minorities, federal and state governments should discontinue this practice against persons under the age of eighteen at the time the offense was committed.

The government should intensify funding for testing programs and "pattern and practice" investigations to assess discrimination, particularly in the areas of housing and employment. Robust enforcement actions should be taken whenever civil rights violations are found.

The Department of Education, in partnership with state and local agencies, should conduct an impact assessment of disciplinary measures in public schools, including the criminalization of school misbehavior, and revisit those measures that are disproportionately affecting racial or ethnic minorities.

Special measures to promote the integration of students in public schools as well as to reduce the achievement gap between white and minority students should be developed in accordance with article 2, paragraph 2 of ICERD.

The federal government and the states of Louisiana, Alabama, and Mississippi should increase their assistance to the persons displaced by Hurricane Katrina, particularly in the realm of housing. The principle that "competent authorities have the primary duty and responsibility to establish conditions, as well as provide the means, which allow internally displaced persons to return voluntarily, in safety and with dignity, to their homes or places of habitual residence"[61] should be respected.

Endnotes

1 Other relevant legislation adopted in this period also included the Voting Rights Act of 1965.

2 U.S. Census Bureau, *2006 American Community Survey.*

3 U.S. Census Bureau, Current Population Survey Annual Social and Economic Supplement, 2003. For additional data, see the Government's responses to Questions Put By the Rapporteur in Connection with the Consideration of the Combined Fourth, Fifth and Sixth Periodic Reports of the United States of America (CERD/C/USA/6) (available at www2.ohchr.org/english/bodies/ cerd/docs/AdvanceVersions/wrusa72.pdf); pp.1–6.

4 On ICCPR, the United States has a reservation on, inter alia, Article 20 on limitations on freedom of expression.

5 See Title V, Section 504 of the Civil Rights Act.

6 See CERD/C/USA/6, para. 153.

7 CERD/C/USA/6, para. 165.

8 See 18 U.S.C. 245. Other statutes related to hate crimes include conspiracy against rights

(18 U.S.C. 241), damage to religious property (18 U.S.C. 247c), criminal interference with the right to fair housing (18 U.S.C. 3631) and criminal interference with voting rights

(42 U.S.C. 1973).

9 Federal Bureau of Investigation, *Hate Crime Statistics* (2000–2007).

10 Department of Education, *How No Child Left Behind Benefits African Americans, Hispanics and American Indians,* http://www.ed.gov/nclb/accountability/ achieve/edpicks.jhtml?src=az.

11 Source: National Center for Educational Statistics.

12 Department of Housing and Urban Development, *The State of Fair Housing 2007,* pp. 4–5.

13 President Bush stated that "Islam is peace. [...] When we think of Islam we think of a faith that brings comfort to a billion people around the world. [...] Women who cover their heads in this country must feel comfortable going outside their homes." http://www.usdoj.gov/crt/ legalinfo/bushremarks.php.

14 See A/HRC/6/17/Add.3.

71

15 http://www.usdoj.gov/crt/legalinfo/nordwg_mission.php.

16 http://www.dhs.gov/xtrvlsec/programs/ gc_1169676919316.shtm

17 See speech by Principal Deputy Assistant Attorney-General Rena Comisac in Jackson, Mississippi on 12 July 2006. Available at http://www.usdoj.gov/crt/speeches/rc_speech_july_12_2006.php.

18 CERD/C/USA/6, para. 255.

19 See, for example, U.S. Citizenship and Immigration Services, *Backlog Elimination Plan: Fiscal Year 2006, 3rd Quarter Update.* Available at http://www.uscis.gov/files/article/ backlog_FY06Q3.pdf.

20 See U.S. Citizenship and Immigration Services. *Welcome to the United States: A Guide for New Immigrants.* Available at http://www.uscis.gov/files/nativedocuments/M-618.pdf.

21 See U.S. Census Bureau, *Annual Estimates of the Population by Sex, Race, and Hispanic Origin for the United States: April 1, 2000 to July 1, 2007* and Bureau of Justice Statistics, *Prison Inmates at Midyear 2007.*

22 Bureau of Justice Statistics, *Contacts between Police and the Public, 2005*, published in April 2007. Available at http://www.ojp.-usdoj.gov/bjs/pub/pdf/cpp05.pdf.

23 Sentencing Project, *Racial Disparity in Sentencing: A Review of the Literature.* Published in January 2005. Available at http://www.-sentencingproject.org/Admin/Documents/ publications/ rd_sentencing-review.pdf.

24 The average sentence for possession of less than 25 grams of powder cocaine is 14 months whereas the average sentence for the possession of less than 25 grams of crack cocaine is 65 months. See The Sentencing Project, *Federal Crack Cocaine Sentencing*, p.2, available at http://www.sentencingproject.org/Admin/Documents/publications/dp_cr acksentencing.pdf. See also Amnesty International, *USA: Amnesty International's briefing to the Committee on the Elimination of Racial Discrimination*, p. 6.

25 Bureau of Justice Statistics, *Capital Punishment Statistics.* Available at http://www.ojp.usdoj.gov/bjs/cp.htm.

26 Amnesty International, *Death by discrimination—the continuing role of race in capital cases*, pp. 5-6.

27 Sickmund, Melissa, Sladky, T.J., and Kang, Wei, 2005, *Census of Juveniles in Residential Placement Databook*. Quoted in USHRN Working Group on Juvenile Justice, 2008, *Children in Conflict with the Law: Juvenile Justice and the U.S. Failure to Comply with Obligations under the Convention for the Elimination of All Forms of Racial Discrimination*, p. 8. Available at http://www2.ohchr.org/english/bodies/cerd/docs/ngos/usa/USHRN14.doc.

28 USHRN Working Group on Juvenile Justice, *Children in Conflict with the Law*, p. 6.

29 Human Rights Watch, *"When I Die, They'll Send Me Home": Youth Sentenced to Life without Parole in California*, p. 26. Published in January 2008. Available at http://hrw.org/ reports/2008/us0108/us0108web.pdf.

30 As an example, see American Civil Liberties Union of Southern California, 2008, *A Study of Racially Disparate Outcomes in the Los Angeles Police Department*.

31 Amnesty International. *Threat and Humiliation: Racial Profiling, Domestic Security and Human Rights in the United States*, p.1. Available at http://www.amnestyusa.org/ racial_profiling/report/rp_report.pdf.

32 The 25 countries are Afghanistan, Algeria, Bahrain, Bangladesh, Egypt, Eritrea, Indonesia, Iran (Islamic Republic of), Iraq, Jordan, Kuwait, Lebanon, the Libyan Arab Jamahirya, Morocco, Oman, North Korea, Pakistan, Qatar, Saudi Arabia, Somalia, the Sudan, Syrian Arab Republic, Tunisia, the United Arab Emirates, and Yemen.

33 See press release by the Department of Homeland Security, "NSEERS 30-Day and Annual Interview Requirements to be Suspended," available at http://www.dhs.gov/xnews/releases/press_release_0306.shtm.

34 Amnesty International. *Threat and Humiliation*.

35 http://www.whitehouse.gov/omb/legislative/sap/110-1/hr1592-sap-h.pdf.

36 See, for example, Human Rights First, *The United States: 2008 Hate Crime Survey*.

37 Gary Orfield and Chungmei Lee, 2007, *Historical Reversals, Accelerating Resegregation, and the Need for New Integration*

Strategies. Available at http://www.civilrightsproject.ucla.edu/
research/deseg/reversals_reseg_need.pdf.

38 U.S. Supreme Court, *Parents Involved in Community Schools
v. Seattle School District*, dissenting opinion by Justice Stephen Breyer.

39 See, for example, NAACP Legal Defense Fund, *Dismantling
the school-to-prison pipeline*, available at http://www.naacpldf.org/
content/pdf/pipeline/Dismantling_the_School_to_Prison_ Pipeline.pdf;
Advancement Project and The Civil Rights Project at Harvard
University, *Opportunities Suspended: The Devastating Consequences of
Zero Tolerance and School Discipline Policies*, p. 6, available at
http://www.advancementproject.org/reports/opsusp.pdf and ACLU, *Race
and Ethnicity in America*, p. 146.

40 ACLU, *Race and Ethnicity in America,* p. 149.

41 Advancement Project and The Civil Rights Project at Harvard
University, *Opportunities Suspended*, p. 6.

42 NAACP Legal Defense Fund, *Dismantling the school-to-prison
pipeline*, p. 7.

43 A recent report by the National Fair Housing Alliance
described paired tests that showed that in 20 percent of tests, African
American or Hispanic testers were denied service or provided limited
service by real estate agents. See *2008 Fair Housing Trends Report*, p.
28. Available at http://www.nationalfairhousing.org. An increase in
steering from 1989 to 2000 was also detected in the Housing
Discrimination Study 2000 conducted by HUD.

44 See Vikas Bajaj and Ford Fessenden, "What's Behind the Race
Gap," *New York Times*, 4 November 2007. Quoted in the shadow report
Residential Segregation and Housing Discrimination in the United States
submitted to CERD by Housing Scholars and Research and Advocacy
Organizations, p.18. http://www2.ohchr.org/english/bodies/ cerd/docs/-
ngos/usa/ USHRN27.pdf.

45 See U.S. General Accounting Office, *Fair Housing:
Opportunities to Improve HUD's Oversight and Management of the
Enforcement Process*. Available at http://www.gao.gov/ new.items/-
d04463.pdf.

46 *Residential Segregation and Housing Discrimination in the
United States*.

47 See CCPR/C/USA/CO/3, para. 22.

48 See U.S. Census Bureau, *Racial and Ethnic Residential Segregation in the United States: 1980-2000.* Available at http://www.census.gov/hhes/www/housing/housing_patterns/pdf/ censr-3.pdf.

49 U.S. Census Bureau, 2007 American Community Survey.

50 Center for Human Rights and Global Justice, *Americans on Hold: Profiling, Citizenship, and the "War on Terror."* Available at http://www.chrgj.org/docs/AOH/AmericansonHold Report.pdf.

51 Quoted in Council of American-Islamic Relations, 2007, *The Status of Muslim Civil Rights in the United States*, p. 6.

52 Louisiana Recovery Authority, *Hurricane Katrina Anniversary Data for Louisiana.* Available at http://lra.louisiana.gov/assets/-docs/searchable/LouisianaKatrinaAnniversaryData082206.pdf.

53 U.S. Census Bureau, 2000 Census and 2006 American Community Survey. In 2000, according to the Census, the white population of New Orleans was 135,956 and the African-American population was 325,947. In 2006, according to the American Community Survey, the white population was estimated at 82,107 and the African-America population at 131,441.

54 For data on the reduction of public housing units, see USHRN, *Hurricane Katrina: A Response to the 2007 Periodic Report of the United States of America*, p. 7.

55 See Advancement Project, *And Injustice for All: Workers' Lives in the Reconstruction of New Orleans.* Available at http://www.advancementproject.org/reports/workersreport.pdf, particularly pp. 11–13.

56 For examples of such cases, see ACLU, *Race and Ethnicity in America*, p. 135.

57 U.S. Census Bureau, 2007 American Community Survey.

58 CCPR/C/USA/CO/3/Rev.1, para. 34.

Appendix

LIST OF OFFICIAL MEETINGS

Federal level
Executive Branch
Department of State
Department of Justice (Civil Rights Division and Federal Bureau of Prisons)
Department of Homeland Security (Office of Civil Rights and Civil Liberties and U.S.
Citizenship and Immigration Services)
Department of Interior (Assistant Secretary for Indian Affairs)
Department of Labor
Department of Education
Department of Housing and Urban Development
Equal Employment Opportunity Commission

Legislative Branch
Chairman of the Committee on the Judiciary, United States House of Representatives
Congressional Black Caucus
Staff of the Committees on the Judiciary and on Foreign Affairs, United States House of Representatives

Judiciary Branch
Justice Stephen Breyer, United States Supreme Court

Local level
Mr. Chad Smith, Principal Chief, Cherokee Nation
New York, NY: New York City Commission on Human Rights
Chicago, IL: Chicago Commission on Human Relations and members of the Mayor's Office
Los Angeles, CA: Office of the Mayor of Los Angeles County, Commission on Human Relations, Men's Central Jail

New Orleans, LA: Mayor C. Ray Nagin
Miami, FL: officials working in the Miami-Date County government
San Juan, Puerto Rico: Ombudsman, Civil Rights Commission.

Chapter 3

All Different, All Equal: From Principle to Practice

Mary Robinson

United Nations High Commissioner for Human Rights
and Secretary-General to the World Conference against Racism

Recognizing the Scale of the Problem

An essential starting point is to recognize the scale of racism and xenophobia in Europe today. We cannot and should not be blind to what is happening around us. Manifestations of racism and xenophobia are now commonplace. The most glaring ones make the headlines—an arson attack on a hostel for asylum-seekers, a particularly savage racial murder. But there are plenty of statistics to show that these are just the tip of the iceberg. Recent arson attacks on synagogues in Erfurt and Düsseldorf are just the most glaring examples of more widespread attacks against the Jewish community in Germany. Racist attitudes in communities and incidents of institutionalized racism in police, immigration, and prison officers are on the rise throughout Europe.

In some ways the problem is the same as it ever was: hatred based on fear; fear of economic competition, fear of loss of identity. In other ways, the patterns of modern racism are worryingly different. We need to pay particular attention to gender and racism and recognize the double discrimination which can occur.

The persistence of racism in Europe is attested in the reports of the UN Committee for the Elimination of Racial Discrimination and in the Council of Europe's European Commission against Racism and Intolerance. We should acknowledge, too, the courageous efforts of NGOs and individual journalists to highlight the root causes and problems.

78

I believe it is important not to stereotype—and thereby somehow distance ourselves from—those we would characterize as racist. Instead, we must look within us—look around at our own families—and acknowledge honestly the seeds that lie hidden within, and about which we must be eternally vigilant.

Among the general aspects which should be noted are:

• An overall increase in intolerance toward foreigners, asylum seekers, and minorities.

• Ill-treatment of members of minority groups by police, immigration, and other officials.

• Discrimination in the workplace and the service sector.

• More people prepared to openly acknowledge that they hold racist views. One survey put the number of French people describing themselves as racist at 38 percent, with 45 percent of Belgians, 23 percent of Germans and 22 percent of British people placing themselves in the same category.

• A rise in support for political parties espousing far-right causes: Austria, Switzerland, and Belgium being examples.

• The emergence of racist attitudes in societies where it had not been so evident before: Finland, Spain, and Ireland, for example.

These trends are alarming, and Europeans should wake up to the threats they pose. The fact that racist attacks and discrimination are being recorded in wealthy countries where there is no threat to livelihoods from refugees and asylum seekers is a worrying new dimension.

These trends are also reminders of the solemn responsibility which Europe bears to lead the fight against racism. Over the last century Europe has experienced the worst excesses of racism and xenophobia. The Holocaust will stand forever as a warning of where anti-Semitism, racial hatred, and the demonization of those perceived as different ultimately leads. And, in case anyone should have thought that such horrors could never happen again, we have only to consider the mass killings, rapes, torture, and expulsions over the past decade in the former Yugoslavia.

This conference provides the opportunity to take stock of the problem of racism and to devise strategies to combat it. We can only do that by first accepting that Europe has a serious problem and by seeking to understand the nature and sources of the problem.

Fortress Europe

In looking at racism in Europe, there is one very significant aspect which must be addressed, and that is the development of what has been described as Fortress Europe. In this context, a true analysis points to the reality of two Europes, increasingly divided by a Brussels-made wall.

The gulf between the rich and the poor in the world is ever widening. Africa, in particular, is experiencing extremes of poverty and exclusion which should shame the developed world into action. But the tendency these days is for developed countries to turn away from the problem. ODA flows are falling, debt relief strategies are inadequate, the international trade system continues to be heavily weighted in favor of the rich. It is as if many in the developed countries have decided to settle for a world divided between haves and have-nots and that the priority must be to protect what they have at all costs. The image of a fortress is appropriate: the sense is of the gates being locked, the drawbridge being drawn up, and everyone who is left outside being allowed to starve and die.

Western Europeans must beware of the fortress mentality. Economically, it is not a sustainable approach in the long-term. Demographically, the population of Western Europe is aging fast. Morally, it cannot be right that millions go hungry, live without clean water or even basic medicines, or die of AIDS at a time when people in the developed countries enjoy unparalleled prosperity, standards of healthcare at an all-time high, and access to the most sophisticated technological advances.

80

Responsibilities of Politicians

Who has the power and the responsibility to effect change? A heavy duty rests on the shoulders of national governments and politicians. To be honest, I see a lot of scope for improvement. Strategies to tackle racism in Western, Central, and Eastern Europe should be coming from the top, from Europe's political leaders. Yet the impression is that it is racists and bigots who make the running in the debate and that some politicians remain silent for fear of antagonizing the few. As Edmund Burke said, "For evil to triumph it is sufficient that good men are silent."

Politicians should lead by example. This is an issue which calls for a strong stance and a transparent approach. Some leaders have had the courage to speak out clearly and show solidarity with victims of racially-motivated attacks. We need more of that—and not only after outrages are committed. We need to hear our political leaders championing diversity, extolling the virtues of multicultural, multi-ethnic societies, defending the vulnerable.

Europe has benefited greatly over the past fifty years from leaders of vision who have determined to move away from past hatreds. I think of Willi Brandt's gesture of atonement in the Warsaw Ghetto, the far-sightedness of the architects of the Treaty of Rome, the Council of Europe, and the European Court of Human Rights. On the world stage, I think of the determination of those postwar leaders who drafted the United Nations Charter, the Universal Declaration of Human Rights, and the Genocide Convention. I think of the courage and magnanimity of Nelson Mandela. We must seek to recapture the spirit that moved those leaders to seek to make the world a better place for all, irrespective of race, gender, or religion.

We can and must do better in the fight against racism and xenophobia. A sustained effort needs to be made at national, regional, and international levels.

National Measures

At the national level, as I have said, I believe that more could be done by governments and political leaders. A serious impediment to tackling the problem occurs where there is broad denial in a country that racism or xenophobia exists at all. Facing up to the reality of the existence of the problem is an important step forward. To tackle it, a wide range of legislative and administrative instruments is available.

A key area is education. While the persistence of racist attitudes is a complex issue, we do know that ignorance and lack of information are root causes. The more that can be done to educate people about the fundamental importance of respecting the rights of others, the better the chance there will be of conquering prejudice. More resources should be put into education, and it should be accorded the high priority it deserves. Surely we can use the opportunities provided by the information revolution to spread the message of the oneness of mankind, of the value of respect, tolerance, and good neighborliness.

Another thing that governments should do is to make full use of the international human rights instruments, and in particular the International Convention for the Elimination of All Forms of Racial Discrimination. The two members of the Council of Europe which have not yet done so—Ireland and Turkey—should ratify the Convention. All should regard the reporting process to the CERD as a positive process which will improve their capacity to combat racism.

And best practices should be followed. Of many such examples, two are worth mentioning. Sweden, as part of its highly developed structure of national institutions, has an Ombudsman against Ethnic Discrimination who places an important emphasis on the employment sector. Given that discrimination so often manifests itself in the workplace, such emphasis can help to shed light on a crucial area.

In Hungary, the Parliamentary Commissioner for National and Ethnic Minority Rights has been active in promoting and protecting the human rights of minorities. One focus has been on the need to put racial discrimination and obstacles to integration of minority communities into curriculum development within educational institutions. Another aspect which the Parliamentary Commissioner has stressed is the importance of addressing minority rights issues not only at federal level but at provincial/ departmental and municipal levels—where much more awareness raising is required. I got this message very strongly in Prague, recently, when I heard concerns from NGOs about the treatment of the Roma community by local officials.

Of the many actions governments should take to combat racism and xenophobia, there are three which I would single out today for special attention: a more sympathetic approach to asylum seekers, tackling contemporary forms of slavery, and ensuring respect for the rights of minorities.

Western Europe's very high level of prosperity makes it inevitable that it will continue to attract asylum seekers and refugees in large numbers. The movement of population from poorer to richer areas is a worldwide trend and it is not about to go away. This is a challenge which should be met with generosity of spirit and respect for the inherent dignity of every human being. But the sense I have is that a generous response is not forthcoming—quite the contrary.

The UN High Commissioner for Refugees has pointed out that the alarming increase in racist attacks on asylum seekers and refugees subjects them to a "continuum of intolerance." The picture is grim: it is intolerance or aggravated discrimination which forces them to leave their countries; intolerance, rejection and abuse which they face along the treacherous road to safety; and, once they have reached a place where they are entitled to expect adequate protection, they are met instead by, at best, suspicion, at worst rejection and physical violence.

The term "asylum seeker" has even become in some countries a term of abuse. Asylum seekers find themselves doubly stigmatized—as "aliens" and as "cheaters," if not "criminals," for no other sin than having entered "Fortress Europe." In public opinion and political discourse there is a disturbing tendency to criminalize asylum seekers, notably by linking their search for protection to the questionable methods of smugglers and traffickers. Some parts of the media have played a very negative part by whipping up hysteria over these issues. This is a dangerous identification of victims with wrongdoers which should be firmly resisted.

Of no less concern is the rise in contemporary forms of slavery and the related issue of trafficking in people. The hundreds of thousands who leave their homes in search of a better life are vulnerable on many fronts, especially if their situation in the host country is irregular. Women and children are the most vulnerable of all. If undocumented, they can become prey to callous, unscrupulous people who force them to work in conditions that amount to forced labor or slavery.

The problem of trafficking is world-wide and growing. It is estimated that between three hundred and six hundred thousand women are smuggled each year into the European Union and between and from Central and Eastern European countries. Human trafficking is a violation in itself, but it can include violations of a whole range of human rights. Poverty, discrimination, and social exclusion are the backdrop for trafficking; it is a phenomenon which destroys thousands of lives and governments throughout Europe, and Europe should be paying more attention to it.

Every country in Europe includes minorities of one kind or another—be they members of minority nationalities, religions, or ethnic groups, indigenous peoples, Roma or Travelers. The protection of minorities and other vulnerable groups was the subject of a regional seminar organized by my office in preparation for the World Conference against Racism. At the seminar held in July in Warsaw, a series of questions was put. How can disparities in access to economic and social opportunities be eliminated so that root causes of prejudice and discrimination can be removed? How can countries establish institutions to monitor themselves so as to detect potential problems in time? How can every country visit and recast its vision of a national identity that embraces and encompasses all parts or groups of the population, that gives to everyone a stake in the future of her or his country?

These are issues which will be pursued vigorously as we prepare for the World Conference. In this, I am mindful of the fact that the United Nations has made the protection of minorities one of the central purposes of its human rights program and that there is a special duty of care on us to protect the rights of these vulnerable groups.

Regional Activities

At the regional level, Europe as a whole is well-placed to give a lead in the fight against racism and xenophobia. The institutions to protect human rights in this region are among the oldest and most sophisticated in existence.

> ➢ I would like to pay tribute to the Council of Europe for the solid contribution it has made and continues to make. Lord Russell Johnston put it succinctly in a lecture delivered on the fiftieth anniversary, pointing out that: "The Council of Europe's myriad of legal and political achievements now affects every possible aspect of our citizen's lives."

> ➢ The reports of the European Commission against Racism and Intolerance provide an important yardstick by which countries can measure progress made and identify what has to be achieved.

> ➢ I pay tribute also to steps taken by the European Union to combat racism and discrimination and note the establishment of the European Monitoring Centre on Racism and Xenophobia and the recent directive implementing the principle of equal treatment between persons irrespective of

racial and ethnic origin, adopted by the Council of the European Union in Luxembourg June 29, 2000.

➤ The European Youth Campaign against Racism and the European Year against Racism were important in that they engaged people's attention to issues of racism. It is vital that we bring young people onboard. Children, it is often said, are color blind—we must find ways of trying to extend that acceptance of difference beyond childhood.

➤ I pay tribute, too, to the work of the OSCE's High Commissioner on National Minorities, who has done a lot through quiet diplomacy to impress on governments the need to give fair treatment to all minorities.

I think it is important, as European institutional arrangements to tackle racism are developed, that attention be paid to complementarity between the different mechanisms. This is some-thing for the institutions themselves to consider, but it is as well to remember that the fight against racism is a common cause, and resources should be used to best advantage.

What I would like to see is each nation examining its record in improving relations between the elements and groups which make up their society. I would like everyone to face up to the origins of racism and discrimination, to come to terms with the legacy of history, including slavery, pogroms, the brutalities of colonialism, genocide. I hope there will be a particular focus on issues of gender and racism. And I would like it to strengthen our resolve to reshape our identity in the modern world as inclusive, multicultural, multiracial communities where everyone is treated on an equal footing.

My aim was to state a self-evident, but often forgotten, truth: that we all constitute one human family. The Visionary Declaration refers to the first mapping of the human genome, an extraordinary achievement which not only reaffirms our common humanity but promises transformations in scientific thought and practice, as well as in the visions which our species can entertain for itself. It encourages us toward the full exercise of our human spirit, the reawakening of all its inventive, creative, and moral capacities, enhanced by equal participation of men and women. And it could make the twenty-first century an era of genuine fulfillment and peace.

The Visionary Declaration calls on us, instead of allowing diversity of race and culture to become a limiting factor in human exchange and development, to refocus our understanding, discern in such diversity the potential for mutual enrichment, and realize that it is the interchange between great traditions of human spirituality that offers the best prospect for the persistence of the human spirit itself.

Europe has the capacity to play a major part in this great enterprise. Do not let it be said that you were found wanting.

Chapter 4

African-American Civil Society and International Politics

Christopher K. Wambu

On October 7, 2003, a very significant forum took place at United Nations Headquarters in New York. The forum's purpose was to brainstorm about how leaders of African America's civil society and the United Nations could collaborate in support of the United Nations' programs for world peace, human rights; sustainable and balanced development; accessible, affordable health; education; and all other areas of international interest. The forum was based on an understanding that all domestic politics were now international and all international politics were now domestic.

African Americans are not new to international affairs or organizations. The early giants—W.E.B. DuBois, Ralph Bunche, Paul Robeson—were all classic examples of progressive inter- nationalists. They were supportive of and critical to the founding of the modern United Nations. They were vanguard thinkers about issues dear to the United Nations like colonialism, human rights, racism, imperialism, and apartheid.

Recently, African Americans have put more emphasis on domestic political matters, perhaps because of the great need in the United States to redress eroding civil rights, increasing economic inequalities, and the resurgence of racial polarization. Yet not too long ago, African Americans played central, effective roles in the movements that helped to end apartheid and colonialism in many parts of the world despite the tendency of America's power elites to disparage, marginalize, or become alarmed by African Americans who question or offer alternatives to U.S. foreign policies, as if international affairs were outside their province. One is reminded, for example, of the firestorm in public opinion that followed Dr. Martin Luther King's forthright sermon at Riverside Church in New York City, a speech that condemned America's role in the Vietnam War. African Americans are expected to deal with only one domestic issue—that is, civil rights—and leave economics and diplomacy, foreign or domestic, to the white establishment.

During the latter part of the twentieth century, the reactionary policies of the mainstream elites who came to power during this period compelled black Americans to narrow their focus to domestic politics, so it should be no surprise that the most common misconception among black people is that domestic issues deserve priority over international issues.

In fact, blacks have already grown from being the vanguards of civil rights crusades to being in the vanguard of political and economic establishments. The United States is a far different place today than it was just twenty to thirty years ago. Blacks have risen to real positions of political power and influence as high-ranking government officials at all levels of government, corporate directors, Hollywood superstars, and sports moguls—even if their political platforms may differ. The math is self-explanatory: there is now a critical mass of influential African Americans across the United States, and there is a steady growth curve that is no longer dictated by seasonal politics but instead represents successes of past struggles, which have culminated in rights and privileges that others have for so long allocated for themselves to the exclusion of black Americans.

Thus, it would be a travesty if the majority of African Americans assessed the presence of individuals like former U.S. Secretaries of State Colin Powell or Condeleeza Rice as temporary phenomena dictated by quixotic Republican politics. African Americans need to see these individuals the way the rest of the world sees them. They are seen as representing the United States; and the fact that they are black simply tells the rest of the world that black Americans are major participants in both domestic and international affairs. The fact that they are black can only increase positive impressions of blacks and help erase the belief that black Americans are marginal citizens.

The presence of blacks in high positions in the United States, which is presently the hegemonic power in the world, sets a trend that suggests a time in the future when qualifiers (e.g., "first black," "only black") will not be needed every time a black person reaches a threshold of power—a time when black people can be less often racially pigeonholed.

Although many African-Americans may differ ideologically with blacks such as Powell and Rice—and they should—Powell's and Rice's presence in key positions of power ought to galvanize the black community into recognizing that they are no longer considered merely insurgents in domestic and international affairs, at least outside the United States.

Unfortunately, many African Americans have invested so much emotional capital in victimhood that, instead of rejoicing about some of these successes, many seem to frown on them and perhaps even consider them aberrations that are merely exceptions to the historical traditions of racial politics and quite temporary, not the start of a new trend.

Yet the evidence on the ground is manifest that African Americans are not merely victims. Every Sunday, hordes of tourists invade Harlem's cultural and religious institutions. It is conceivable that black Americans do not associate this attention with political power. But the fact that many Europeans choose to visit Abyssinian Baptist Church instead of St. Patrick's is a political asset. It is part of a larger precept that defines black people's significance on the world stage.

Many international dignitaries have trekked to this historical black institution and used its pulpit to speak to the world. Fidel Castro of Cuba, U.N. Secretary General Kofi Annan, and various African and European heads of state have been accorded this platform to address America and the world. Dr. Calvin Butts, the senior pastor of Abyssinian Baptist Church, now occupies a larger and much more universal pulpit than before, a fact that he seems to be aware of, as was his distinguished predecessor, Congressman/Reverend Adam Clayton Powell, son of Abyssinian Baptist Church's legendary pastor of the same name. This "bully-pulpit" phenomenon is continually replicated all over the country in other black churches, at historically black colleges and universities, in cultural institutions, and at national professional and fraternal conferences where African Americans are called upon to project a force beyond the United States' borders.

What can African Americans bring to the table? In a fragmented world, black Americans, if audacious enough, could be a voice of reason, balance, and advancement in a public arena that has become vulgarized and polarized across the board by right-wing ideologues who have captured center stage. Many over-arching African-American values wrought from their historical experiences confronting disparities in the United States often connect more with the rest of the world than do the values and concerns of conservative white Americans. Undoubtedly, African Americans are not monolithic; but the contradictions in American life are profound, and African Americans continue to be disproportionately affected by the disparities.

Add to that that there is no known political resentment toward African Americans as a group outside the United States. While the rest of the world sees most of America's besetting sin as snobbery, very little antipathy is applied to blacks, though people outside the United States are struck by what seems to be an American-nurtured, limited knowledge about the world outside the United States.

Further, having long been societal and economic underdogs, African Americans are well-positioned to translate and address America's moral and immoral concepts. Black Americans do not have to condone terrorism and religious chauvinism in order to be fair-minded when evaluating current anti-American currents in the world. In some ways, black Americans possess a much more refined and legitimate moral clarity about these and other similar issues than any other group. Black Americans have rarely participated, on a global scale, in those activities that seem to attract political hostilities abroad.

Black Americans are also better situated to discuss poverty, given their firsthand experience with an economic and social distortion that plagues much of the world's peoples. Americans talk a good game about wanting to alleviate poverty in the world, but when economic policies—such as opening its borders for truly fair trade—seemingly threaten its current unfair worldwide trade advantage, there is an outcry.

Even close to home, there was never a serious effort during the time when the North American Free Trade Agreement was being negotiated to alleviate the economic imbalances between the United States and Mexico, for example, which inevitably heightened disparities in Mexico. Blacks in the United States have experienced poverty and the negative consequences of unfavorable terms of trade, including the decimation of local manufacturing, lost jobs, fallen wages, neighborhood erosion, poor education, costly and inaccessible health care and housing, and generations of family members unable to climb out of impoverishment.

Looking at the United States today, the conservative elite appears to suffer from a perception gap. It purposely maintains extremely selective and narrow practices supported by its narrow perceptions. It is indoctrinated with moral and political chauvinism, reinforced by a lack of curiosity about the rest of the world, believing wrongly that America's hegemonic self-interests and narrow world view represent an elemental common denominator and that all the world should subscribe to these principles. This suggests a sort of willful ignorance perhaps driven by misguided moral concerns and provincial politics. This line of moral punctiliousness is always selective and often economically and politically driven.

As we begin to construct solutions or ways to effectively address and evolve away from these practices, African Americans who are just as religiously observant could help to reduce the antipathy toward America because they are less doctrinaire. They could help to reduce the uneasy feelings Europeans have about American foreign policy, which they see as driven by a messianic

92

zeal that is dangerous because it is anchored not in facts, but in faith; not by truth, but on ideology. African Americans have great faith in God, but they also have a deep appreciation of human equality and freedom and respect for reason. They are more politically tolerant and less vitriolic in disagreements.

Blacks and other progressives should seriously seek to invalidate the right-wing's hostilities toward the rest of the world. Each of us is entitled to a say, but the all-out attack on the United Nations, for example—the only world body—requires a sober response. There is a need in America to mediate the incongruity of how the world sees America and how America sees herself. It is a tragedy to disregard the rest of the world. If America chooses to leapfrog back to isolationism in international affairs, well, fine, but the world will move on, albeit without America's approval.

African Americans need to write papers that make known their views about international affairs and recommend new American strategies for national security and peace. They also need to reappropriate national symbols and insist that their critiques and contributions are also patriotic and in the best interests of America's future.

African Americans need to address the negative effects of unilateralism, commonly practiced by the Bush administration. They need to challenge America's doctrine on the preemptive use of force and its preference for temporary, one-issue-oriented, short-term coalitions when the need is for long-term alliances based on long-term constructive interests.

African Americans need to construct messages that tone down the current administration's belligerent approach to the so-called "axis of evil," which is counterproductive because of its ability to trigger energized pursuits of nuclear weapons out of fear of invasion.

Africa is experiencing a decade of democracy that is sweeping the continent, but there is an ingrained unrealistic public expectation—particularly in the United States—that democracy will take hold immediately against a backdrop of serious long-term social and economic inequalities on the continent. African Americans could assist in solidifying these long-overdue democratic gains while encouraging the U.S. government to enter into a constructive engagement with African countries that goes beyond the conservative view of the world as black or white.

African Americans can assist in molding a constructive image of international organizations like the United Nations that in the past have been dismissed by American conservatives. They can help in building partnerships between international organizations and domestic economic, political, and cultural institutions.

There are many endeavors that could benefit from collaborations between the United Nations Organizations (UNO's), black churches, universities and colleges, national and local elected officials, business and professional organizations, and cultural institutions. Black Americans have built a formidable phalanx of institutions that could be used to contribute to the world through UNO partnerships. Black Americans have skilled manpower and financial resources, and they are media savvy and bold. They could assist the UNO's, Africa, and the world in navigating the tumultuous current of American politics.

Conclusion

In the United States, every ethnic group except African Americans and American Indians is expected to have an opinion about and input into that part of international affairs that interests them. Even corporations and NGOs are allowed to have opinions that are both domestic and global in scope.

African Americans need to overcome this state of political paralysis, inertia in diplomacy, and their overarching view of themselves as victims. We are aware of past constraints—legal and extra-legal—that fostered the black community's political impotency in international affairs. Unquestionably, there have been threats, ridicule, disparaging responses, silence, and worse whenever African Americans dared to contribute to or engage in world affairs.

94

But black Americans cannot afford to be an auxiliary force in foreign affairs. There is great need for more pluralism in U.S. foreign policy. The incongruity of American foreign policy—especially its relationship with international organizations—could use a corrective from African Americans because, as experience demonstrates, that policy now suffers from distorted misconceptions about the world dictated by xenophobic strictures.

African Americans are well-situated to figure out the necessary permutations to aid and improve relations between the United States and the rest of the world, to improve and assist the functions of the UNO's, to aid in reversing negative images of the United Nations in the United States, and finally, to help extirpate the bad feelings that seem to exist between the United States and international organizations. Black Americans could coordinate the current negotiations between American pharmaceutical industries and the third world over the pricing of AIDS drugs, for example. They could assist in addressing debt issues that have paralyzed third world economics. Above all, they, alongside the UNO's, could be partners in assuring skeptical Europeans, Asians, and Africans that the whole of the United States of America does not subscribe to cowboy unilateralism in diplomacy. With United Nations Organizations, African Americans could promote democracy as an end in itself, a means to foster peace and solidarity among world nations.

Chapter 5

European Public Opinions about Immigration and Migrants

James S. Jackson and Toni C. Antonucci

Introduction

People in most advanced industrialized countries are living longer; life expectancy is increasing (Jackson 2003). At the same time, the demographic distribution of the population in many nations, especially in advanced countries, has changed from a pyramid-shaped distribution with many more younger than older people to a beanpole-shaped population distribution with relatively equal numbers of people in each generation. Given the employment and social security structures in most Western Advanced Industrial Nations (AIN), it is imperative that larger numbers of younger people participate actively in the labor force in order to contribute to the economic well-being of these societies and to directly provide financial assistance (through direct payroll exchanges) to those who are in various states of retirement in older ages. In most cases the only source of large enough numbers of young workers is through immigration from other countries, primarily less advanced and more traditional countries.

In this paper we focus on the attitudes of native populations toward immigrants, recognizing that the reception these immigrants receive will significantly influence both how well they adapt to their new countries and how successfully they contribute to societal economic well-being. We capitalize on unique data which detail the attitudes and beliefs of Western Europeans from the fifteen European Union countries toward immigrants (Jackson, Brown, Brown, and Marks 2001; Lemaine, Ben Brika, and Jackson 1997). We believe these attitudes will fundamentally influence the experience of immigrants, their families, and the communities within which they live.

To facilitate this investigation, we have developed a heuristic model, presented in Figure 1, which outlines several broad societal and individual factors hypothesized to influence beliefs, attitudes and behaviors of the majority population toward immigrants. In the paragraphs below we outline each component of the model reflecting on their effects on older people. We begin with the proposition that macro contextual factors influence an individual's feelings and behaviors toward immigrant groups.

Macro contextual factors refer to generalized characteristics, at both the national and the individual level, which influence how people view the target group. These factors include such characteristics as education, income, historical time and period, ethnic, family, or geographic background. In essence, these characteristics or factors set the overall stage for how immigrants will be viewed (Blumer 1958). For example, people with higher levels of education and income are more inclined to appreciate the potential contribution of diverse populations. They are more likely to perceive immigrants as broadening and enriching their environment and often because of their positions do not feel directly in competition with immigrants, as may individuals of lower income and education (Fetzer 2000; Esses, Jackson, and Armstrong 1998; Wagner and Zick 1995). Although historical time and period can be influential at a global level, individual countries can also be affected by events or population shifts that in turn affect their attitudes about immigration and migrants. For example, a country with a pyramid population structure—that is, fewer older people and many younger people—may not be as concerned about the amount of resources immigrants would consume and therefore may be more welcoming to new immigrants. Another country with a beanpole shaped population structure, that is, having similar numbers of older and younger people and consequently fewer people actively contributing to the economy may already be feeling the strain of providing for their elders; thus, they may be somewhat less welcoming to older immigrants while welcoming younger migrants. Historical context and personal history also influence how people feel about immigration and migrants

(Maddens, Billiet, and Beerten 2000). Israel provides a unique example. As a relatively young country, it is predominantly made up of immigrants. Nevertheless, people who immigrated to Israel as young adults and have worked for the intervening fifty or more years on a kibbutz are more likely to be perceived by other collective members to have earned the care and support they will need in their old age. On the other hand, others who immigrate as older people to join their children might be perceived as less deserving of the support of the kibbutz, since they have not contributed to the resources of the kibbutz during their younger years.

Additional specific family background characteristics can influence how individual immigrants are received. Having a highly educated family background, being from a specific geographic or ethnic subgroup, or having a particularly needed skill are all likely to influence how any one individual or group is received. Each of these characteristics provides a general context within which immigrant experiences need to be interpreted. They can also combine to have unfortunate affects. To illustrate, being a Muslim immigrant in the United States was not overly distinctive nationally prior to the September 11, 2001 attack on the World Trade Center. Since that time, however, most Muslims report significantly elevated negative responses from other Americans. Thus, a specific religion and ethnic background have combined in this particular historical period to produce an unfortunate and unique circumstance and consequent macro environmental context within which all representative members, whether young or old, are evaluated. As these examples demonstrate, the objective facts or characteristics of immigrants to particular countries must be placed within the macro, broader historical context in order to understand how they are perceived and received by the host country. We turn next to a consideration of social, cognitive and affective resources.

Social, cognitive and affective sources also affect how the immigrant is perceived. These sources refer to those collective social, cognitive, and emotional factors that influence how one

98

interacts with immigrants, what one believes about immigrants, and how one reacts to immigrants (Esses et al. 1998; Essed 1991). For example, patriotism or national pride might be defined in such a way as to make sure the country remains as isolated and "pure" as possible, suggesting a general rejection of immigrants; or, alternatively, it might be defined as a country that welcomes all immigrants. At the same time, there can be collective beliefs about specific immigrant groups as hard-working, "good" people, while others are simply criminals fleeing the authorities or deported by them. Groups of all types, including nations, often have complex but widely held beliefs about specific others. Thus, people might consider all immigrants as "in-group" members, essentially the approach adopted by Israel in arguing that Jews worldwide have the right to be Israelis; while others argue that only a very carefully defined group, identified by whatever characteristic (e.g., genes or geography) can be appropriately considered "in-group" members (Duckitt and Mphuthing 1998; Bobo and Hutchings 1996). This in-group/out-group identification is critical because it is often associated with feelings of threat (Esses et al. 1998; Jackson and Ingelhart 1995; Jackson, Brown, and Kirby 1998; Noiriel 1996). Members of one's own group tend to be considerably less threatening than members of another group or the "out-group." People who identify immigrants as an out-group may come to feel threatened by them, imagining that they will threaten their jobs, their security, and in the case of older people specifically, might worry that they will drain the country of needed public services (Pettigrew, Jackson, Ben Brika, Lemaine, Meertens, Wagner, and Zick 1998; Quillian 1995). It is the case that cognitive and affective sources can be the source of stereotypes or affective reactions to any specific group (Gaertner and Dovidio 1986). Thus, a stereotype might be developed which identifies members of a specific immigrant group as lazy or hard working; law abiding or criminal. These cognitions can be associated with an affective or emotional reaction to the group that can be either positive or negative, creating warm and welcoming reactions to the group, or

99

cold and rejecting ones (Agnew et al. 2000; Bobo 1999; Glick and Fiske 2001).

As diagrammed in Figure 1, both the macro environmental context and the social, cognitive, and affective resources are hypothesized to influence social and political civility. These refer to the generally accepted patterns, customs, and rules of interaction with immigrants, influenced a great deal by basic values of the society (Schwartz 2006). For example, if immigrants and older people are labeled out-group members and negatively stereotyped, they will be received with much less social or political civility on multiple dimensions (Maddens et al. 2000; Lloyd and Waters 1991). A significant amount of literature has shown that contact, values, ideology, and the political climate all affect how well the individual or group member will be received (Allport 1954; Pettigrew 1998a; 1998b; Van Dick, Wagner, Pettigrew, Christ, Wolf, Petzel, Castro, and Jackson 2004). Generally speaking, more contact is associated with more positive attitudes but not if that contact leads to negative experiences (Agnew, Thompson, and Gaines 2000). Similarly, if the characteristics of the group are valued—for example, the wisdom of the old or the skill of an ethnic group—they will be received more positively—that is, with greater social and political civility. With respect to immigrants, it is also clear that the ideology and political climate in the receiving country will greatly influence either positively or negatively the norms which are adopted for interacting with them. If the political climate is conservative, immigrants from countries with similar views may be more readily welcomed, whereas if the political climate is liberal or permissive, the opposite is likely to be the case. Older, religious immigrants to a nonreligious country or a nonobservant one may be much less well-received than older religious immigrants who have immigrated to a country with similar religious customs and values. Even when values and ideologies differ, it is sometimes the case that if social distancing is resisted and receiving country members have constructive interactions with the immigrating group, positive social and political norms can be achieved (Van Dick et al. 2004).

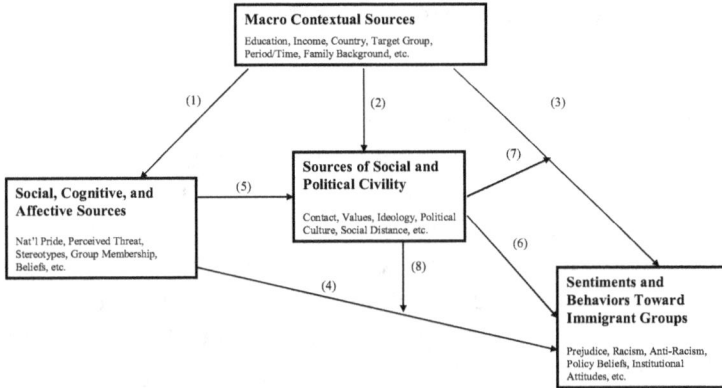

Figure 1: Sources of Sentiments and Behaviors Toward
Minority Ethnic, and Immigrant Groups

As this heuristic model indicates, these three factors—the macro contextual sources; social, cognitive, and affective influences; and social and political civility—are all hypothesized to influence either directly or indirectly sentiments and behaviors toward immigrant groups which are manifest in various ways, including racism, prejudice, institutional beliefs and policy (Jackson et al. 2001). In the following pages, we present an overview of attitudes and beliefs about immigrants and consider how several characteristics noted in the heuristic model outlined above might influence these views.

With the data available to us we are able to address representative examples of each element of our heuristic model. Hence, we examine (1) what is the macro-environmental context within which immigrants to the European Union are received; (2) are there social, cognitive, and affective factors which distinguish attitudes about immigrants; (3) what are the social and political norms of civility concerning these immigrant groups, and what factors influenced the development of these norms; (4) are resultant attitudes concerning immigrants informed by those factors explicated in our heuristic model; (5) what is the likely

101

prognosis for future relationships. We depend heavily on data from 1997, although in some cases we present population trend data over the period 1988 through 2000 for some selected items. Before turning to the data, however, we provide a brief overview and description of the Eurobarometer project.

Methods
The surveys of the European Union (EU) are a long running set of opinion polls that are conducted twice yearly (and at special periods) in the spring and fall on nationally representative samples of the EU. These surveys, in varied form, have been conducted since 1970. In 1974, the Commission of the European Communities initiated the Eurobarometer series to provide a regular monitoring of social and political attitudes of the publics within the EU. Over the years, these Eurobarometer surveys have focused on special topics such as public attitudes toward guest workers and a number of similar, timely public concerns (see Lemaine et al. 1997).

The analyses reported in this chapter are based upon survey data collected from approximately fifteen thousand respondents living in households in fifteen Western European countries (i.e., Belgium, Denmark, Germany, Greece, Spain, France, Ireland, Italy, Luxembourg, the Netherlands, Portugal, the United Kingdom, Austria, Sweden, and Finland) from the 1997 Eurobarometer (47). A total of 12,141 respondents weighted to reflect the European Union population were included in the analyses reported in this chapter

Results
In this section, we summarize the attitudes and beliefs of majority members of the fifteen European Union countries toward immigrant groups. We begin with a consideration of beliefs concerning the presence and numbers of immigrants in their country which can be considered an element of the macro environmental context within which immigrants are received.

102

Attitudes about Immigration and Immigrants: Macro Environmental Context

Western Europeans from the fifteen Eurobaramenter European Union countries were asked if they believed there were "too many, a lot but not too many, or not many immigrants" in their country. The highest proportion of people, 45 percent, report that there are a lot but not too many people of other races, cultures, or religions in their country, while an almost equal proportion of people, 41 percent of the population, report that there are too many such people. Only 14 percent of the respondents felt that there were not many people of other races, cultures, and religions in their country. Figure 2 presents the trends over time in the percentages of EU citizens perceiving that there are "too many" non-nationals in their country. France, one of the larger of the EU countries, is presented as a contrast. As shown, the peak of feeling overwhelmed by non-nationals occurred in 1991 (about 56 percent), remained steady through 1993, and then decreased to 1988 levels by 1994 and remained about 40 percent over the last period shown. This trend was paralleled by the data from France.

Figure 2: Perception of Number of Non-Nationals in Own Country

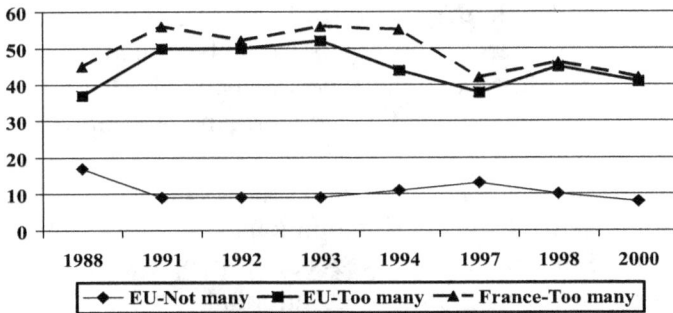

A large number of people who believe their countries have already reached their limits in terms of the number of immigrants currently

103

in their country and those who further agree that increasing the current number of immigrants in the country would be problematic. Only 35 percent of the majority population disagrees with the statement that the country has already reached its limits, while 65 percent tend to agree with this statement. Similarly, only 28 percent of the population disagreed with the statement that there is a limit to how many people (immigrants) a society can accept, while the overwhelming majority, 71 percent, of the respondents agreed with this statement.

Respondents in each of the fifteen countries were asked if they agreed with the statement that people who were full members of a minority group were so different from others that they could never be fully accepted members of the society. Responses are presented in Table 1. A combined average of all European Union countries indicates that approximately 38 percent of the population agreed with this statement. It can be noted, however, that agreement actually varied quite widely from country to country, with 56 percent of the Belgians agreeing with this statement but only 23 percent of the Finns and Spaniards agreeing. A slightly different wording suggests that these beliefs vary by minority group. As indicated in Table 1, when people were asked whether the extent to which minority group members would be fully accepted into the society depended upon the specific minority group to which they belonged, across all the European Union countries, 63 percent of the respondents agreed with this statement. Once again, however, there was considerable variance by country. For example, 81 percent of the Germans but only 48 percent of the Italians agreed with this statement.

Respondents from the fifteen European Union member countries also had differing opinions about how immigrants should integrate into their country. Asked if people would have to give up aspects of their religion or culture that conflicted with the laws of the host country, on average, as indicated in Table 1, 59 percent of the respondents agreed. There was considerable variance across the different countries with fully 90 percent of the Danes agreeing with this statement but only 28 percent of the Italians and 29 percent of the Spaniards agreeing. Asked in a manner reflecting assimilation rather than integration, however, respondents were much less likely to feel assimilation was necessary for acceptance. Thus, if the question is asked, "Must people give up their culture in order to be fully accepted into the society of the host culture," on average, only 24 percent of the respondents from the fifteen countries agreed, (see Table 1) with the highest agreement, 44 percent, from the Belgians and the lowest, 11 percent, from the Italians.

Table 1: European Attitudes about Immigration and Immigrants: Macro Environmental Context

Attitude	European Average Percent
Minorities Can Never be Fully Accepted	38%
Acceptance Depends Upon the Group	63%
Minorities Must Give up Parts of Their Culture that Conflict with Law	69%
Minorities to be Fully Accepted Must Give Up Their Own Culture	24%

A comparison of the percentage of individuals, who believe minority groups should be integrated, assimilated, or neither is presented in Table 1. As shown, only 24 percent of the averages across countries agree with the requirement of assimilation—that is, one must give up one's culture. Approximately 36 percent agree with the requirement of integration, giving up only those parts of one's culture that are in conflict with the laws of the host country. Fully 39 percent of respondents averaged across all European Union countries disagree with both assimilation and integration as a requirement for full acceptance into the society of the host country. These percents vary widely by country. Some examples are illustrative of the considerable variation. While as few as 10 percent of the Italians agree with the requirement of assimilation, as many as 44 percent of the Belgians agree. On the other hand, only 16 percent of the Spaniards but as many as 65 percent of the Swedes agree with the requirement of integration, although as few as 8 percent of the Danes and as many as 67 percent of the Spaniards disagree with both assimilation and integration.

How Immigrants Affect Society: Social, Cognitive, and Affective Sources

A series of questions probed the degree to which the majority population in European Union countries felt that minorities affected their society in a negative manner. For example, as shown in Table 2, 63 percent of the European Union respondents felt that minorities tended to increase the rate of unemployment in their country. On the other hand, only 37 percent felt that the government provided minorities with preferential treatment.

Table 2: Perceptions of How Minorities/Immigrants Affect Society: Social, Cognitive & Affective Sources

Attitude	European Average Percent
Minorities Increase Unemployment	63.2%
Minorities Keep Sectors of Economy Going	39.7%
Minorities Receive Preferential Government Treatment	33.7%
Their Presence Causes Insecurity	44.5%
Their Religious Practices Threaten Way of Life	28.7%
Minorities Abuse System of Social Benefits	58.9%
Minorities Harm Quality of Country's Education System	52.8%
Minorities Enrich Education	73.2%
Job Discrimination Should be Banned	86.9%
Minorities Face Job Discrimination	70.6%
Employers Should Only Look at Qualifications	87.6%
Minorities Do Jobs Not Wanted by Others	68.4%
Minorities Pay More Than They Take from Social Security	21%
Minorities Enrich Cultural Life	58.2%
Minorities Help in International Sports	41.6%
Authorities Should Improve Status of Minorities	71.4%
Minorities Are Discriminated Against in Housing	67.3%

Approximately 44 percent agreed that the presence of minorities is a cause of insecurity and only 29 percent agreed that the religious practices of minorities threatened their own way of life. However,

59 percent felt that minorities tended to abuse the system of social benefits and 53 percent of the respondents felt that the quality of the education system suffers because of the presence of minorities.

When asked about various situations reflecting the rights of minorities, people do tend to be in favor of supporting basic rights and liberties. As shown in Table 2, over 85 percent of those asked felt that discrimination against minorities in the job market should be against the law and 70 percent believed that minorities are discriminated in the job market. Almost everyone—87 percent— agreed that employers should only take qualifications into consideration among job applicants.

Another set of questions asked about how minorities influenced their social and economic environments. These responses are summarized in Table 2. Only 40 percent of the respondents agreed that minorities keep large sectors of the economy going, but 68 percent of the respondents agreed that minorities do jobs that other people do not want to do. Interestingly, many saw a positive side with respect to education. Seventy-three percent of the respondents agreed that education can be enriched by the presence of minorities. Only 21 percent felt that minorities paid more into the social system than they receive. Over half, 58 percent, agreed that minorities enrich cultural life, and 42 percent of the respondents felt that their country would do less well in sports without minorities.

There seems to be general agreement that authorities should improve the situation for minorities. As shown in Table 2, 71 percent of the European Union respondents feel that the authorities should improve the situation of minorities, and over half of the respondents, 57 percent, agreed that minorities get poorer housing because of discrimination against them. Figure 3 shows the trend from 1991 through 1998 in the nonacceptance of southern Mediterranean immigrants. As with the perceptions of "too many" non-nationals in their countries, public opinion against these immigrants peaked in the mid-nineties and then fell to the early 1990 levels by the end of the decade.

Figure 3: Non-Acceptance of People Coming from Countries South of the Mediterranean

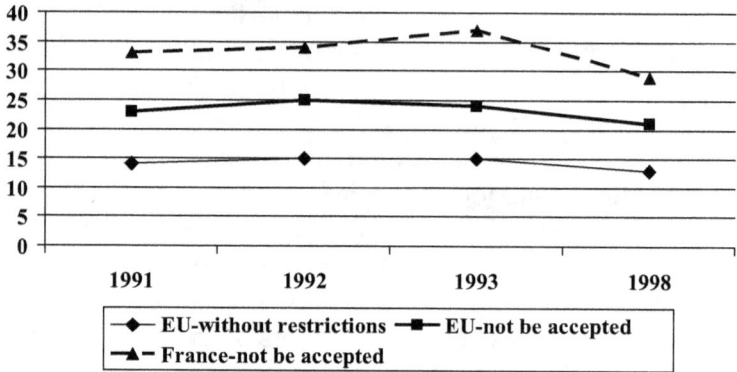

Figure 4: Non-Acceptance of People Seeking Political Asylum

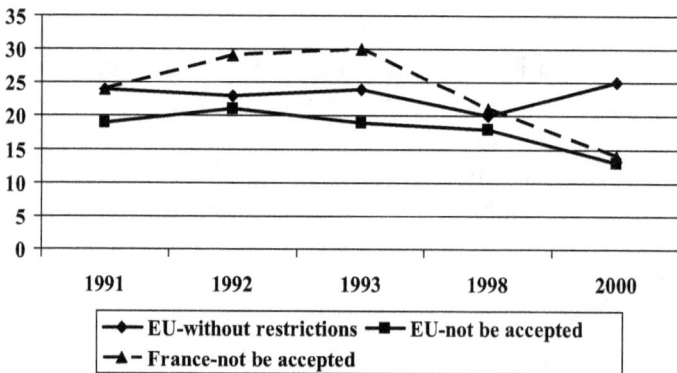

Views About and Relationships with Immigrants: Social and Political Civility

A second set of questions inquired about the majority European Union respondents' views and relationships with minority members. Asked about whether they felt that minority group members wanted to become full members of the majority society, only 16 percent of the respondents disagreed with this statement while over 84 percent of the respondents agreed with it.

People were also asked about their friendships with minority group members. Specifically, respondents were asked if they had none, some, or many friends who were members of minority groups. While 55 percent of people in the majority culture reported that they had no minority friends, only 6 percent said that they had many. Approximately 30 percent of the majority European Union respondents indicated that they had some friends who were members of a minority group.

A series of questions suggests that most people believe that the fundamental rights of minorities should be preserved (Council of Europe 1998). These responses are summarized in Table 3. The majority of people felt that when persecuted, people should be provided with political asylum under all circumstances (55 percent). Figure 4 shows the trend from 1991 through 2000 in the numbers of EU residents agreeing that people should be accepted in their countries without restrictions for reasons of political asylum. As shown in prior trends, the negativity about political asylum peaked in the mid-nineties and then fell to early 1990 levels by the end of the decade.

Almost everyone (91 percent) agreed that people should be treated equally before the law, should have religious liberty (82 percent), should have the right to their own language or culture (83 percent), and the right to free speech (81 percent). There was less agreement (64 percent) that under all circumstances people should be granted freedom of association, that is, the right to associate with and meet with whomever they wished.

There was general agreement, as indicated in Table 3, that other fundamental rights should be granted under all circum-

109

stances. These include the right to housing (85 percent), to live with family (86 percent), and to be protected from discrimination (87 percent). Over 92 percent of the respondents agreed that under all circumstances minorities should be granted the right to education. Somewhat fewer people agreed (66 percent) that minorities should have the right to vote under all circumstances. Interestingly, responses were about equally divided concerning protection from religious persecution. Approximately 54 percent agreed that religious asylum should be granted under all circumstances while 46 percent felt that it depended on the circumstances.

Table 3: Fundamental Rights of Minorities/Immigrants: Social & Political Civility

Fundamental Rights Under All Circumstances	European Average Percent
Asylum for Political Views	56.4%
Asylum for Religious Views	54.5%
Equality Before Law	90.8%
Religious Liberty	82.3%
Language and Culture	82.6%
Freedom of Association	63.9%
Freedom of Speech	81.4%
Housing	85.2%
Live with Family	86.2%
Discrimination Protection	87.2%
Education	92.1%
Vote	66.3%

Rights and Relocation Issues: Sentiments and Behaviors Toward Immigrant Groups

Respondents made clear distinctions between immigrants from non-European Union countries and, as suggested in their responses summarized in Table 4, tended to feel less of a commitment to them. There was, however, a wide range of responses from what might be interpreted as quite restricted to quite liberal. Over one-fifth of all EU respondents felt that all immigrants should be sent back to their country of origin, "even those born here" (21 percent), and "even those who are legally here" (21 percent). Twice as many (43 percent) felt that legal immigrants should be sent back if they were unemployed, and considerably more (65 percent) felt that all illegal immigrants should be sent back regardless of circumstances. On the other hand, 68 percent of the respondents did feel that whether or not immigrants should be deported should be determined by individual circumstances.

Table 4: Rights and Relocation Issues: Sentiments & Behaviors Toward Minority/Immigrant Groups

Sentiments and Behaviors toward Non-EU Minorities/Immigrants	European Average Percent
Send Back all Immigrants	21.5%
Send Back Illegal Immigrants	20.6%
Send Back Legal Immigrants if Unemployed	42.8%
Send Back All Illegal Immigrants Without Exception	65.5%
Circumstances should Determine if Illegal Immigrants are Sent Back	68.1%

Although not shown, there were different responses concerning deportation of legal immigrants among the specific fifteen European Union countries. While on average about 43 percent of all respondents felt that legal immigrants should be sent back if unemployed, this figure ranged from 59 percent among the Italians to 18 percent among the Swedes. These responses are also influenced by the age, education, and gender of the respondent. In general, older people, people with lower levels of education, and men about as often as women felt that even legal immigrants should be deported if they were not employed. Responses to this question also varied by the respondent's political views. The data indicate that people against the European Union (53 percent) and people from the political right (65 percent) were much more likely

111

to endorse the view that legal immigrants who are unemployed should be sent back to their country of origin.

Discussion

These data reveal that there is considerable variation among majority members of the European Union concerning attitudes and beliefs about immigrants in their country. The attitudes of many European Union members are generally negative toward immigration (Hira 1991; Miles 1993; Pettigrew 1998b; Miles 1993). At the same time, most European Union members endorse civil liberties for their own population, although they tend to be less open to these liberties for immigrants (Lloyd and Waters 1991; van Dijk 1997).

The trends found in Figures 2 through 4 indicate that attitudes toward immigrants over the beginning to mid-1990s showed a negative increase but a decrease by the end of the decade. Although we are sure that this trend is the product of many factors, most European countries introduced punitive anti-immigration policies in the mid-1990s. We argue that it is important for European citizens to maintain an adherence to positive set of political and social values (e.g., egalitarianism and openness) (Schwartz 2006). These set of values are sorely tested when perceived large numbers of non-national minorities, especially those from south of the Mediterranean, enter their countries as permanent residents. The introduction of severe restrictions on immigration as well as tightening of social welfare policies for these residing within these countries addresses the threat inherent in the types of attitudes and beliefs. Given that the government had responded to the concerns of European citizens by introducing these negative measures, attitudes, as expressions of the underlying political and social values of European citizens, returned to the low levels of the beginning of the decade. Thus, European immigration attitudes are responsive to government interventions and may have played a significant role in the development of these policies

The growth of aging populations worldwide is creating a demand for immigration among people of all ages, but increasingly so among advanced industrial nations as they attempt to maintain economic competitiveness. Unfortunately, it appears as though citizens of advanced industrialized nations, such as those in Western Europe, may become increasingly intolerant of increased immigration, especially as population aging takes place in receiving countries with significantly greater resources.

Additional research is needed to examine the direct linkages between basic western values, immigrant attitudes and beliefs, public policies, and the adjustment of immigrant/minority populations in Europe (Jackson 2003). Similarly, additional attention is needed from family researchers to examine the increased pressure for family and kin reunification which may lead older people to immigrate in order to reunite with their children and other relatives in these countries. Since this is most likely to be from less to more economically and socially resourceful countries, the potential for negative attitudes and receptivity of these host countries may have enormous negative influences on both individuals and families, as well as the broader societal context for all residents.

References

Agnew, C. R., Thompson, V. D., Gaines, S. O., Jr. (2000). Incorporating proximal and distal influences on prejudice: Testing a general model across outgroups. *Personality and Social Psychology Bulletin,* 26(4), 403–418.

Allport, G.W. (1954). *The Nature of Prejudice* (2nd ed.). Reading, MA: Addison-Wesley Press.

Blumer, H. (1958). Race prejudice as a sense of group position. *Pacific Sociological Review,* 1, 3–7.

Bobo, L. (1989). Keeping the linchpin in place: Testing the multiple sources of opposition to residential integration. *Revue Internationale de Psychologie Sociale,* 2(3), 269–273.

Bobo, L. (1999). Prejudice as group position: Micro-foundations of a sociological approach to racism and race relations. *Journal of Social Issues*, *55*(3), 445–472.

Bobo, L., and Hutchings, V. L. (1996). Perceptions of racial group competition: Extending Blumer's theory of group position to a multiracial context. *American Sociological Review, 61*, 951–972.

Council of Europe (1998). *Legal measures to combat racism and intolerance in the member states of the Council of Europe.* Report prepared by the Swiss Institute of Comparative Law, Lausanne. Council of Europe: Strasbourg, France.

Duckitt, J. and Mphuthing, T. (1998). Group identification and intergroup attitudes: A longitudinal analysis in South Africa. *Journal of Personality and Social Psychology, 74*(1), 80–85.

Essed, P. (1991). *Understanding Everyday Racism: An Interdisciplinary Theory.* Newbury Park: Sage.

Esses, V. M., Jackson, L.M. and Armstrong, T.L. (1998). Intergroup competition and attitudes toward immigrants and immigration: An instrumental model of group conflict. *The Journal of Social Issues, 54*(4), 699–724.

Fetzer, J. S. (2000). Economic self-interest or cultural marginality? Anti-immigration sentiment and nativist political movements in France, Germany and the USA. *Journal of Ethnic and Migration Studies, 26*(1), 5–23.

Gaertner, S. L. and Dovidio, J. F. (1986). The aversive forms of racism. In J. Dovidio and S. L. Gaertner (Eds.). *Prejudice, Discrimination and Racism.* San Diego, CA: Academic Press.

Glick, P. and Fiske, S. (2001). An ambivalent alliance: Hostile and benevolent sexism as complimentary justifications for gender inequality. *American Psychologist, 56*(2), 109–118.

Hira, S. (1991). Holland: The bare facts. *Race and Class, 32* (3), 119–123.

Jackson, J. S. (2003). Conceptual and methodological linkages in cross-cultural groups and cross-national aging research. *Journal of Social Issues, 58*(4), 825–835.

Jackson, J.S., Brown, T.N., Brown, K., and Marks, B. (2001). Contemporary immigration policy orientations among dominant group members in Europe. *Journal of Social Issues, 57* (3), 431–456.

Jackson, J. S., Brown, K. T., and Kirby, D. (1998). International perspectives on prejudice and racism. In J. L. Eberhardt and D. T. Fiske (Eds.), *Racism: The Problem and the Response* (pp. 101–135). Newbury Park: Sage Publications.

Jackson, J.S. and Inglehart, M.R. (1995). Reverberation theory: Stress and racism in hierarchically structured communities. In S. E. Hobfoll and M. W. deVries (Eds.), *Extreme Stress and Communities: Impact and Intervention,* (pp. 353–373). Dordrecht, the Netherlands: Kluwer Academic Publishers.

Lemaine, G., Ben Brika, J. and Jackson, J.S. (1997). *Racism and xenophobia in Europe. First results presented at the closing conference of the European Year Against Racism.* Luxembourg, December 18–19. European Commission, Directorate General V: Brussels, Belgium.

Lloyd, C. and Waters, H. (1991). France: One culture, one people? *Race and Class, 32* (3), 49–65.

Maddens, B., Billiet, J. and Beerten, R. (2000). National identity and the attitude toward foreigners in multi-national states: The case of Belgium. *Journal of Ethnic and Migration Studies, 26*(1), 45–60.

Miles, R. (1993). *Racism after 'Race Relations'.* London: Routledge.

Noiriel, G. (1994). "Civil rights" policy in the United States and the policy of "integration" in Europe: Divergent approaches to a similar issue. *Journal of Policy History,* 6 (1), 120–139.

Noiriel, G. (1996). The French melting pot immigration: Citizenship and national identity. Contradictions of modernity, 5. Minneapolis: University of Minnesota Press.

Pettigrew, T. F. (1998a). Applying social psychology to international social issues. *Journal of Social Issues, 54*(4), 663–675.

Pettigrew, T. F. (1998b). Reactions toward the new minorities of Western Europe. *Annual Review of Sociology, 49*, 77–103.

Pettigrew, T F., Jackson, J. S., Ben Brika, J., Lemaine, G., Meertens, R.. W., Wagner, U., and Zick, A. (1998). Outgroup prejudice in Western Europe. *European Review of Social Psychology, 8*, 241–273.

Quillian, L. (1995). Prejudice as a response to perceived group threat: Population composition and anti-immigrant and racial prejudice in Europe. *American Sociological Review, 60*, 586–611.

Räthzel, N. (1990). Germany: One race, one nation? *Race and Class, 32* (3), 31-46.

Schwartz, S. H. (2006). Value orientations: Measurement, antecedents and consequences across nations. In (Eds.) R. Jowell. C. Roberts, R. Fitzgerald and G. Eva. *Measuring attitudes cross-nationally- lessons learned from the European Social Survey*. London: Sage.

Van Dick, R., Wagner, U., Pettigrew, T. F., Christ, O., Wolf, C. Petzel, T., Castro, V. S., and Jackson, J. S. (2004). The Role of Perceived Importance in Intergroup Contact. *Journal of Personality and Social Psychology, 87*(2), 211–227

van Dijk, T. A. (1997). Political discourse and racism: Describing others in western parliaments. In S.H. Riggins (Ed.), *The Language and Politics of Exclusion: Others in Discourse*, pp. 31–64. Thousand Oaks, CA: Sage Publications.

Wagner, U. and Zick, A. (1995). The relation of formal education to ethnic prejudice: Its reliability, validity, and explanation. *European Journal of Social Psychology*, 25(1), 41–56.

Chapter 6

The Ways Europeans View Foreigners' Impact on Society: A Cross-National Comparison

Moshe Semyonov and Anastasia Gorodziesky

Foreigners in Europe

Throughout the second half of the twentieth century, immigrants have begun arriving in European countries in ever increasing numbers. As Europe has become home to millions of overseas labor migrants, guest workers, ex-colonials, immigrants, and refugees, the ethnic fabric of many European societies has dramatically changed (Lahav 2004; Sassen 1996; Castle and Miller 1993; Pettigrew 1998). The emergence of new ethnic communities in the host countries has not only changed the ethnic composition of European societies but also led to increased ethnic tension between minority and majority members. Many citizens have begun viewing the "foreigners" as a serious social problem, and questions about the terms of inclusion of immigrants within the national community of the receiving state have become more crucial than ever before (Baldwin-Edwards and Schain 1994; Schnapper 1994; Soysal 1994).

In Table 1, we display the distribution of the foreign populations across twenty-one European countries in 2001. The data reveal that in 2001 percent foreign population as well as non-EU foreign population has become quite substantial in many European countries. The presence of foreigners is quite apparent in old-immigrants-importing countries such as Switzerland, Luxemburg, United Kingdom, Belgium, Germany, Austria, France, and Sweden. In East European countries such as Poland, Hungary, and Slovenia, and in the new-immigrant importing countries such as Ireland, Italy, Spain, Portugal, and Finland, the numbers of the foreign populations, although increasing, have not become substantial yet.

Table 1: The distribution of the foreign populations across 21 European countries in 2001[1]

Nation	% Non EU[3]	% All Foreigners[2]
Belgium	2.9	8.4
Denmark	3.9	4.8
Germany	6.7	8.9
Greece	6.5	7.0
Spain	1.8	3.0
France	3.5	5.6
Ireland	1.2	3.6
Italy	2.1	2.7
Luxembourg	5.1	36.8
Netherlands	2.9	4.2
Austria	8.4	9.1
Portugal	1.2	1.6
Finland	1.4	1.8
Sweden	3.4	5. 5
UK	2.8	4.2
Norway	2.3	4.1
Switzerland	8.5	19.7
Czech	1.2	2.1
Poland	0.1	0.1
Hungary	0.6	1.3
Slovenia	1.3	2.2

Sources: Eurostat: Yearbook 2003; Living conditions in Europe, Statistical pocketbook, 1998-2000, 2003 edition; Demographic statistic 2002. OESD: "Trends in international migration," 2001, 2002.
2. Mean of percentage of foreigners (non nationals) in 2000 and 2001
3. Mean of percentage of Non EU foreigners in 2000 and 2001

Studies of attitudes toward foreigners and immigrants in Europe reveal increased hostility toward foreigners coupled by increased support for restrictive policies on inclusion of immigrants in society. In effect, despite the dire need and growing demand for workers in European countries—mostly for low-paying manual and service jobs that the local populations are not willing to take—anti-foreigner sentiment is rising in an era of unprecedented global migration. Recent research in West European societies shows a high level of anti-foreigner sentiment, xeno-phobia, ethnic tension, racism, and even ethnic violence, even in societies that only recently have begun hosting immigrants. Immigrants and foreigners are perceived not only as outsiders to the social, cultural, and political spheres, but also as a threat to economic success, national identity, and the social order of the host society, even in countries with low numbers of foreigners (Pettigrew 1998; Coenders 2001; Scheepers et al 2002; Lahav 2004; Gijsberts et al. 2004; Semyonov et al. 2006).

As more foreigners have established permanent residence in European countries, many citizens have begun raising questions regarding the legal status of the foreigner populations and their place in society. Foreigners are viewed as a serious "social problem" and as a threat to future economic stability and to the national identity of society. In fact, as more migrants have made Europe their home, the "immigration problem" has become rele-vant more than ever because it has been transformed from a labor market problem to one of national identity (Castles and Kosack 1985; Faist 1994; Schnapper 1994; Fetzer 2000; Baumgartl 1995) and questions of national identity tend to mobilize more sentiments against foreigners than questions of labor market competition. Subsequently, exclusionary efforts toward outsiders seem to appeal to the ethnic solidarity of the majority population and to prompt anti-ethnic and anti-foreigner sentiments.

The definition of the foreign population in European coun-tries is not a simple but rather a complex matter. Foreigners have arrived to various European host countries from a wide variety of countries of origin. Their legal and civilian statuses also differ across countries. Some arrived as labor migrants and some were recruited as guest workers; others are ex-colonials, and many others are refugees and asylum seekers. In Switzerland, for example, many labor migrants have arrived from the former Yugoslavia and Turkey, India and China, and many asylum seekers arrived from Sri Lanka. These immigrants and asylum

120

seekers cannot become citizens of Switzerland. In the Scandinavian countries, most immigrants used to come from neighboring countries, but the recently flows of immigrants have begun arriving from Pakistan and the former Soviet Union. In Germany, many ethnic Germans (mostly from the former Soviet Union) can become German citizens upon arrival in Germany, while many sons and daughters of Turk and Yugoslav immigrants find it difficult to become citizens, and currently many of them are not German citizens. In Italy and Spain, the foreign populations are composed of labor migrants from North Africa, sub-Saharan Africa, Latin America, and Asia. The United Kingdom has received large numbers of immigrants and ex-colonials from India, Pakistan, and the West Indies, and the Netherlands received large numbers of Surinamers and Malaysians. Likewise, France and Belgium have become home to ex-colonial immigrants from the sub-Sahara and from North Africa and in recent years to migrants from Southeast Asia. Yet, despite variations in country of origin and ethnic background and despite variations in civilian status across countries, they are considered outsiders. From a theoretical point of view, they can be viewed as out-group populations, and as such, they often become a target for discrimination, prejudice, hostility, and even violence in their host countries (e.g., Pettigrew 1988; Semyonov et al. 2006).

In the following analysis, we examine public views of the impact foreigners exert on society and some trends in such views. The availability of the European Social Survey (ESS) and the Eurobarometer Surveys provide us with opportunity to compare across a large number of countries public attitudes toward the impact that foreign populations exert on European societies as well as trends in such attitudes. In the data presented in this chapter, we will first examine change in public views of the impact foreigners exert on the country in which they live between 1988 and 2000 for twelve European countries (based on analysis of the Eurobarometer Surveys in 1988 and 2000), and second, compare views on the impact foreigners have on society across twenty-one

121

European countries in 2002/3 (based on analysis of the recent European Social Survey).

Change in Attitudes toward Foreigners across Twelve Countries

The analysis reported in this section is based on data gathered in the 1988 and 2000 Eurobarometer surveys in twelve countries. In both points in time, representative samples of twelve national populations (aged fifteen and over) were interviewed regarding the impact that foreigners living in the country have on society. The questions address the following three issues: impact of foreigners on the welfare system, impact of foreigners on unemployment, and impact of foreigners on delinquency and violence (for detailed definitions and exact wording of the three items, see Appendix A). Responses for the three items were also combined to construct the index of anti-foreigner sentiment. According to the coding scheme, when a respondent expresses a negative attitude toward foreigners, the item is coded one, and when a respondent does not express a negative attitude, it is coded zero. When all three items are summed, the values of the index can range from zero (no negative response or positive attitude on all items) to three (negative attitude on all items). In order not to exclude from the analysis respondents who did not provide answers for all of the three items, the index was weighted and is expressed in terms of percent of the items on which a respondent expresses negative attitude (out of all items on which a respondent provides answers). The values of the index, thus, range from zero (no negative response on any of the items) to one hundred (negative responses on all items).

Table 2 (columns 1–6) presents percentage of respondents who expressed negative attitudes toward foreigners in each one of the three items by country for two time points, 1988 and 2000. Columns 7 and 8 in Table 1 display the mean value of the index of anti-foreigner sentiment in 1988 and 2000. In Figure 1-4 we list the values of each item for the twelve countries at the two time-points for illustrative purpose.

122

Table 2: Percentage of Respondents Who Expressed Negative View Toward Foreigners and Mean Value (standard deviation) of the Index of Anti-Foreigner Sentiment, by Country and by Year[1]

Nation	Foreigners abuse social benefits		Foreigners increase un-employment		Foreigners cause delinquency and violence		Anti-Foreigner Sentiment Index	
	(1) 1988	(2) 2000	(3) 1988	(4) 2000	(5) 1988	(6) 2000	(7) 1988	(8) 2000
France	32.1	71.4	34.3	59.6	22.8	55.7	29.7 (35.9)	61.6 (4.6)
Belgium	34.1	71.9	38.7	71.5	24.1	61.5	32.3 (37.6)	67.6 (38.1)
Netherlands	20.3	57.7	25.2	56.9	10.2	50.7	18.5 (28.5)	54.9 (39.1)
Germany	15.2	65.5	29.1	67.8	11.4	53.4	18.5 (28.4)	62.8 (37.6)
Italy	8.5	49.8	40.9	50.8	13.4	44.9	20.9 (25.7)	49.0 (39.3)
Luxembourg	29.1	54.4	22.5	53.4	12.6	45.7	21.4 (29.7)	50.9 (37.9)
Denmark	25.3	58.2	29.0	51.6	18.2	65.0	24.2 (32.8)	58.3 (37.6)
Ireland	5.6	71.4	21.8	55.7	2.4	49.4	9.9 (18.1)	57.1 (37.8)
UK	20.7	69.7	35.6	58.9	14.8	40.1	23.7 (31.4)	56.5 (39.6)
Greece	15.0	58.6	45.1	88.1	26.1	80.0	28.7 (32.1)	77.0 (30.5)
Spain	2.8	44.4	25.9	46.7	9.4	37.4	12.7 (21.8)	42.5 (39.3)
Portugal	11.6	62.0	31.1	67.0	9.8	52.1	17.5 (29.5)	60.2 (38.9)
Europe[2] 12 countries	17.3	61.5	33.4	59.3	14.9	49.4	21.9 (30.3)	56.7 (39.7)

Source: Eurobarometer Surveys: (30) for 1988; (53) for 2000.
2. Total percent in Europe is computed through using weight variables that includes an adjustment of each national sample in proportion to its share in the total population of the European Community

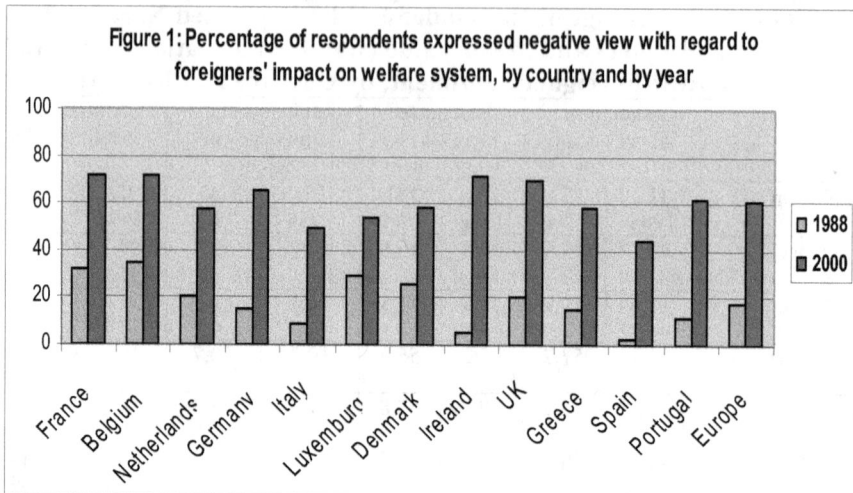

Figure 1: Percentage of respondents expressed negative view with regard to foreigners' impact on welfare system, by country and by year

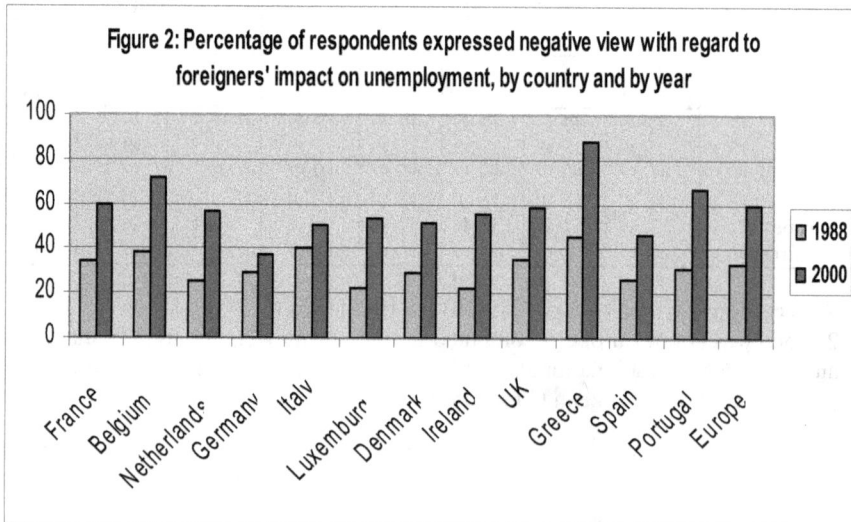

Figure 2: Percentage of respondents expressed negative view with regard to foreigners' impact on unemployment, by country and by year

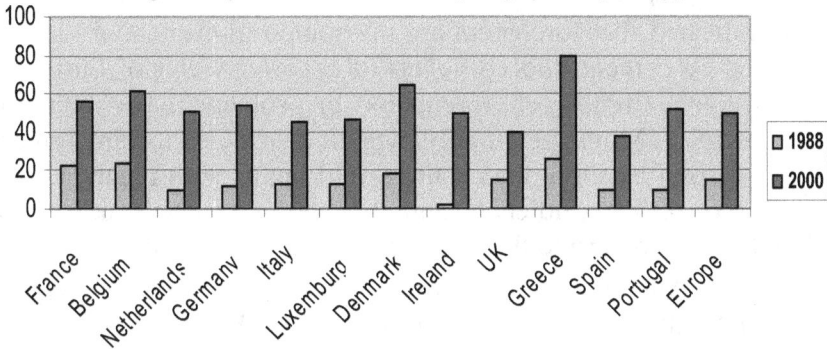

Figure 3: Percentage of respondents expressed negative view with regard to foreigners' impact on violence and delinquency, by country and by year

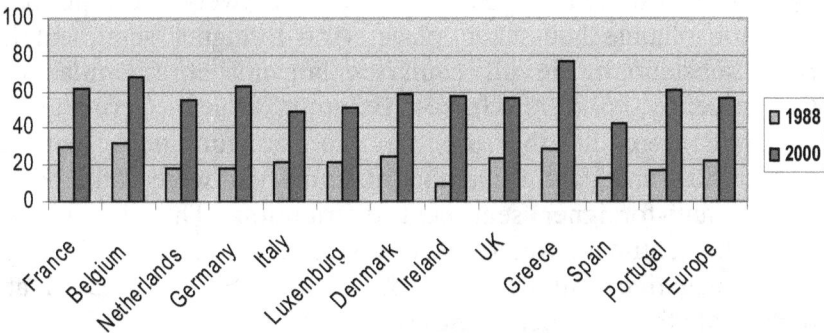

Figure 4: Mean Values of Anti-Foreigner Sentiment Index, by Country and by Year

According to the data, in 1988 third of Europeans reported that presence of foreigners in their countries increases unemployment, about 20 percent reported that foreigners abuse the welfare system of social benefits and about 15 percent indicated that the presence of foreigners is a source of delinquency and violence. In

2000, that percent of Europeans that reported that the presence of foreigners increases unemployment reached almost 60 percent, the percent of Europeans that suggested that foreigners abuse the welfare system exceeded 60 percent, and the percent of Europeans that indicated that foreigners are the source of crime and violence reached 50 percent. Indeed, levels of negative views of Europeans toward the impact of foreigners on society have increased dramatically. More specifically, negative attitudes toward foreigners had risen by more than a three-fold factor with regard to their impact on crime, violence, and the welfare system and almost doubled with regard to their impact on unemployment.

The data also reveal considerable variations across countries in levels of anti-foreigner attitudes. By the year 2000, anti-foreigner sentiment was most pronounced in places such as Greece, Belgium, Germany, France, and Portugal and least pronounced in countries such as Spain, Italy, and Luxembourg. In 1988, anti-foreigner attitudes were most evident in old immigration countries such as France, Belgium, United Kingdom, and Denmark and least evident in new immigration countries such as Ireland, Spain, and Portugal. Apparently, within a twelve-year period, a dramatic change had taken place. Anti-foreigner sentiment had risen substantially in all countries but not at a similar rate. Consequently, in 2000, Greece, Belgium, France, Germany, and Portugal were at the top of the anti-foreigner sentiment distribution, and Italy, Luxembourg, and Spain were at the bottom of the anti-foreigner sentiment distribution. The rise in anti-foreigner sentiment was especially steep in Ireland and Portugal, where negative attitudes toward foreigners had increased at a higher rate than in other countries.

Table 3: Mean (Std. Deviation) of the Responses Regarding Views of the Impact Foreigners Exert on Society and of the Index[1]

Nation	Impact on health and welfare systems	Impact on job creation/scarcity	Impact on crime's problems	Impact Foreigners Exert on Society Index
Belgium	6.06 (2.05)	5.72 (1.94)	7.06 (2.00)	6.29 (1.59)
Denmark	5.92 (2.09)	4.40 (1.76)	6.74 (1.98)	5.70 (1.52)
Germany	6.21 (2.02)	5.86 (1.98)	7.11 (2.03)	6.39 (1.60)
Greece	7.01 (2.46)	7.42 (2.28)	8.19 (1.79)	7.54 (1.80)
Spain	5.29 (2.09)	5.23 (2.15)	6.75 (1.84)	5.76 (1.57)
France	5.65 (2.35)	5.10 (2.33)	6.51 (2.32)	5.75 (1.85)
Ireland	6.39 (2.22)	5.87 (2.31)	5.87 (1.19)	6.04 (1.62)
Italy	4.98 (2.13)	5.37 (2.40)	6.43 (2.29)	5.61 (1.65)
Luxembourg	5.65 (2.47)	5.04 (2.31)	7.16 (2.28)	5.99 (1.77)
Netherlands	5.76 (2.05)	4.93 (1.66)	7.16 (1.87)	5.96 (1.40)
Austria	5.61 (2.30)	5.29 (1.93)	6.72 (2.01)	5.89 (1.74)
Portugal	4.59 (2.34)	6.27 (2.09)	6.92 (1.86)	5.97 (1.67)
Finland	5.91 (2.16)	4.97 (1.93)	6.61 (1.75)	5.84 (1.50)
Sweden	5.30 (2.04)	3.91 (1.85)	6.57 (2.28)	5.25 (1.59)
UK	6.17 (2.13)	5.63 (2.04)	6.41 (1.87)	6.05 (1.65)
Norway	5.30 (1.94)	4.52 (1.73)	7.37 (1.81)	5.74 (1.33)
Switzerland	5.93 (1.94)	5.21 (1.75)	7.17 (1.79)	6.12 (1.36)
Czech Republic	6.47 (2.09)	6.28 (2.15)	7.61 (1.74)	6.80 (1.61)
Poland	5.92 (2.02)	6.13 (2.26)	6.70 (1.99)	6.27 (1.69)
Hungary	6.46 (2.02)	6.63 (2.25)	7.26 (2.15)	6.80 (1.73)
Slovenia	5.64 (1.94)	5.88 (2.11)	6.48 (2.06)	6.01 (1.59)
Overall Mean	5.79 (2.19)	5.57 (2.21)	6.78 (2.08)	6.05 (1.70)

Source: 2002/3 European Social Survey.
2. Total mean in Europe is computed through using weight variables that includes an adjustment of each national sample in proportion to its share in the total population of the Europe.

Additional and More Recent Comparative Data

The European Social Survey provides us with the opportunity to compare a larger number of European countries (twenty-one countries) and to study more recent data on the attitudes toward foreigners (the data were gathered in 2002–2003). Here, we focus on three questions addressed to respondents regarding their views of the impact foreigners exert on society that are most comparable to the three items available in the Eurobarometer data. Specifically, we focus on the respondents' attitudes toward foreigners' impact on job creation, health and welfare services, and crime problems. Foreigners are defined as people who come to live here from other countries. The responses are measured on an eleven-point scale ranging from zero (positive) to ten (negative). The detailed definition and exact wording of each item is provided in Appendix A.

The data displayed in Table 3 and in Figures 5–8 reveal that, in general, Europeans are more likely to view the impact that foreigners exert on the three aspects of social and economic life in their country in negative than in positive terms. In all twenty-one countries, negative views are most pronounced with regard to foreigners' impact on crime (mean value across Europe is 6.78) than on employment and the welfare system. Yet, the views on all three items are generally negative.

With regard to the impact foreigners exert on crime problems, respondents in Greece, Czech Republic, Hungary and Norway express the most negative views while respondents in Ireland, Slovenia and United Kingdom expressed somewhat less but still quite negative views toward foreigners' impact on the crime problems in society. Negative attitudes toward foreigners impact on the health and welfare systems are most pronounced in Greece, Ireland, Czech Republic, and Hungary (mean values are 7.01, 6.39, 6.47, and 6.46, respectively) and least pronounced in Italy and Portugal (where the impact of foreigners is not viewed on average in negative terms with mean values reaching 4.98 and 4.59, respectively). In general, the data reveal the moderate level of

128

negative attitudes toward foreigners' impact on the health and welfare systems in the "old immigration" West European countries. Negative views toward foreigners' impact on jobs were most pronounced in Greece and Portugal but were also quite pronounced in East European countries such as Poland and Hungary. In these countries, respondents tend to suggest that foreigners (people who come to live in their country) are more likely to take jobs from workers than to help to create new jobs. In

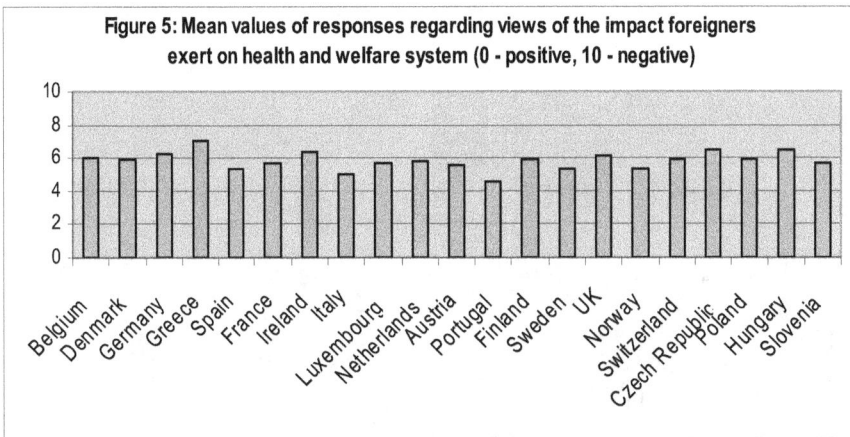

Figure 5: Mean values of responses regarding views of the impact foreigners exert on health and welfare system (0 - positive, 10 - negative)

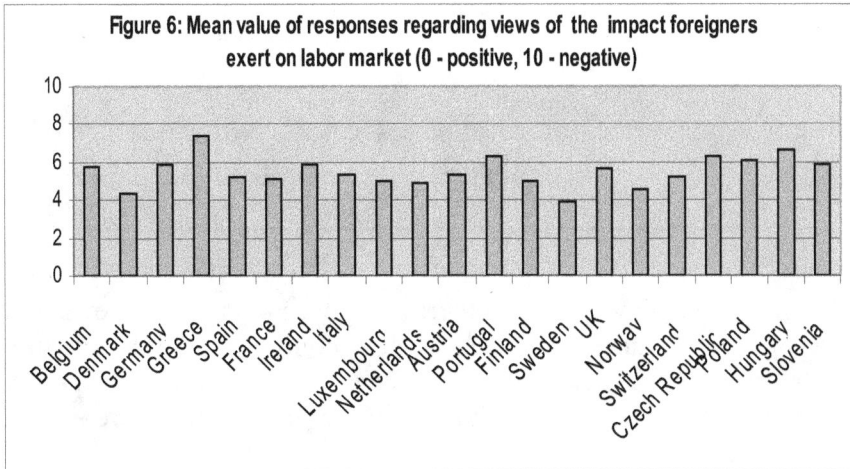

Figure 6: Mean value of responses regarding views of the impact foreigners exert on labor market (0 - positive, 10 - negative)

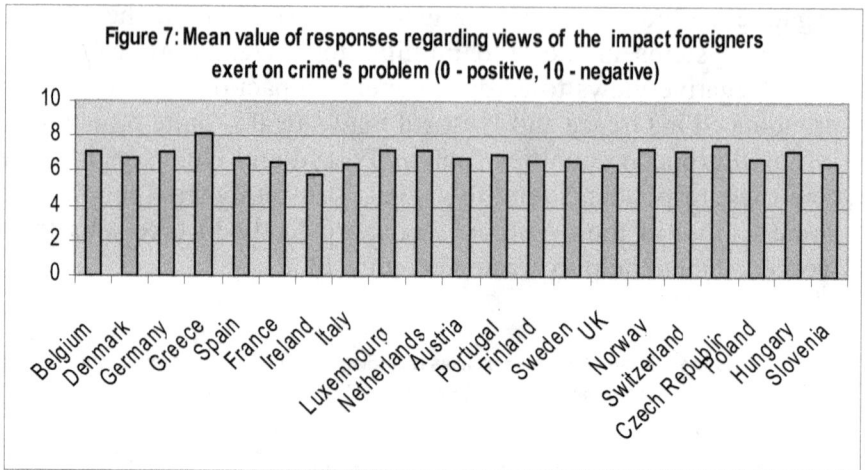

Figure 7: Mean value of responses regarding views of the impact foreigners exert on crime's problem (0 - positive, 10 - negative)

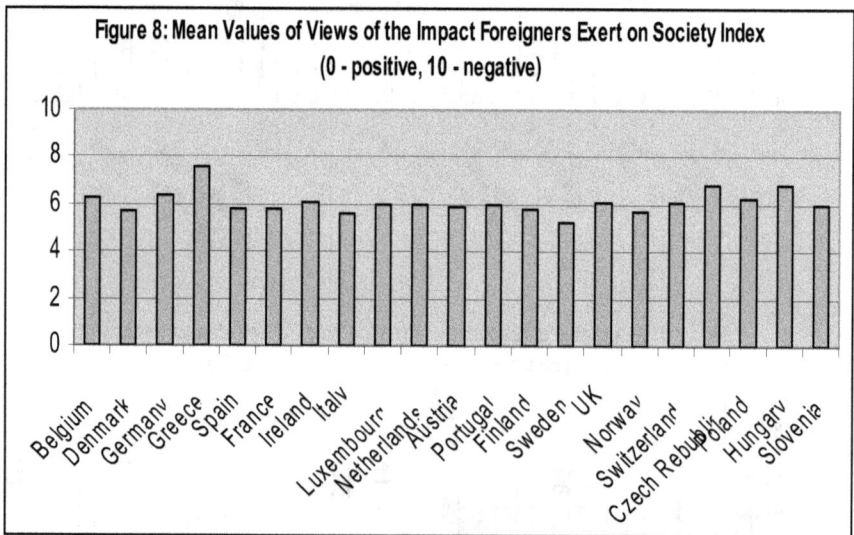

Figure 8: Mean Values of Views of the Impact Foreigners Exert on Society Index (0 - positive, 10 - negative)

France, Luxembourg, the Netherlands, and Finland, the views with regard to foreigners' impact on the economy and jobs creation were, on average, neutral, and in places such as Sweden, Denmark, and Norway, the views with regard to job creation were even slightly positive.

130

Conclusions

The data presented in this chapter clearly reveal that negative views toward foreigners had dramatically increased toward the end of the twentieth century. Currently, anti-foreigner sentiments are widely spread across European countries, even in countries with a relatively low presence of foreign populations. Foreigners and immigrants are not viewed by the majority of the native population in positive terms. Rather they are believed to exert negative impact on society. The native populations tend to suggest that foreigners are exploiting the welfare and health systems, that they take jobs away from the local populations, and that they are one of the causes of crime and delinquency in society. Indeed, they are viewed as a source of competitive threat.

Studies on sources of prejudice and discrimination suggest that negative views toward out-group populations are more prevalent among persons who have low education, are unemployed, and who hold conservative political ideology. The net of individual-level attributes of the populations studies reveals that negative views toward out-group populations tend to be more pronounced in places with high proportions of the out-group population and in places with depressed economic conditions. Thus, in an era when the foreign population is consistently rising and becoming a source of tension and even violence, the issue discussed here should become a major focus of both social scientists and policy makers.

Appendix A:		
Variables, Definitions and Measurements, and Data Source		
Variables	**Definition**	**Source**
Anti-Foreigner Sentiment	Percent of items on which respondents express negative view toward foreigners. The items are expressed as follows: "Foreigners exploit our social welfare system." "The presence of foreigners in our country increases unemployment." "The presence of foreigners is one of causes of delinquency and violence."	Eurobarometer Surveys: (30) for 1988 (Reif and Melich); (53) for 2000 (Hartung).
Views of the Impact Foreigners Exert on Society	Measured on 0–10 scale: 0 = positive, 10 = negative The items are expressed as follows:	European Social Survey for 2002/3
	"Most people who come to live here work and pay taxes. They also use health and welfare services. On balance, do you think people who come here take out more than they put in or put in more than they take out?"	
	"Would you say that people who come to live here generally take jobs away from workers in [country], or generally help to create new jobs?"	
	"Are [country]'s crime problems made worse or better by people coming to live here from other countries?"	

References

Baldwin-Edwards, Martin and Martin A. Schain. 1994. "The Politics of Immigration: Introduction." Pp: 1-16 in *The Politics of Immigration in Western Europe*, edited by M. Baldwin-Edwards and M. A. Schain. Essex: Frank Class and Co.

Baumgartl, Bernd and Adrian Favell (editors). 1995. *New Xenophobia in Europe*. London: Kluwer Law International.

Castles, Stephen and Godula Kosack. 1985. *Immigrant workers and class structure in Western Europe*. London: Oxford University Press

Castles, Stephen and Mark J. Miller. 1993. *The Age of Migration. International Population Movements in the Modern World.* New York: Guilford Press.

Coenders, Marcel. 2001. *Nationalistic Attitudes and Ethnic Exclusionism in a Comparative Perspective: An Empirical Study of Attitudes Toward the Country and Ethnic Immigrants in 22 Countries.* Ph.D. dissertation. ICS. Nijmnegen University.

European Social Survey 1-2002. ESS data file. Retrieved from http://ess.nsd.uib.no.

Faist, Thomas. 1994. "How to define a foreigner? The symbolic politics of immigration in German partisan discourse, 1978–1992." Pp: 50–71 in *The Politics of Immigration in Western Europe*, edited by M. Baldwin-Edwards and M. A. Schain. Essex: Frank Class and Co.

Fetzer, Joel S. 2000. *Public Attitudes toward Invigoration in the United States, France, and Germany.* New-York: Cambridge University Press.

Gijsberts , Mérove, Louk Hagendoorn and Peer Scheepers. 2004. *Nationalism and Exclusion of Migrants. Cross-National Comparisons.* Aldershot: Ashgate

Hartung, Halard. *Eurobarometer 53: Racism, Information Society, General Services, and Food Labeling, April-May 2000* [Computer File]. 3rd ICPSR version. Brussels, Belgium: INRA (Europe) [producer], 2000. Cologne, Germany: Zentralarchiv fur Empirische Sozialforschung/Ann Arbor, MI: Inter-University Consortium for Political and Social Research [distributors], 2002.

Lahav, Galliya. 2004. *Immigration and Politics in the New Europe. Reinventing Borders.* Cambridge: Cambridge University Press

Pettigrew, Thomas F. 1998. "Reaction toward the new Minorities of Western Europe." *Annual Review of Sociology* 24: 77–103.

Reif, Karlheinz and Anna Melich. *Eurobarometer 30: Immigrants and Out-Groups in Western Europe, October-November 1988* [Computer File]. Conducted by Fairs et Opinions, Paris. 2nd ICPSR ed. Ann Arbor, MI: Inter-University Consortium for Political and Social Research [producer and distributor], 1992.

Sassen, Saskia. 1996. "Loosing Control: Sovereignty in an Age of Globalization." *The 1995 Columbia University Schoff Memorial Lectures.* New York: Columbia University Press.

133

Scheepers, Peer, Merove Gijberts, and Marcel Coenders. 2002. "Ethnic Exclusionism in European Countries: Public Oppositions to Civil Rights for legal Migrants as a Response to Perceived Threat." *European Sociological Review* 18:17–34.

Schnapper, Dominique. 1994. "The Debate on Immigration and the Crisis of National Identity." Pp: 127–139 in *The Politics of Immigration in Western Europe,* edited by M. Balwin-Edwards and M. Schain. Essex: Frank Cass and Co.

Semyonov, Moshe, Rebecca Raijman and Anastasia Gorodzeisky. Forthcoming 2006. "The Rise of Anti-Foreigner Sentiment in European Societies, 1988–2000." *American Sociological Review.*

Soysal, Yasemin N. 1994. *Limits of Citizenship. Migrants and Postnational Membership in Europe.* Chicago: The University of Chicago Press.

Chapter 7

Anti-Semitism and Islamophobia:
Education for Tolerance and Understanding

Shashi Tharoor, Former Under-Secretary-General of the United Nations

Anti-Semitism is a blot on the record of humanity. It has a long and ugly history. It has wrought unfathomable havoc and destruction on millions of ordinary people, and not only in the twentieth century.

The recent rise in anti-Semitism is most definitely a threat to people everywhere, and fighting it is the responsibility of everyone. As George Santanya said it so eloquently, "Those who cannot remember the past are condemned to repeat it." And this Organization was created to ensure that the history of the first half of the twentieth century is not repeated.

I am glad of having references made to other aspects and variations of racism. I'll never forget one of my closest friends at the United Nations—in fact, one of my mentors early in my career—is a holocaust survivor. He actually was one of the few people to survive both Auschwitz and Mauthausen and who devoted his entire life to the United Nations, particularly working for the High Commissioner for Refugees. He and I were talking one day—he still bears the notorious tattoo on his arm—about racism. And he said, "You know something"—his name is Tom Luke, he lives in Geneva—"the first face I saw opening the window and letting in light into the concentration camp where I was lying at death's door was that of a black American soldier." He said to me, "Racism is impossible. That black face was the face of freedom."

And I think it was a stark reminder of how all sorts of discrimination in this world—all sorts of humiliations visited upon people because of what they cannot help but be—lie deep in the behavior patterns of people who ought to know better. That, I think, is why we speak of education. Not education in the sense of learning the high technology that tells you what sort of gas to pump into the concentration chamber, but rather the education of values, the education of mutual respect, the education that enables people to recognize the dignity in others who are not like them, and that is an education that I think we at the United Nations, and in my department in particular, rededicate ourselves to today.

It is true that the United Nations has not always lived up to its ideals by facing up squarely against anti-Semitism. I hope today's seminar will be the first of many efforts by our organization to do this, to face up squarely and, as I have said, my own department will use the tools of education and civic outreach as our major weapons.

But we also understand, and I know Anne Bayefsky and Felice Gaer and many others have said this, that action is also needed, action in the political sphere. And I have to say there are a number of suggestions that have to be made, many of which are for Member States, some of which are for the Secretary-General himself, few of which, I am sorry to say, fall within the remit of my own department—the Department of Public Information.

But, having organized this seminar, we have an obligation to help try and take this to the next step, and so what I am going to do is to ask my staff to compile all the suggestions that have been made, both from the podium and from the floor, to convey those to the Secretary-General as suggestions emerging from this meeting. For our own part, we will contact some of the panellists who have come up with some of these ideas, and others who have expressed interest in working with us, to see whether we can't constitute an informal, I wouldn't even call it something as pompous as a working group, but just an informal sounding board if you like, to decide how best we can follow up on some of the things, that we in my department can do, while conveying to the Secretary-General those things that he, within his authority, can do.

But don't forget that his own major suggestion this morning in his speech, that our Member States might draw a leaf from the

136

OSCE's book and use the U.N.'s unique legitimacy to explicitly afford Jews the protection that they have extended to other victims of prejudice, that suggestion too is beyond his authority. It is only the Member States who can actually act upon it.

I don't want to say that we are in any way trying to shirk the responsibilities that we have so openly welcomed today, but I do want to ask for some realism on the part of everyone in this room in terms of your expectations of how change can be brought about. It is often a slow process, but it is a process on which we are resolutely embarked, and if it is only a first step and it is a small step, please do not be impatient and assume that the end of the journey must come tomorrow. It will take time. There will be others who have other views, there will be a process that needs to be gone through, but we have at least opened today a new chapter that I hope will mean that the next time some of you come to this building, you will see it as much your home as those of the many, many countries of the world who take the U.N. as a forum to express their complaints and dissatisfactions, but also, above all, their hopes for the future.

You know, sometimes amongst all of the criticism of the U.N., there used to be a bumper sticker in this country, and I suspect some of you probably, judging by some of the things I've heard today, may have welcomed that bumper sticker that said, "Let's get the U.N. out of the U.S. and the U.S. out of the U.N." Well, whenever I saw that bumper sticker, I was reminded of a dreadful old story about Adam and Eve in the Garden of Eden, where Adam found that Eve was becoming a bit indifferent to him. So Adam said to Eve, "Eve, is there someone else?"

Now you think about that for a minute, because it's exactly the question you can ask about the United Nations. Is there another organization in which all of us, irrespective of our nationality, our race, our gender, our value system, our religious faith, can come, knowing that there is a universality that the world brings to this place that alone can bring about change, where people of all these backgrounds can work together for common objectives in the name of our common humanity, a place where we can dream the same dreams together? There is not. This is the one organization we have, let's work together in it and with it to achieve the objectives that we all share.

***

Every one of us has many identities. Sometimes religion obliges us to deny the truth about our own complexity by obliterating the multiplicity inherent in our identities. It's true that fundamentalism, and Islamic fundamentalism, is no exception, does so because in many ways fundamentalism reflects a passion for pure belonging, a yearning intensified by the threatening tidal wave of globalization, as well as by the nature of Middle Eastern politics, in the Islamic case, which I think have been elements that have infused undercurrents in at least some of the discussions today.

Of course there is something precious and valuable in a faith that allows a human being to see herself at one with others stretching their hands out toward God around the world. But can we, and I am asking the question because I don't expect an answer but for you to think some more, can we separate religion from identity? Can we dream of a world in which religion has an honored place, but where the need for spirituality, for a connection to the divine, will no longer be associated with a need to belong?

If we can accept the truth that we each have multiple identities—that you can be a good Muslim, a good Jordanian, a good Arab, a good human being, all at once, the same person—and that each of these identities can live in harmony with other identities, then we might resist intolerance more effectively.

There have been references to terrorism today, and we know there have been references to bigotry as well. But terrorism and bigotry both emerge from blind hatred of an Other, with a capital O, and that in turn is the product of three factors: fear, rage, and incomprehension. Fear of what the Other might do to you, rage at what you believe the Other has done to you, and incomprehension about who or what the Other really is; these three elements fuse together in igniting the deadly combustion that assaults, and even destroys, people whose only sin sometimes is that they feel none of these things themselves.

Let me repeat that mantra—fear, rage, and incomprehension. Isn't that also how the world responded, certainly the United States responded, after the attacks of 9/11? And not surprisingly, I might say, that perhaps most of us in this room may have responded that way too.

What is reprehensible and just plain wrong is when we attach these understandable emotional responses to the same blind hatred of the Other that is the source of terrorism, when we direct our anger not at the perpetrators of these crimes but at everyone who shares their color, their hair color, their ethnicity, who believes in the teachings they claim to be following.

The ends to both terrorism and to Islamophobia are to be found in the same place. If they are to be tackled and ended, we will have to deal with each of these factors by attacking the ignorance that sustains them. We will have to know each other better, have to learn to see ourselves as others see us, learn to recognize hatred and deal with its causes, learn to dispel fear and above all just learn about each other.

I know this is no small challenge, but we have heard a lot today that I think has given us all food for thought in taking this all forward. But since we have heard so much reference to Judaism, to Christianity, as well as of course today to Islam, let me perhaps end with a story from a different religious tradition, that of Hinduism, which Dr. Jayaraman had also mentioned earlier today.

I am after all, as some of you know, also an Indian writer, so I think I should end by telling you an Indian story. It's a tale from our ancient Puranas; it is a typical Indian story of a sage and his disciples, in which the sage asks his disciples, "When does the night end?" And the disciples say, "Well, at dawn, of course."

139

The sage says, "I know that, but when does the night end and the dawn begin?" Well the first disciple, who is from the tropical south of India where I come from and Dr. Jayaraman comes from, replies: "Oh, I know, when the first glimmer of light across the sky reveals the palm fronds on the coconut trees swaying in the breeze, that is when the night ends and the dawn begins."

The sage says no, so the second disciple, who is from the cold north of my country, ventures: "Oh, I know, when the first streaks of sunshine make the snow and ice gleam and glitter white on the mountaintops of the Himalayas, that is when the night ends and the dawn begins."

The sage says, "No, my sons. When two travelers from opposite ends of our land meet and embrace each other as brothers, and when they realize they sleep under the same sky, see the same stars and dream the same dreams—that is when the night ends and the dawn begins." That's a two-thousand-year-old story.

There has been many a terrible night in the century that has just passed. I think one lesson we can all take away from today's meeting, and from the series on Unlearning Intolerance, is let us preserve the diversity of the human spirit to ensure that we will all have a new dawn in the century that has just begun.

Chapter 8

America's Human Development Report on Race

Cedric Herring and Alice Palmer

Competing views about the nature and extent of racism and racial discrimination lead to different recommendations about what, if anything, we need to be doing. These disagreements have obvious implications for debates about equal opportunity policies (such as affirmative action), employment policies, debates about poverty and underemployment, and racial differences in income, incarceration rates, and access to education and health care.

America's prosperity during the 1990s showed all too clearly that there is no automatic link between economic growth and human development. Even today, for example, it is possible to read about such seemingly contradictory occurrences as "jobless recoveries," the "working poor," "corporate downsizing" despite growing profits, industrial relocation in spite of reduced production costs, "permanent contingent" workers, etc. Often, these contradictory occurrences compound racial and ethnic disparities in such domains as health, education, employment, security, political involvement, and socioeconomic status.

Below, we present some data that we have been analyzing for *America's Human Development Report on Race*. This project explicitly speaks to race and public policy concerns and informs policy with respect to several quality-of-life issues in the United States. We have developed social indicators that we hope are not only useful to scholars and researchers but also to activists and policy makers who want to arm themselves to address racism and racial disparities in American society. The project has been modeled (loosely) on the international *Human Development Report* that is produced annually by the United Nations Development

141

Programme. We present our findings in the hope that they will be useful to scholars, activists, and policymakers.

What Is Human Development, and What Is the Project About?

Human development is about more than the rise or fall of national incomes or the gross domestic product. It is about creating an environment in which people can develop to their full potential and lead productive, creative lives in accord with their needs and interests. We take the position that people are the real wealth of a nation. Development is about expanding the choices people have to lead lives that they value. And it is thus about much more than economic growth, which is only a means of increasing the choices available to people. Fundamental to increasing choices is building human capabilities, the range of things that people can do or be in life. The most basic capabilities for human development are (1) to lead long and healthy lives, (2) to be knowledgeable, and (3) to have access to the resources needed for a decent standard of living and to be able to participate in the life of one's community. Without these basics, many choices are simply not available, and many opportunities in life are not really accessible.

We also take the position that, with the right policies, the United States can advance faster in human development than in economic growth, and if the United States ensures that growth favors the poor and the disadvantaged, it can do much more with that growth to promote human development.

The United Nations Human Development Programme's Human Development Index (or HDI) measures only the average national achievement in a country. Disaggregating a country's HDI by race and ethnicity can shed light on stark disparities. The United States, for example, consistently ranks among the top 5 countries in terms of human development, or quality of life. But the question is what does this mean for the standard of living for people of color? Our project makes it possible to determine what the disparities are in terms of human development by racial and ethnic subgroups.

142

Measuring Human Development

The Human Development Index is a composite measure of human development. It measures the overall achievement in a country in three basic dimensions of human development: longevity, knowledge, and standard of living. It is measured by life expectancy, educational attainment (adult literacy and combined primary, secondary, and tertiary enrollment), and adjusted income per capita in purchasing power parity. The HDI is a summary, not a comprehensive measure of human development.

Initial Meetings

As mentioned earlier, this project began with an initial meeting between Lord Meghnad Desai (Professor and Chair of the Centre for the Study of Global Governance at the London School of Economics and a lead consultant to the United Nations Development Programme in the preparation of their international *Human Development Report)* and approximately twenty scholars, policy analysts, and policymakers. In that meeting, those assembled discussed the scope, subject matter and content, resource needs, data needs and availability, division of labor, timeframes for completion, and related topics for the project.

Subsequent meetings consisted of consultations with key opinion leaders about the kinds of quality of life indicators they find useful in informing decisions that they must make or in processing information that they must analyze. We also held working meetings with scholars who formed the core of the research team and subsequent planning meetings with Lord Desai. We found that there was great interest in and commitment to such a project. In subsequent meetings, the team worked through the process of identifying indicators that are integrative, comprehensive, comparable across locales, multidisciplinary in scope, and useful to policymakers and others concerned about issues on the public agenda.

So, what are we doing in concrete terms? We compiled data from several sources, but especially from the Current Population

143

Surveys. We generated statistics for over two hundred American cities on things such as mean years of educational attainment, percent with bachelor's degrees, percent below the poverty line, mean household income, per capita income, mortality rates, infant mortality rates, and neo-natal mortality rates by race/ethnicity for each of these cities. We used this information to create a database that now contains these summary statistics.

We used the information in the database to generate eight indexes that reflect (1) education, (2) income, and (3) health—the three dimensions that the UN HDI taps. We took these eight indexes that reflect the three dimensions and combined them into an overall Human Development Index Score for each racial and ethnic group for each of the more than two hundred cities.

The following charts, graphs, and tables summarize the findings from our analysis.

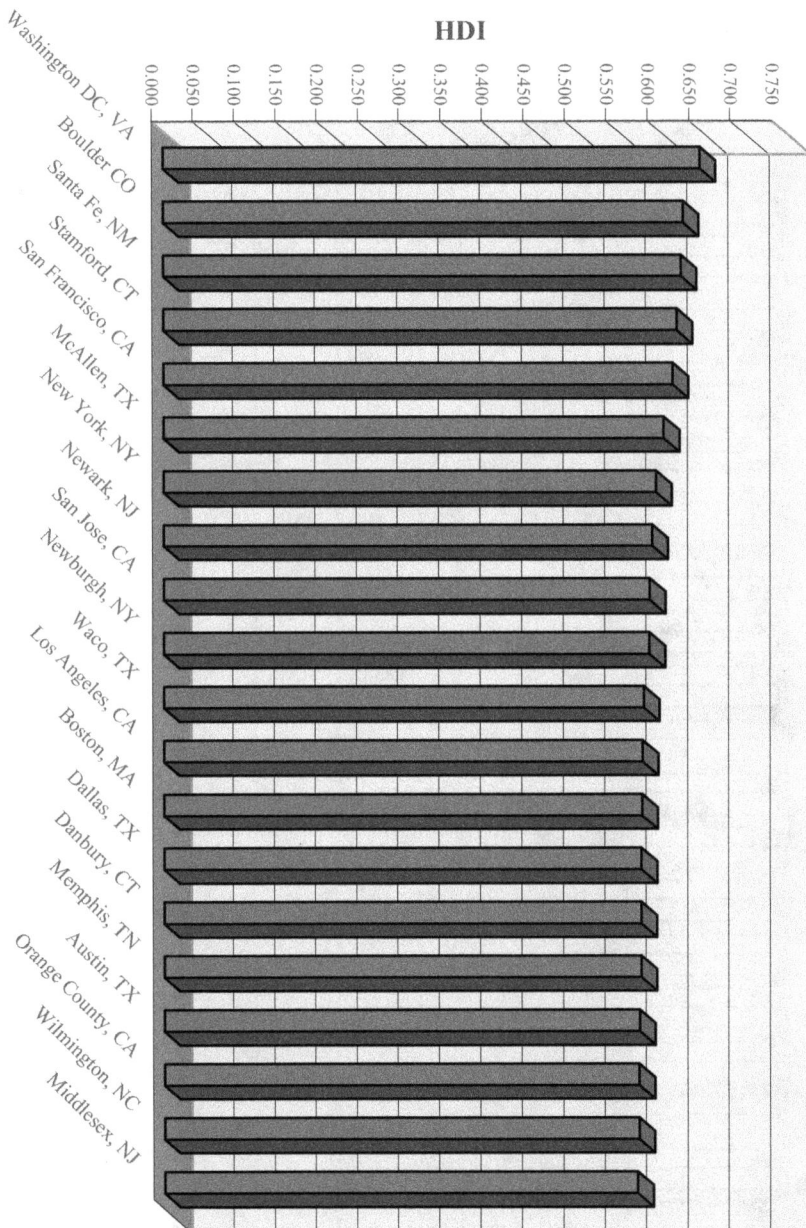

Human Development Index (HDI) for Whites by City
Top 20 Cities

HDI

Washington DC, VA
Boulder CO
Santa Fe, NM
Stamford, CT
San Francisco, CA
McAllen, TX
New York, NY
Newark, NJ
San Jose, CA
Newburgh, NY
Waco, TX
Los Angeles, CA
Boston, MA
Dallas, TX
Danbury, CT
Memphis, TN
Austin, TX
Orange County, CA
Wilmington, NC
Middlesex, NJ

0.000 0.050 0.100 0.150 0.200 0.250 0.300 0.350 0.400 0.450 0.500 0.550 0.600 0.650 0.700 0.750

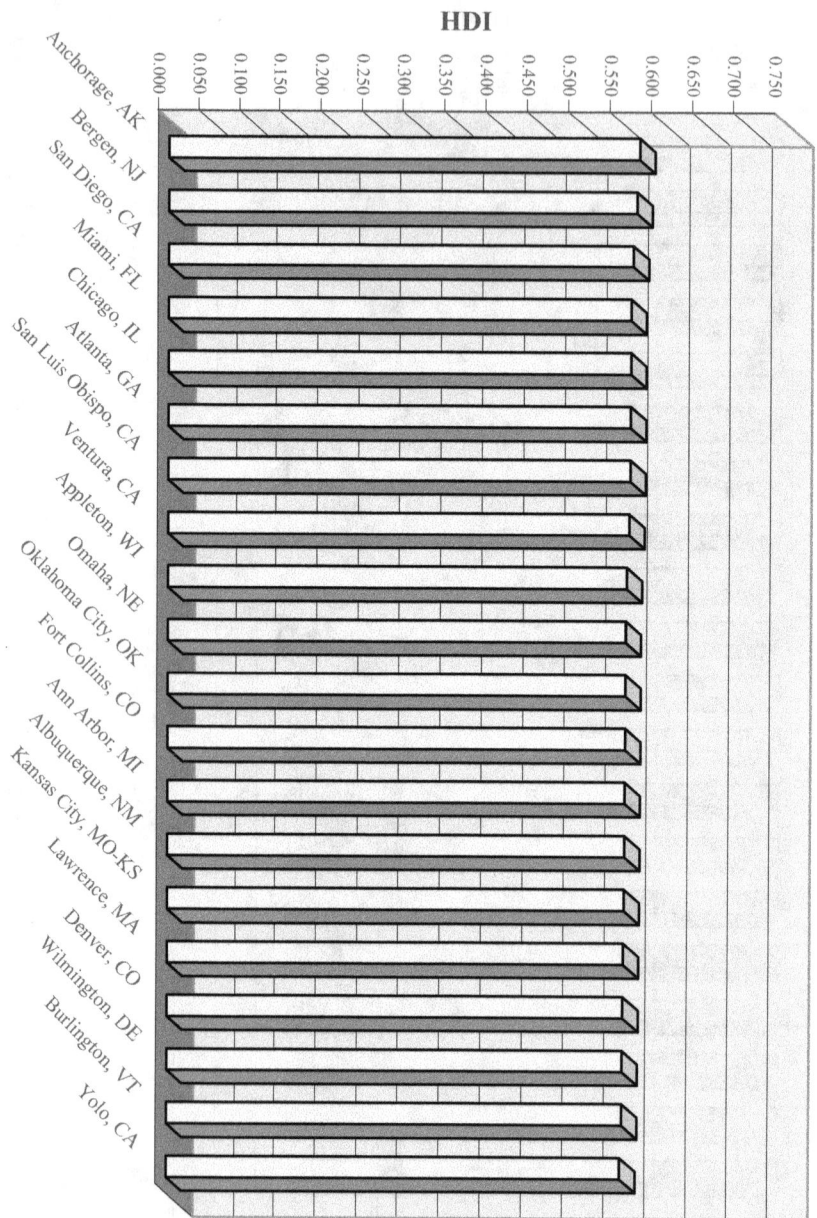

Human Development Index (HDI) for Whites by City Cities Ranked 21-40

HDI

Anchorage, AK
Bergen, NJ
San Diego, CA
Miami, FL
Chicago, IL
Atlanta, GA
San Luis Obispo, CA
Ventura, CA
Appleton, WI
Omaha, NE
Oklahoma City, OK
Fort Collins, CO
Ann Arbor, MI
Albuquerque, NM
Kansas City, MO-KS
Lawrence, MA
Denver, CO
Wilmington, DE
Burlington, VT
Yolo, CA

0.000
0.050
0.100
0.150
0.200
0.250
0.300
0.350
0.400
0.450
0.500
0.550
0.600
0.650
0.700
0.750

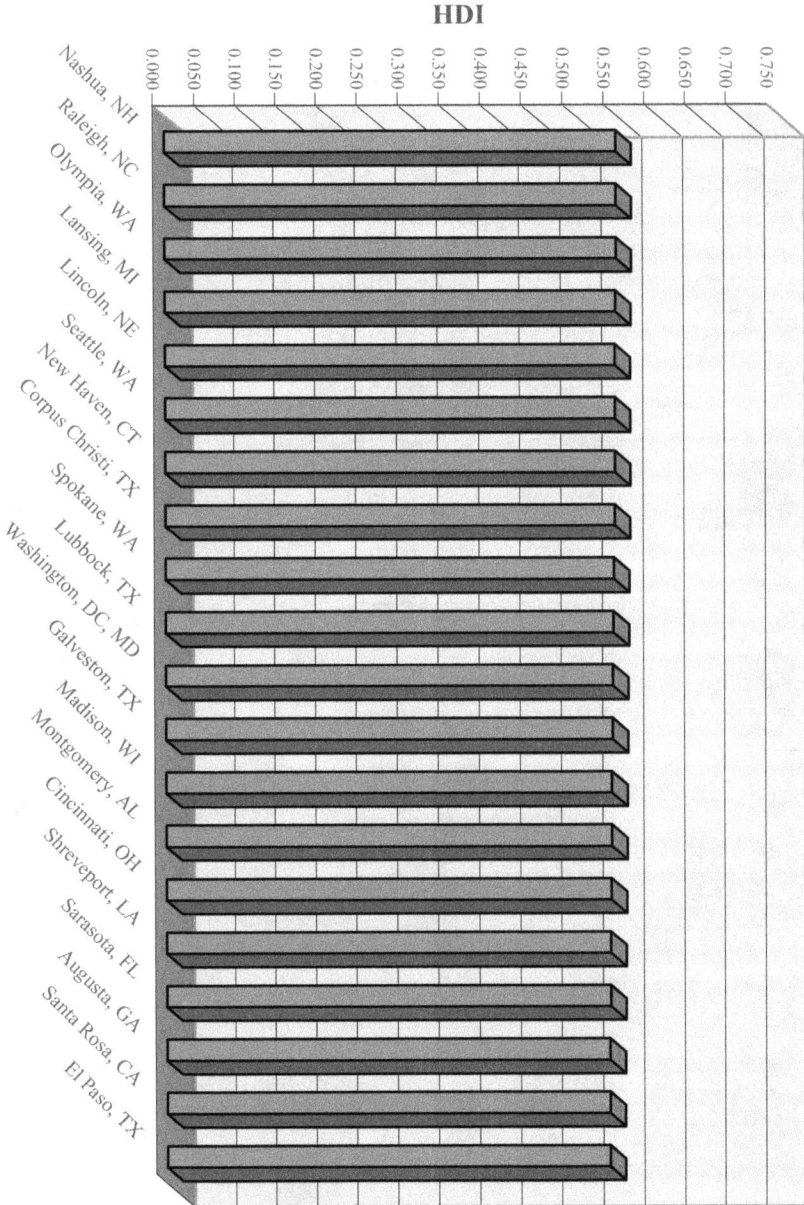

Human Development Index (HDI) for Whites by City
Cities Ranked 41-60

HDI

Nashua, NH
Raleigh, NC
Olympia, WA
Lansing, MI
Lincoln, NE
Seattle, WA
New Haven, CT
Corpus Christi, TX
Spokane, WA
Lubbock, TX
Washington, DC, MD
Galveston, TX
Madison, WI
Montgomery, AL
Cincinnati, OH
Shreveport, LA
Sarasota, FL
Augusta, GA
Santa Rosa, CA
El Paso, TX

0.000 0.050 0.100 0.150 0.200 0.250 0.300 0.350 0.400 0.450 0.500 0.550 0.600 0.650 0.700 0.750

HDI

Human Development Index (HDI) for Whites by City
Cities Ranked 61-80

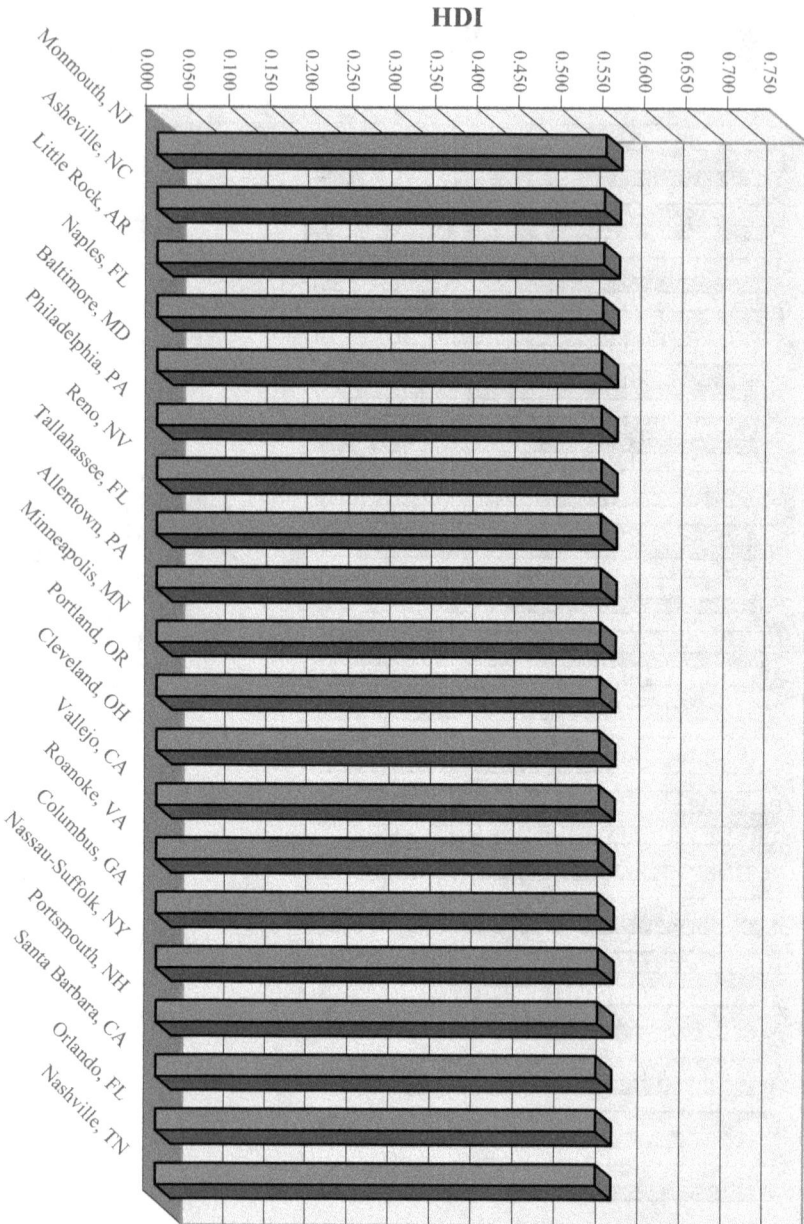

0.000
0.050
0.100
0.150
0.200
0.250
0.300
0.350
0.400
0.450
0.500
0.550
0.600
0.650
0.700
0.750

Monmouth, NJ
Asheville, NC
Little Rock, AR
Naples, FL
Baltimore, MD
Philadelphia, PA
Reno, NV
Tallahassee, FL
Allentown, PA
Minneapolis, MN
Portland, OR
Cleveland, OH
Vallejo, CA
Roanoke, VA
Columbus, GA
Nassau-Suffolk, NY
Portsmouth, NH
Santa Barbara, CA
Orlando, FL
Nashville, TN

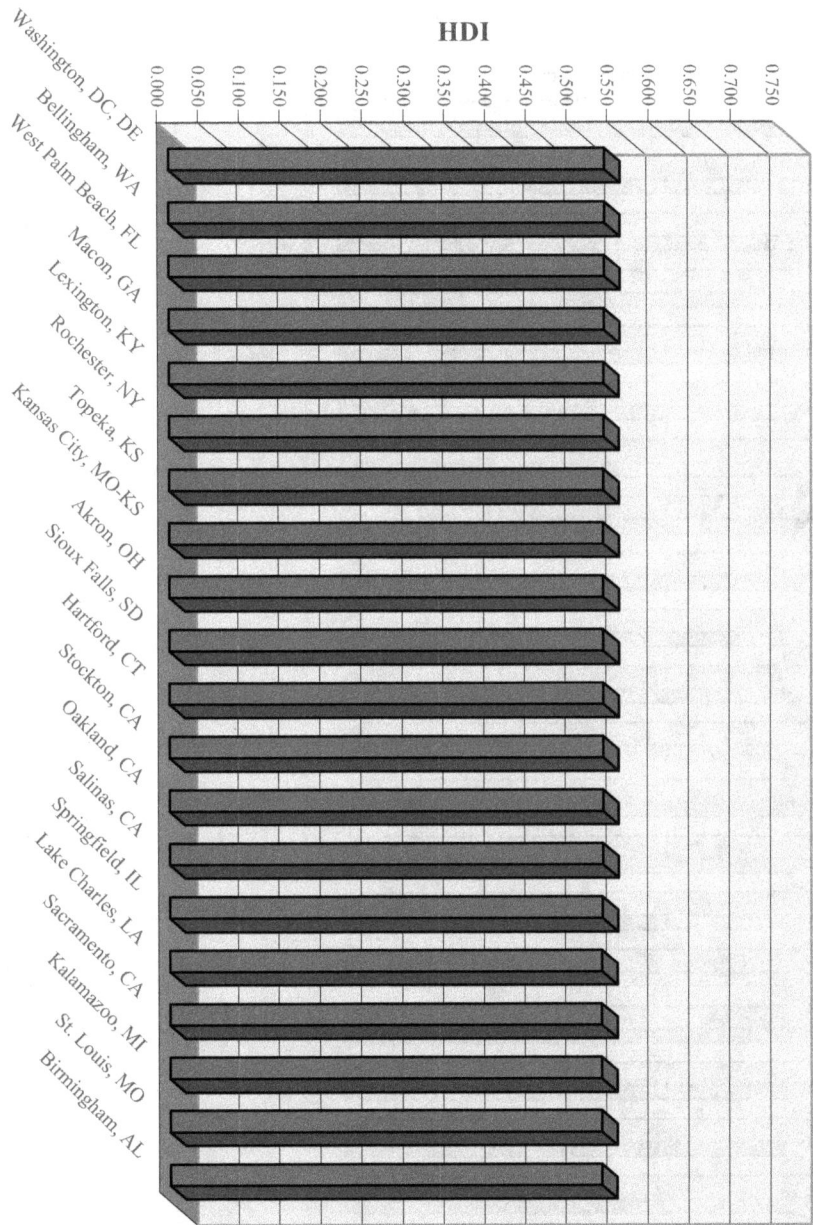

**Human Development Index (HDI) for Whites by City
Cities Ranked 81-100**

HDI

Washington, DC, DE
Bellingham, WA
West Palm Beach, FL
Macon, GA
Lexington, KY
Rochester, NY
Topeka, KS
Kansas City, MO-KS
Akron, OH
Sioux Falls, SD
Hartford, CT
Stockton, CA
Oakland, CA
Salinas, CA
Springfield, IL
Lake Charles, LA
Sacramento, CA
Kalamazoo, MI
St. Louis, MO
Birmingham, AL

0.000
0.050
0.100
0.150
0.200
0.250
0.300
0.350
0.400
0.450
0.500
0.550
0.600
0.650
0.700
0.750

Human Development Index (HDI) for Whites by City
Cities Ranked 101-120

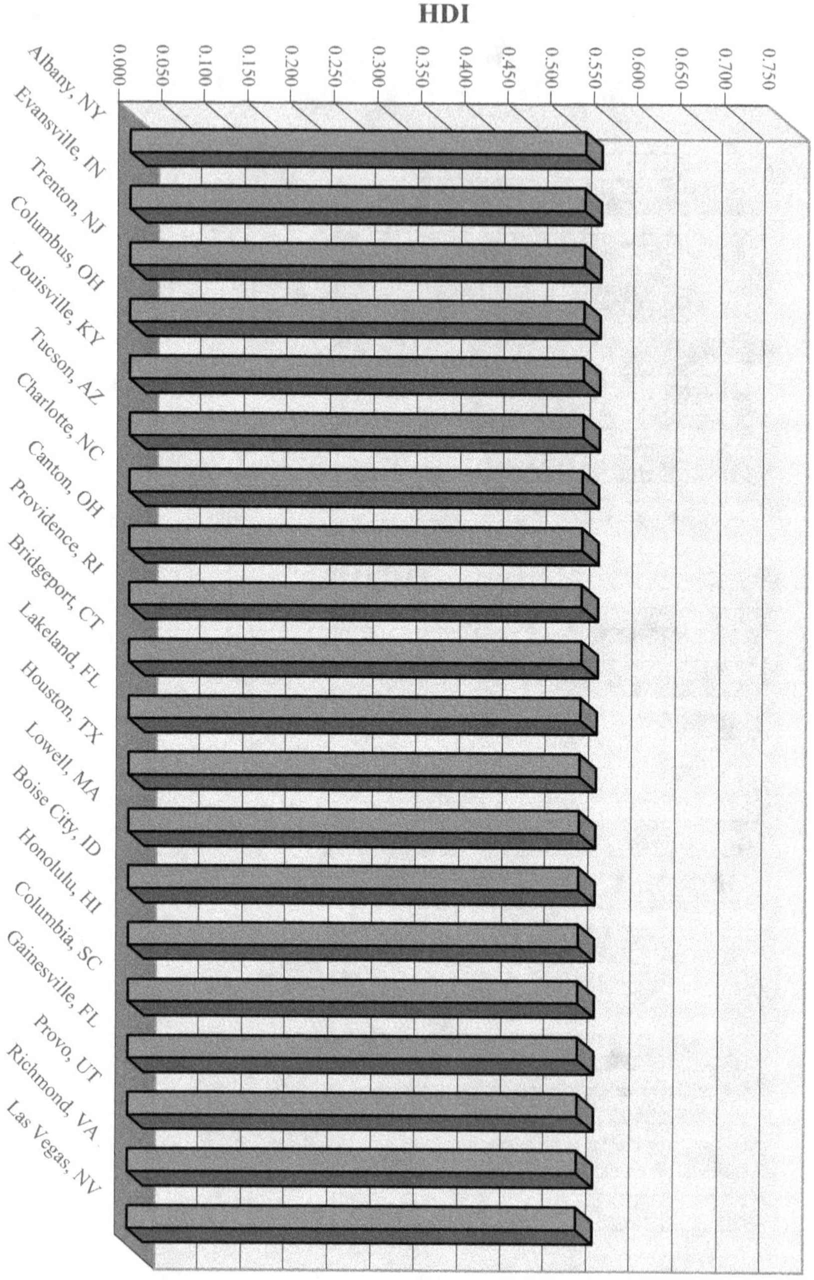
HDI
0.000
0.050
0.100
0.150
0.200
0.250
0.300
0.350
0.400
0.450
0.500
0.550
0.600
0.650
0.700
0.750
Albany, NY
Evansville, IN
Trenton, NJ
Columbus, OH
Louisville, KY
Tucson, AZ
Charlotte, NC
Canton, OH
Providence, RI
Bridgeport, CT
Lakeland, FL
Houston, TX
Lowell, MA
Boise City, ID
Honolulu, HI
Columbia, SC
Gainesville, FL
Provo, UT
Richmond, VA
Las Vegas, NV

HDI

Human Development Index (HDI) for Whites by City
Cities Ranked 121-140

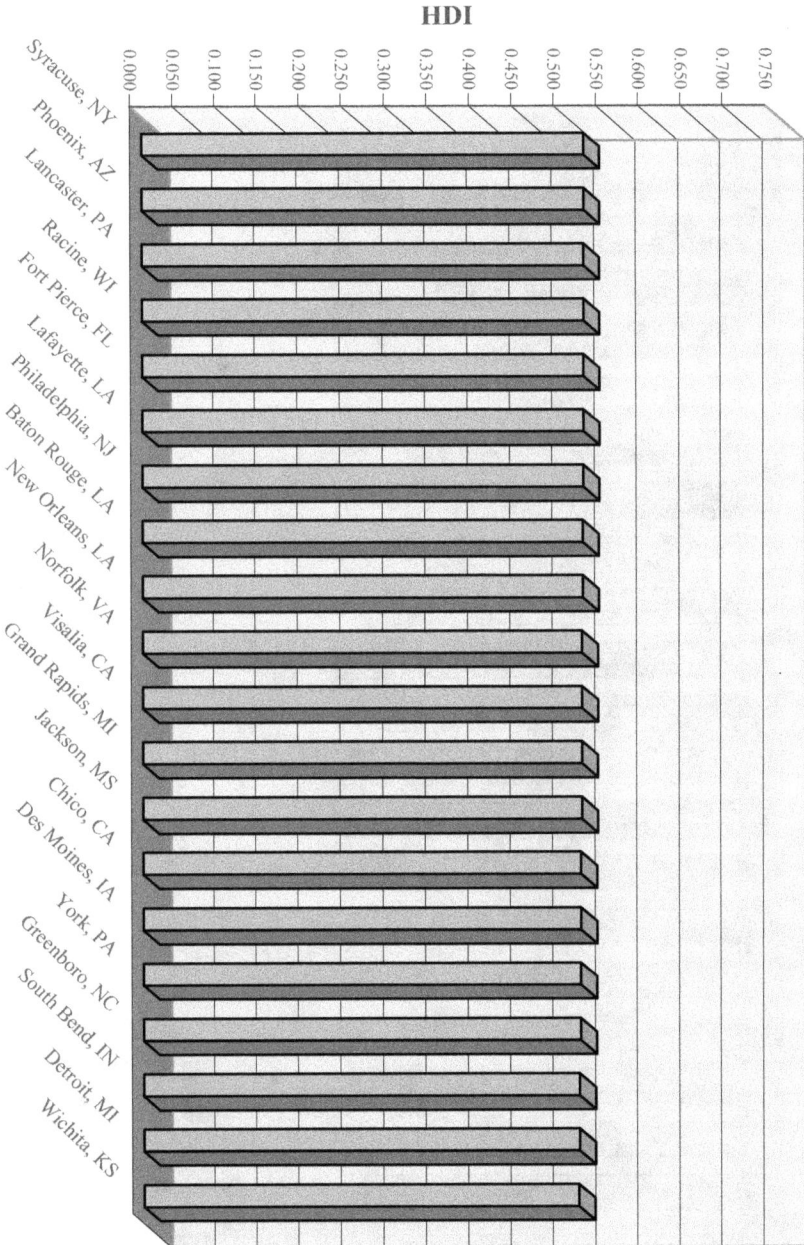

Syracuse, NY
Phoenix, AZ
Lancaster, PA
Racine, WI
Fort Pierce, FL
Lafayette, LA
Philadelphia, NJ
Baton Rouge, LA
New Orleans, LA
Norfolk, VA
Visalia, CA
Grand Rapids, MI
Jackson, MS
Chico, CA
Des Moines, IA
York, PA
Greenboro, NC
South Bend, IN
Detroit, MI
Wichita, KS

0.000
0.050
0.100
0.150
0.200
0.250
0.300
0.350
0.400
0.450
0.500
0.550
0.600
0.650
0.700
0.750

HDI

Human Development Index (HDI) for Whites by City
Cities Ranked 141-160

Colorado Springs, CO
Vineland, NJ
Buffalo, NY
Punta Gorda, FL
Charleston, SC
Knoxville, TN
Panama City, FL
Milwaukee, WI
Dayton-, OH
Augusta, SC
Davenport, IA
Toledo, OH
Tulsa, OK
Flint, MI
Wheeling, WV
Mobile, AL
Indianapolis, IN
New London, CT
Utica, NY
Portland, ME

0.000
0.050
0.100
0.150
0.200
0.250
0.300
0.350
0.400
0.450
0.500
0.550
0.600
0.650
0.700
0.750

Human Development Index (HDI) for Whites by City
Cities Ranked 161-180

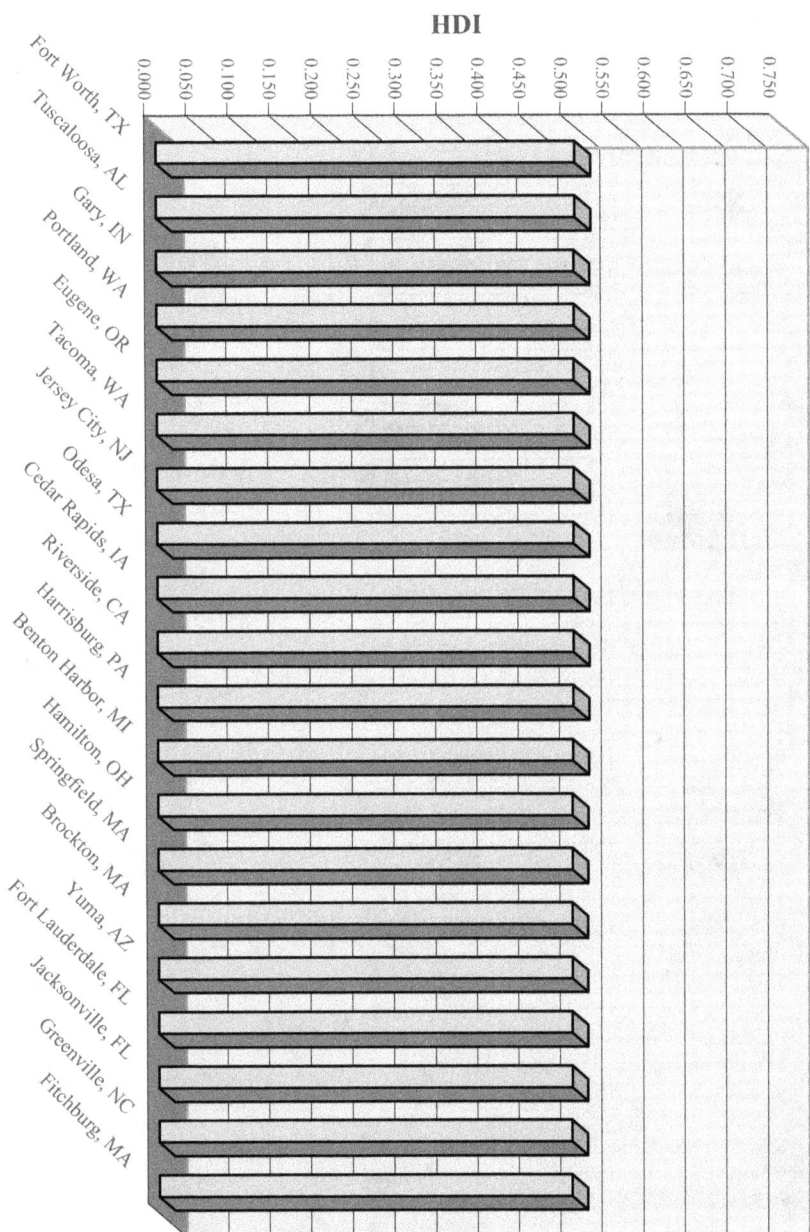

HDI

Fort Worth, TX	
Tuscaloosa, AL	
Gary, IN	
Portland, WA	
Eugene, OR	
Tacoma, WA	
Jersey City, NJ	
Odesa, TX	
Cedar Rapids, IA	
Riverside, CA	
Harrisburg, PA	
Benton Harbor, MI	
Hamilton, OH	
Springfield, MA	
Brockton, MA	
Yuma, AZ	
Fort Lauderdale, FL	
Jacksonville, FL	
Greenville, NC	
Fitchburg, MA	

Axis values: 0.000, 0.050, 0.100, 0.150, 0.200, 0.250, 0.300, 0.350, 0.400, 0.450, 0.500, 0.550, 0.600, 0.650, 0.700, 0.750

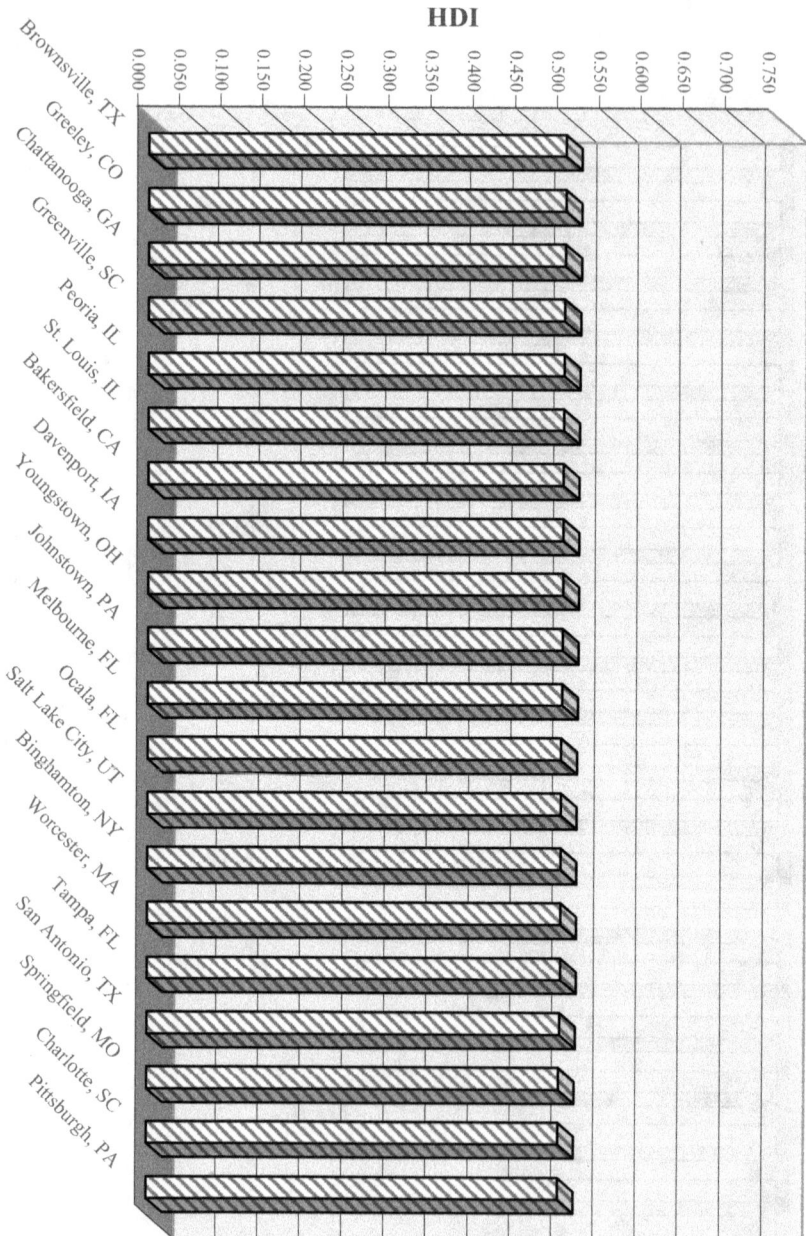

Human Development Index (HDI) for Whites by City
Cities Ranked 181-200

HDI

Brownsville, TX
Greeley, CO
Chattanooga, GA
Greenville, SC
Peoria, IL
St. Louis, IL
Bakersfield, CA
Davenport, IA
Youngstown, OH
Johnstown, PA
Melbourne, FL
Ocala, FL
Salt Lake City, UT
Binghamton, NY
Worcester, MA
Tampa, FL
San Antonio, TX
Springfield, MO
Charlotte, SC
Pittsburgh, PA

0.000
0.050
0.100
0.150
0.200
0.250
0.300
0.350
0.400
0.450
0.500
0.550
0.600
0.650
0.700
0.750

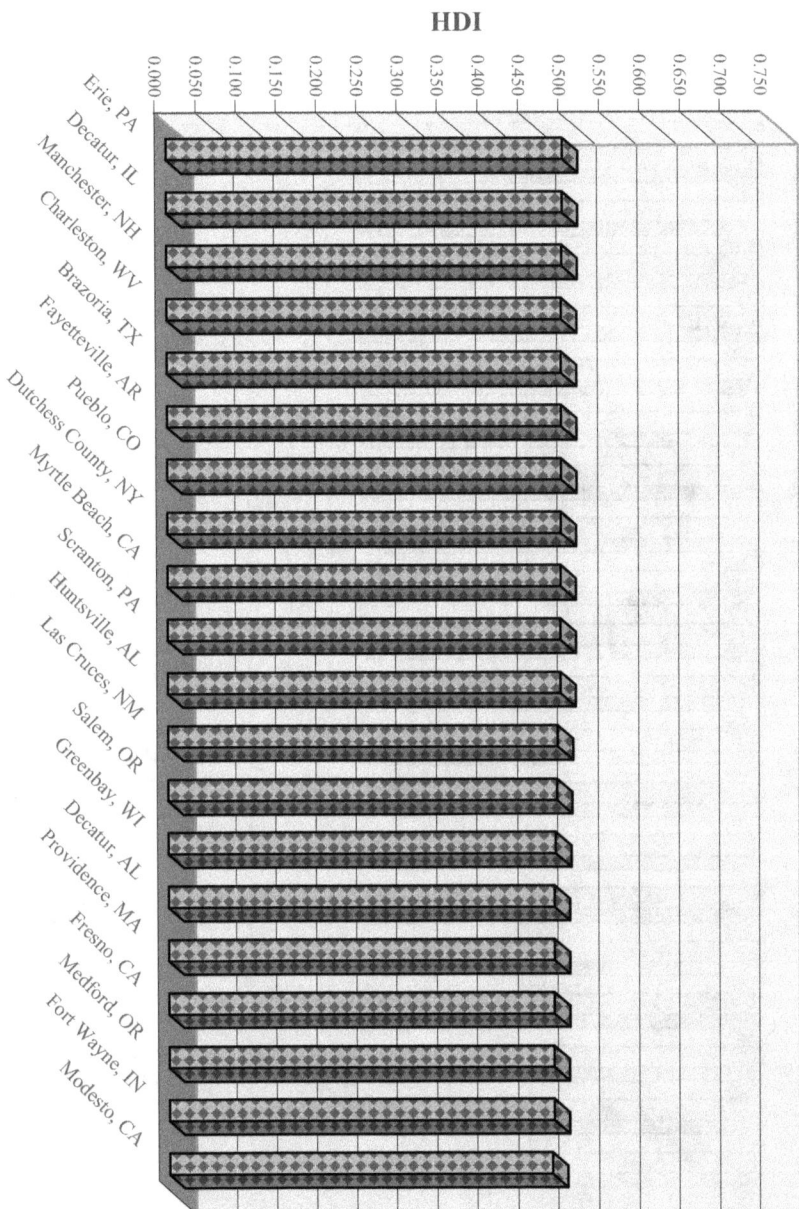

HDI

Human Development Index (HDI) for Whites by City
Cities Ranked 201-220

Erie, PA
Decatur, IL
Manchester, NH
Charleston, WV
Brazoria, TX
Fayetteville, AR
Pueblo, CO
Dutchess County, NY
Myrtle Beach, CA
Scranton, PA
Huntsville, AL
Las Cruces, NM
Salem, OR
Greenbay, WI
Decatur, AL
Providence, MA
Fresno, CA
Medford, OR
Fort Wayne, IN
Modesto, CA

0.000
0.050
0.100
0.150
0.200
0.250
0.300
0.350
0.400
0.450
0.500
0.550
0.600
0.650
0.700
0.750

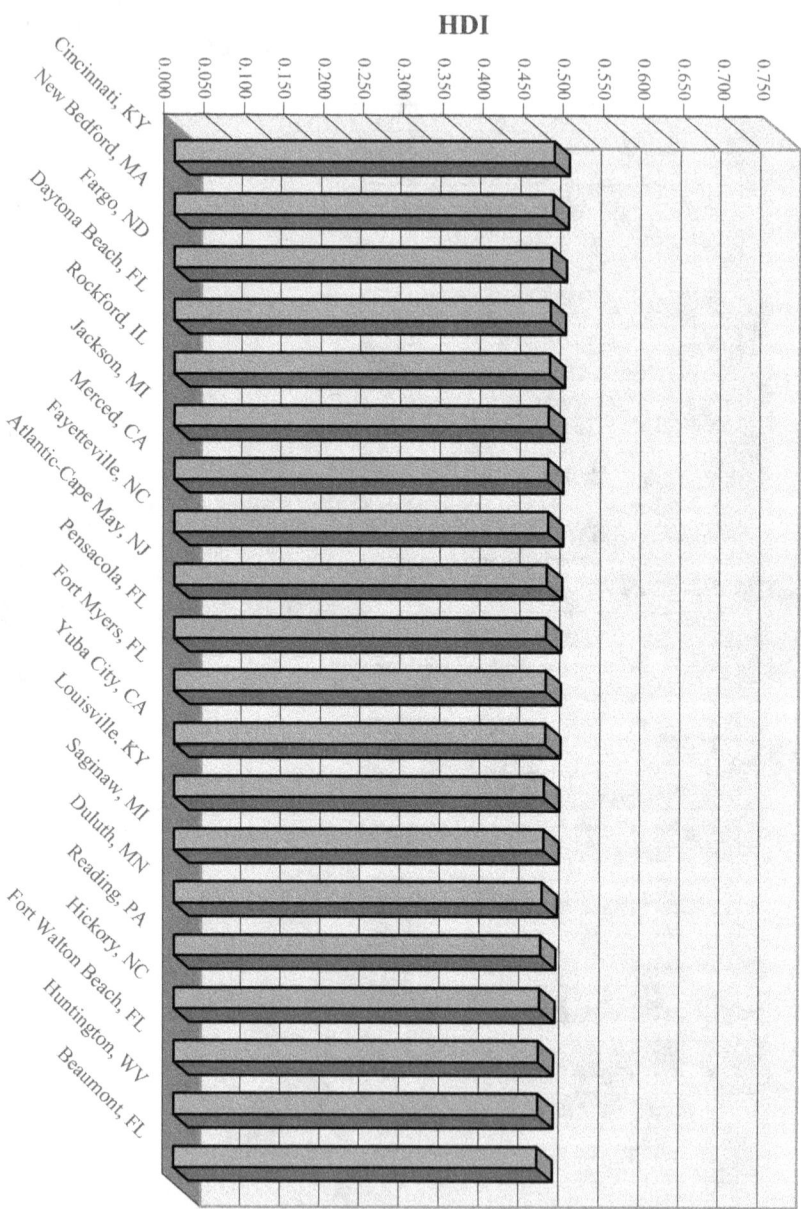

HDI

Human Development Index (HDI) for Whites by City
Cities Ranked 221-240

Cincinnati, KY
New Bedford, MA
Fargo, ND
Daytona Beach, FL
Rockford, IL
Jackson, MI
Merced, CA
Fayetteville, NC
Atlantic-Cape May, NJ
Pensacola, FL
Fort Myers, FL
Yuba City, CA
Louisville, KY
Saginaw, MI
Duluth, MN
Reading, PA
Hickory, NC
Fort Walton Beach, FL
Huntington, WV
Beaumont, FL

0.000
0.050
0.100
0.150
0.200
0.250
0.300
0.350
0.400
0.450
0.500
0.550
0.600
0.650
0.700
0.750

156

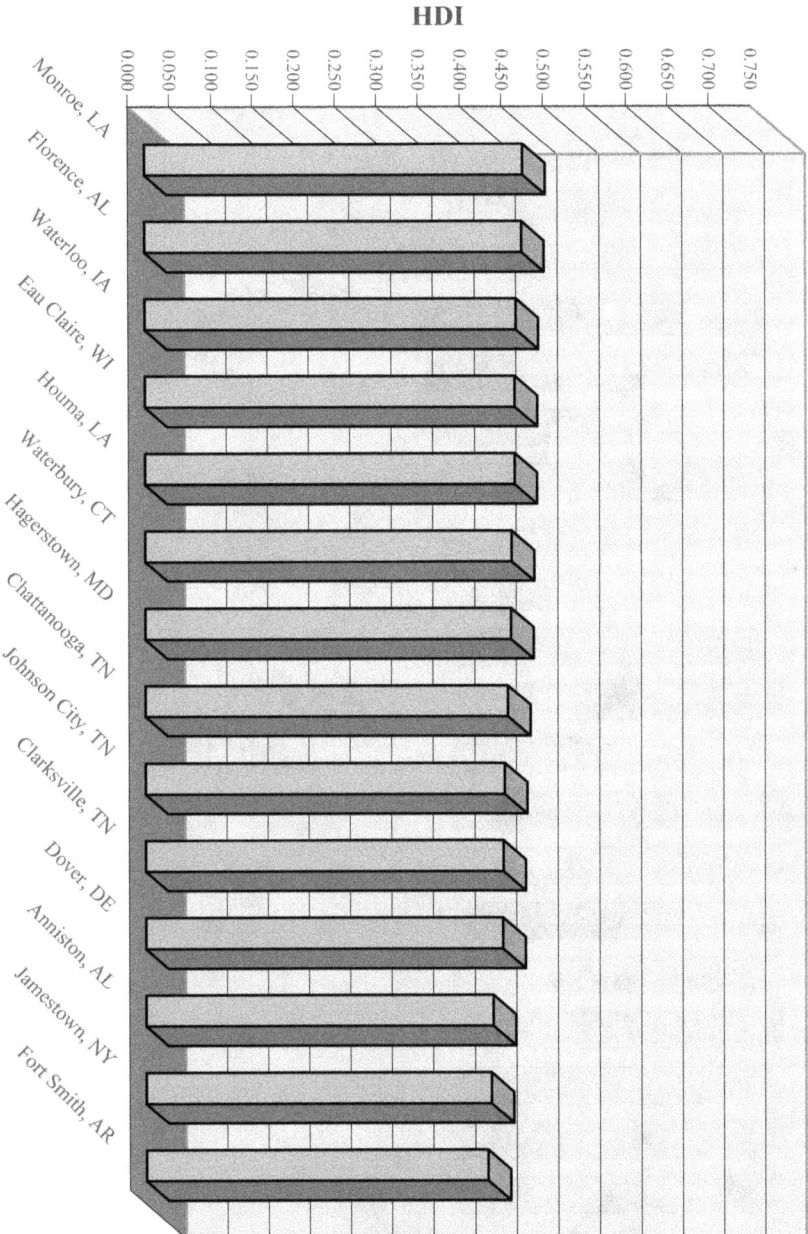

Human Development Index (HDI) for Whites by City
Cities Ranked 241-254

Human Development Index (HDI) for Blacks by City
Top 20 Cities

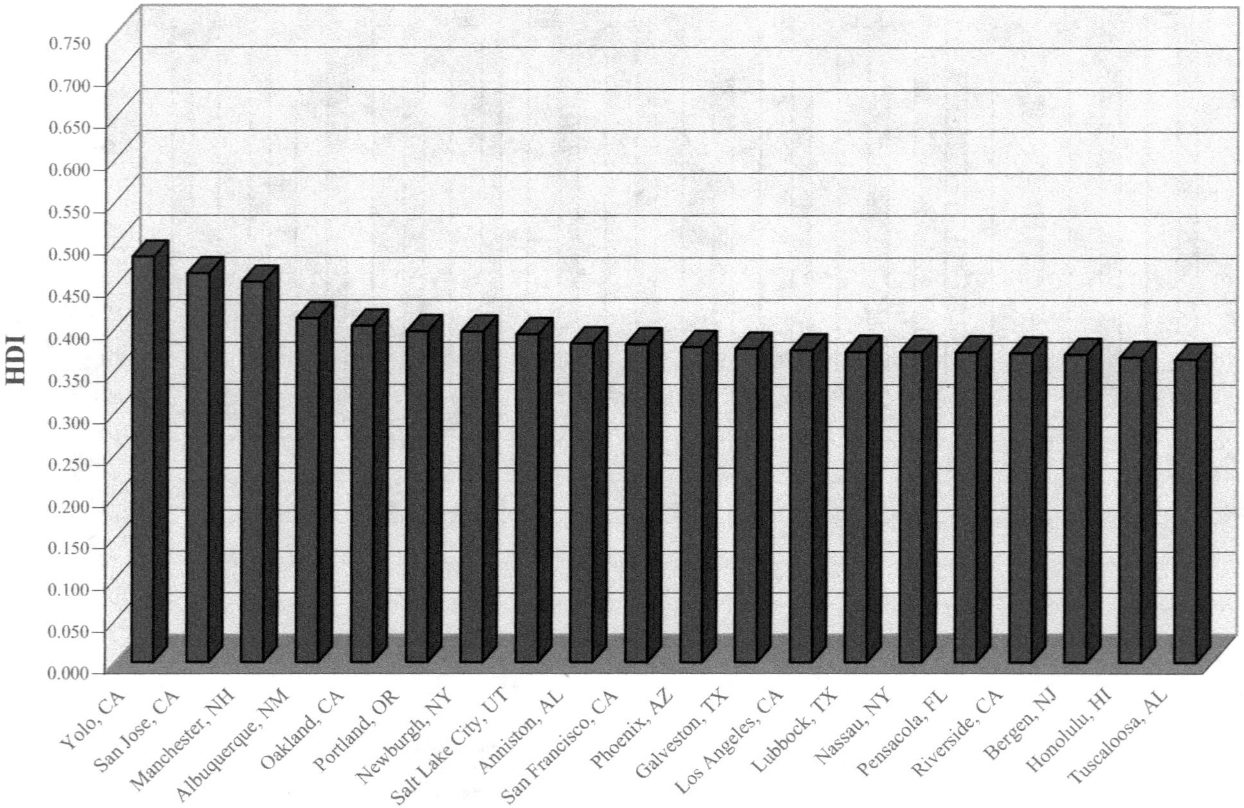
HDI
0.750
0.700
0.650
0.600
0.550
0.500
0.450
0.400
0.350
0.300
0.250
0.200
0.150
0.100
0.050
0.000
Yolo, CA
San Jose, CA
Manchester, NH
Albuquerque, NM
Oakland, CA
Portland, OR
Newburgh, NY
Salt Lake City, UT
Anniston, AL
San Francisco, CA
Phoenix, AZ
Galveston, TX
Los Angeles, CA
Lubbock, TX
Nassau, NY
Pensacola, FL
Riverside, CA
Bergen, NJ
Honolulu, HI
Tuscaloosa, AL

Human Development Index (HDI) for Blacks by City
Cities Ranked 21-40

HDI

Middlesex, NJ	
Orange County, CA	
Anchorage, AK	
Fort Worth, TX	
New Haven, CT	
Houston, TX	
Tacoma, WA	
Dallas, TX	
Toledo, OH	
Little Rock, AR	
Portland, OR	
Newark, NJ	
Ann Arbor, MI	
Springfield, MA	
Kansas City, MO	
Charleston, WV	
Raleigh, NC	
Syracuse, NY	
San Antonio, TX	
Sioux Falls, SD	

0.000 0.050 0.100 0.150 0.200 0.250 0.300 0.350 0.400 0.450 0.500 0.550 0.600 0.650 0.700 0.750

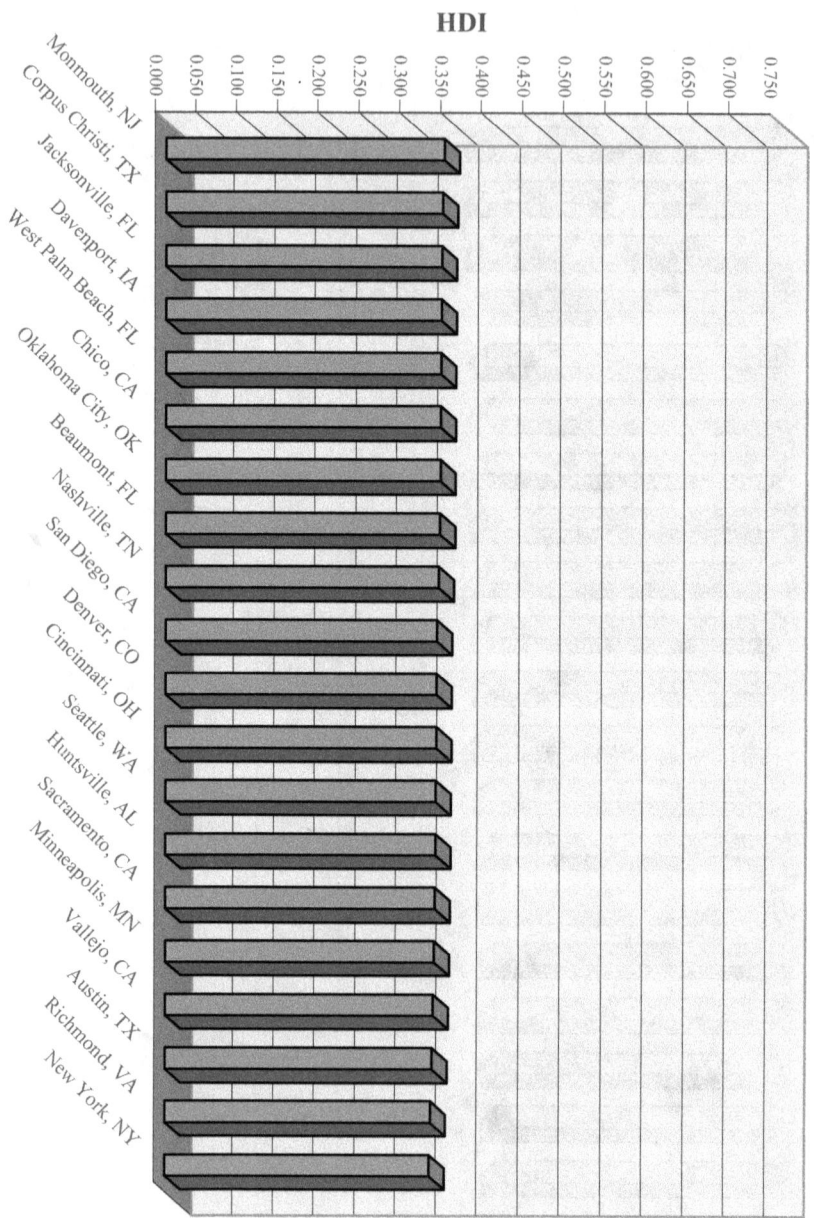

HDI

Human Development Index (HDI) for Blacks by City
Cities Ranked 41-60

Monmouth, NJ
Corpus Christi, TX
Jacksonville, FL
Davenport, IA
West Palm Beach, FL
Chico, CA
Oklahoma City, OK
Beaumont, FL
Nashville, TN
San Diego, CA
Denver, CO
Cincinnati, OH
Seattle, WA
Huntsville, AL
Sacramento, CA
Minneapolis, MN
Vallejo, CA
Austin, TX
Richmond, VA
New York, NY

0.000
0.050
0.100
0.150
0.200
0.250
0.300
0.350
0.400
0.450
0.500
0.550
0.600
0.650
0.700
0.750

Human Development Index (HDI) for Blacks by City
Cities Ranked 61-80

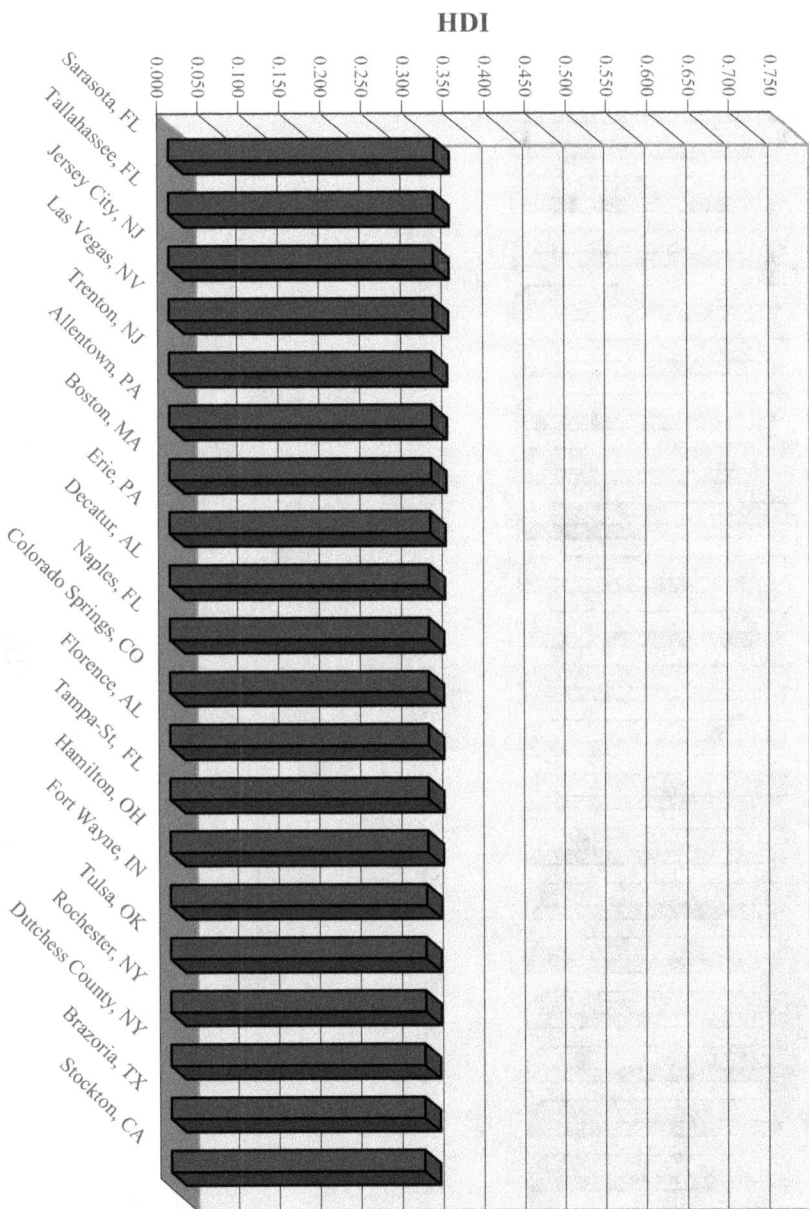

HDI

Sarasota, FL	
Tallahassee, FL	
Jersey City, NJ	
Las Vegas, NV	
Trenton, NJ	
Allentown, PA	
Boston, MA	
Erie, PA	
Decatur, AL	
Naples, FL	
Colorado Springs, CO	
Florence, AL	
Tampa-St, FL	
Hamilton, OH	
Fort Wayne, IN	
Tulsa, OK	
Rochester, NY	
Dutchess County, NY	
Brazoria, TX	
Stockton, CA	

Scale: 0.000, 0.050, 0.100, 0.150, 0.200, 0.250, 0.300, 0.350, 0.400, 0.450, 0.500, 0.550, 0.600, 0.650, 0.700, 0.750

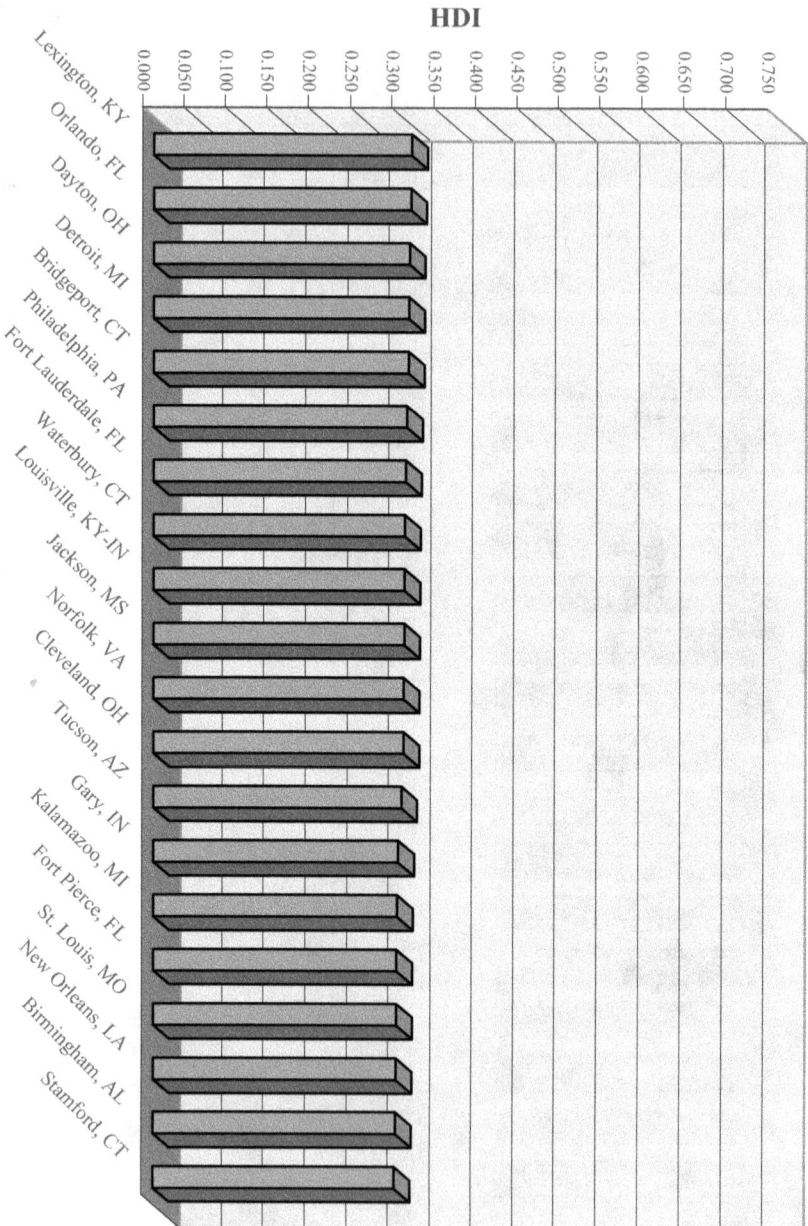

Human Development Index (HDI) for Blacks by City
Cities Ranked 81-100

HDI

Lexington, KY
Orlando, FL
Dayton, OH
Detroit, MI
Bridgeport, CT
Philadelphia, PA
Fort Lauderdale, FL
Waterbury, CT
Louisville, KY-IN
Jackson, MS
Norfolk, VA
Cleveland, OH
Tucson, AZ
Gary, IN
Kalamazoo, MI
Fort Pierce, FL
St. Louis, MO
New Orleans, LA
Birmingham, AL
Stamford, CT

0.000
0.050
0.100
0.150
0.200
0.250
0.300
0.350
0.400
0.450
0.500
0.550
0.600
0.650
0.700
0.750

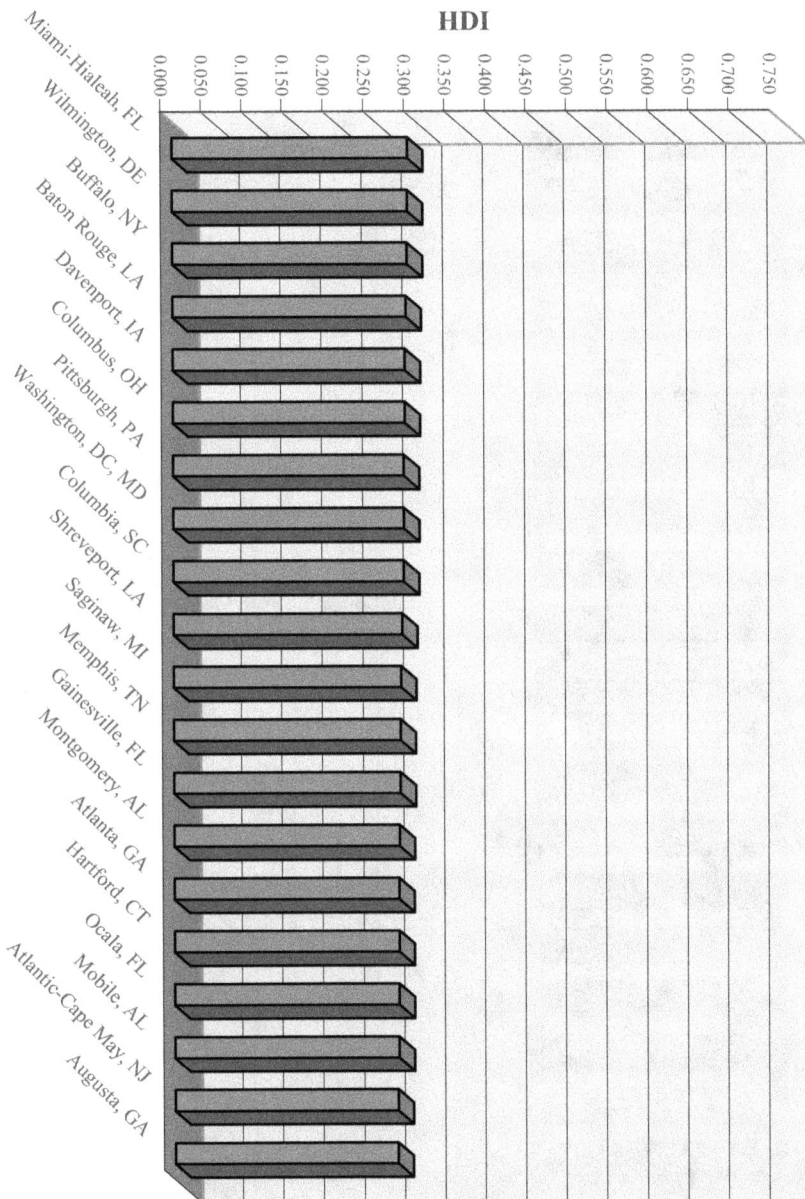

HDI

Human Development Index (HDI) for Blacks by City
Cities Ranked 101-120

Miami-Hialeah, FL
Wilmington, DE
Buffalo, NY
Baton Rouge, LA
Davenport, IA
Columbus, OH
Pittsburgh, PA
Washington, DC, MD
Columbia, SC
Shreveport, LA
Saginaw, MI
Memphis, TN
Gainesville, FL
Montgomery, AL
Atlanta, GA
Hartford, CT
Ocala, FL
Mobile, AL
Atlantic-Cape May, NJ
Augusta, GA

0.000
0.050
0.100
0.150
0.200
0.250
0.300
0.350
0.400
0.450
0.500
0.550
0.600
0.650
0.700
0.750

Human Development Index (HDI) for Blacks by City Cities Ranked 121-140

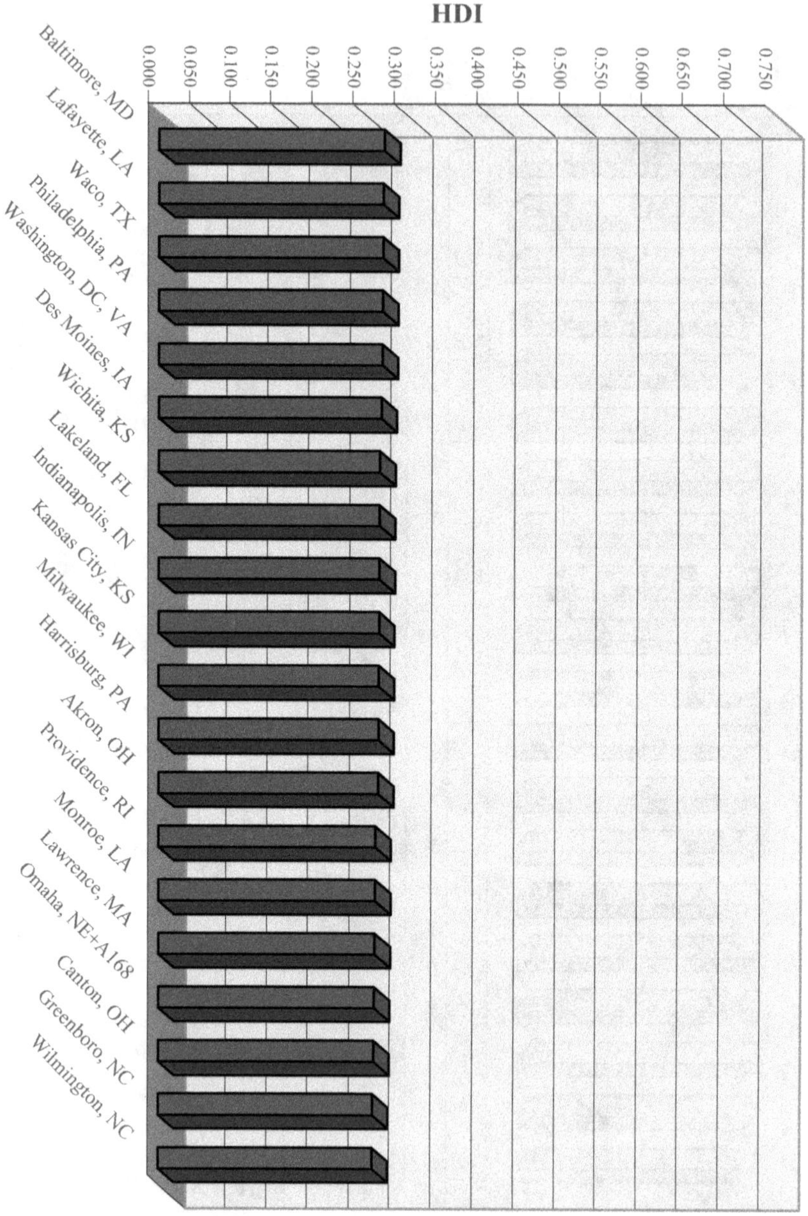
HDI
0.000
0.050
0.100
0.150
0.200
0.250
0.300
0.350
0.400
0.450
0.500
0.550
0.600
0.650
0.700
0.750
Baltimore, MD
Lafayette, LA
Waco, TX
Philadelphia, PA
Washington, DC, VA
Des Moines, IA
Wichita, KS
Lakeland, FL
Indianapolis, IN
Kansas City, KS
Milwaukee, WI
Harrisburg, PA
Akron, OH
Providence, RI
Monroe, LA
Lawrence, MA
Omaha, NE+A168
Canton, OH
Greenboro, NC
Wilmington, NC

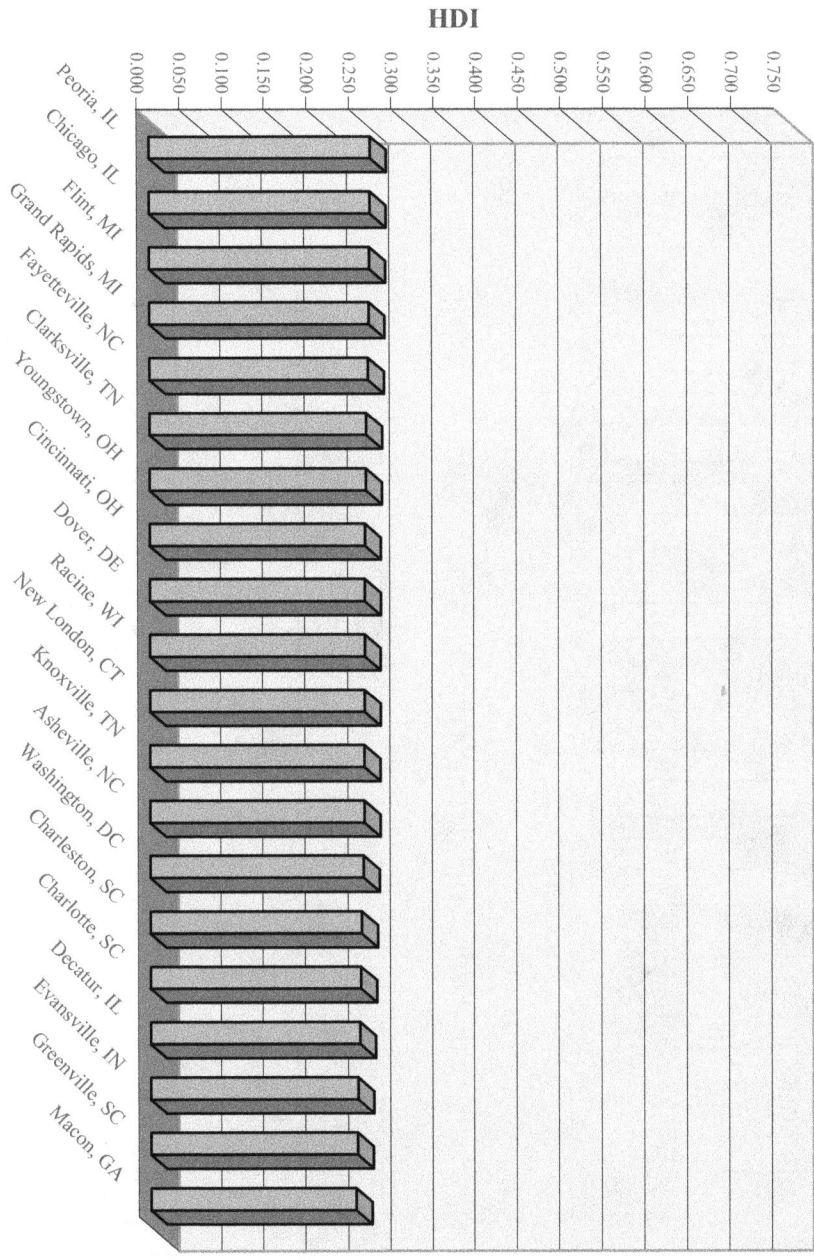

Human Development Index (HDI) for Blacks by City
Cities Ranked 141-160

HDI

Peoria, IL
Chicago, IL
Flint, MI
Grand Rapids, MI
Fayetteville, NC
Clarksville, TN
Youngstown, OH
Cincinnati, OH
Dover, DE
Racine, WI
New London, CT
Knoxville, TN
Asheville, NC
Washington, DC
Charleston, SC
Charlotte, SC
Decatur, IL
Evansville, IN
Greenville, SC
Macon, GA

0.000
0.050
0.100
0.150
0.200
0.250
0.300
0.350
0.400
0.450
0.500
0.550
0.600
0.650
0.700
0.750

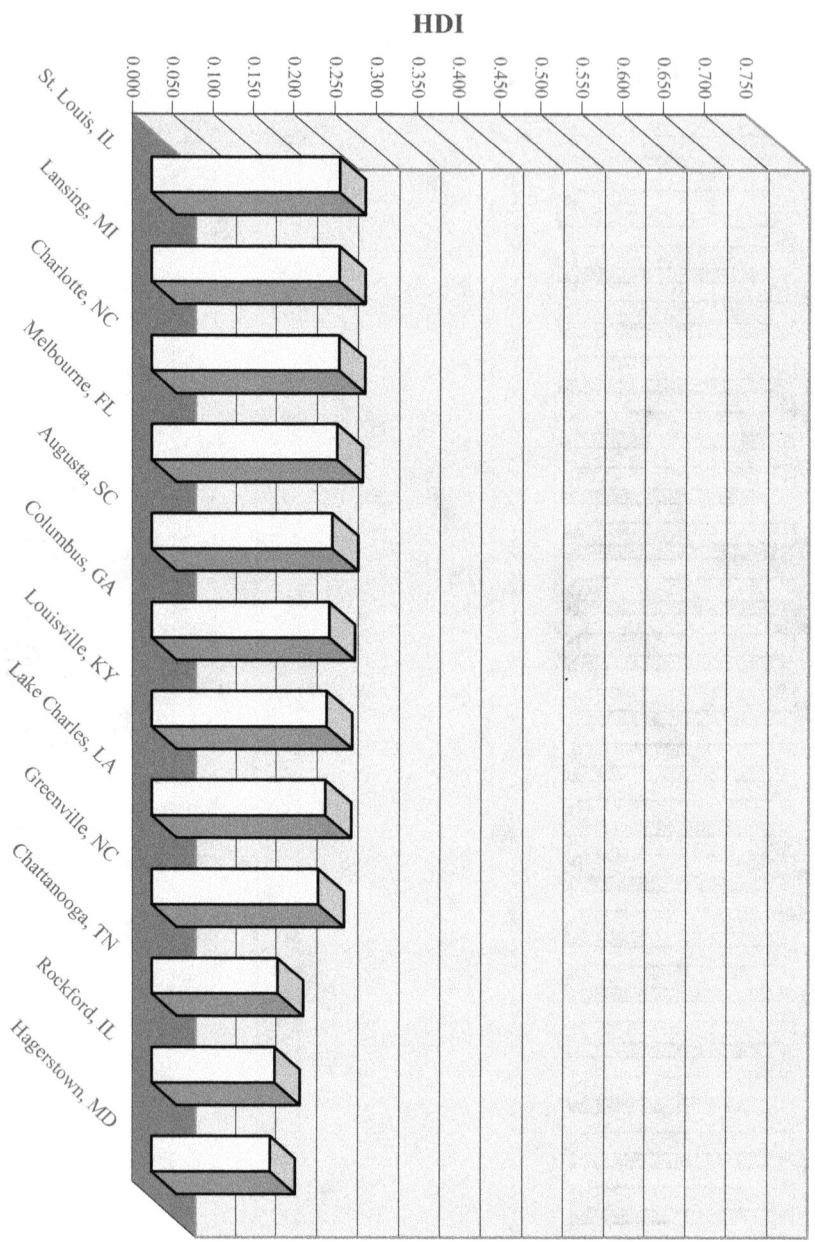

Human Development Index (HDI) for Blacks by City
Cities Ranked 161-172

Human Development Index (HDI) for Hispanics by City
Top 20 Cities

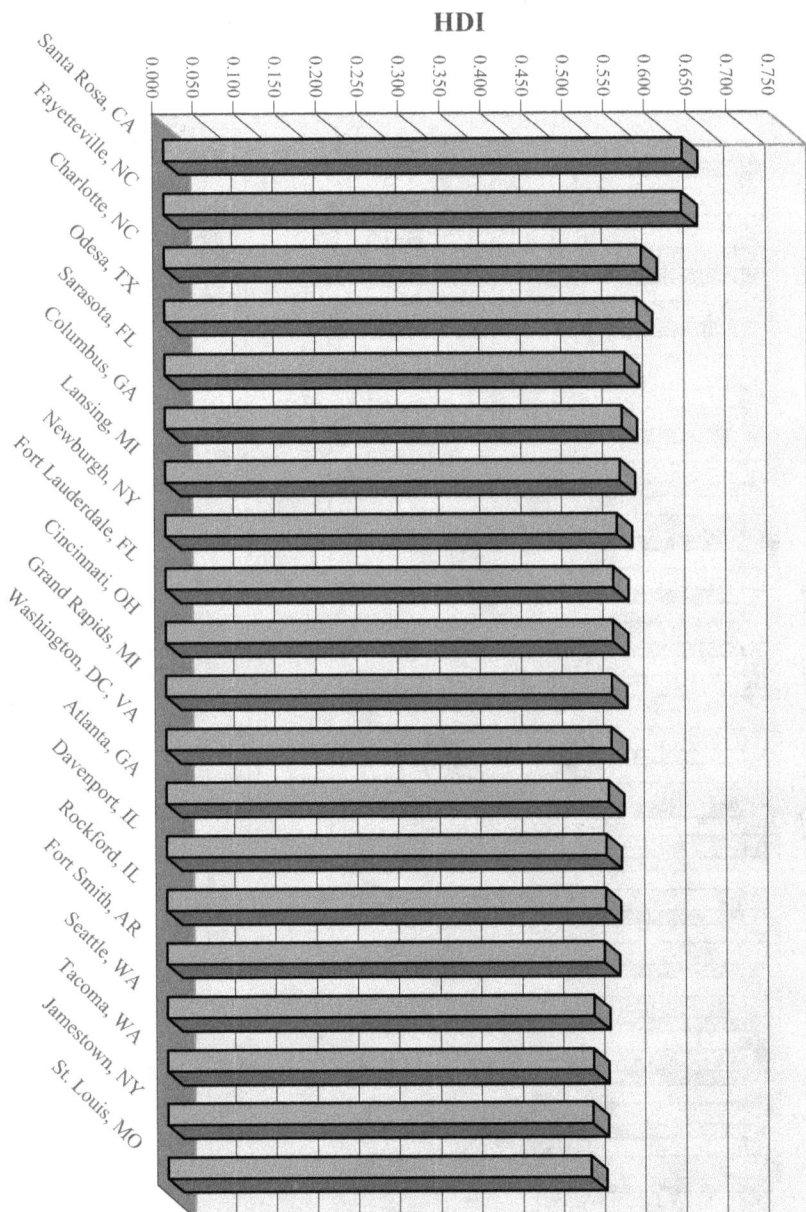

HDI

City	
Santa Rosa, CA	
Fayetteville, NC	
Charlotte, NC	
Odesa, TX	
Sarasota, FL	
Columbus, GA	
Lansing, MI	
Newburgh, NY	
Fort Lauderdale, FL	
Cincinnati, OH	
Grand Rapids, MI	
Washington, DC, VA	
Atlanta, GA	
Davenport, IL	
Rockford, IL	
Fort Smith, AR	
Seattle, WA	
Tacoma, WA	
Jamestown, NY	
St. Louis, MO	

Scale: 0.000, 0.050, 0.100, 0.150, 0.200, 0.250, 0.300, 0.350, 0.400, 0.450, 0.500, 0.550, 0.600, 0.650, 0.700, 0.750

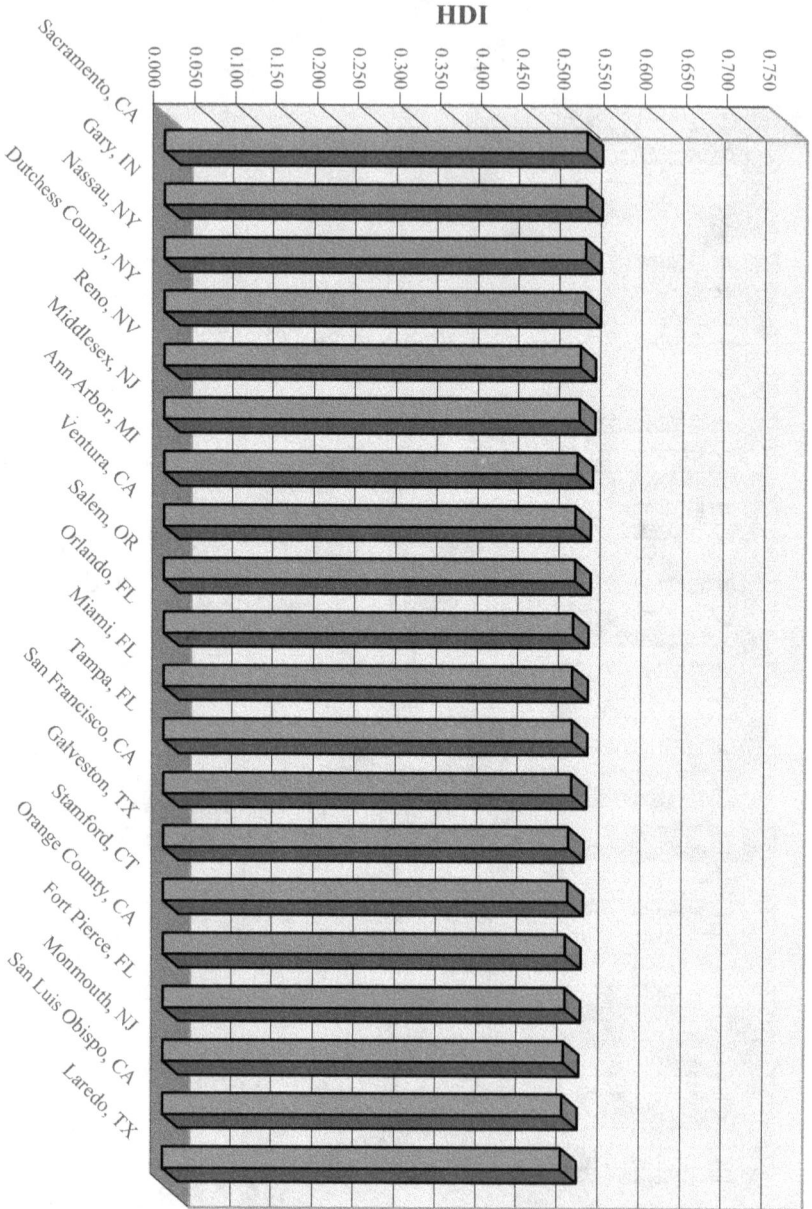

Human Development Index (HDI) for Hispanics by City
Cities Ranked 21-40

HDI

Sacramento, CA
Gary, IN
Nassau, NY
Dutchess County, NY
Reno, NV
Middlesex, NJ
Ann Arbor, MI
Ventura, CA
Salem, OR
Orlando, FL
Miami, FL
Tampa, FL
San Francisco, CA
Galveston, TX
Stamford, CT
Orange County, CA
Fort Pierce, FL
Monmouth, NJ
San Luis Obispo, CA
Laredo, TX

0.000 0.050 0.100 0.150 0.200 0.250 0.300 0.350 0.400 0.450 0.500 0.550 0.600 0.650 0.700 0.750

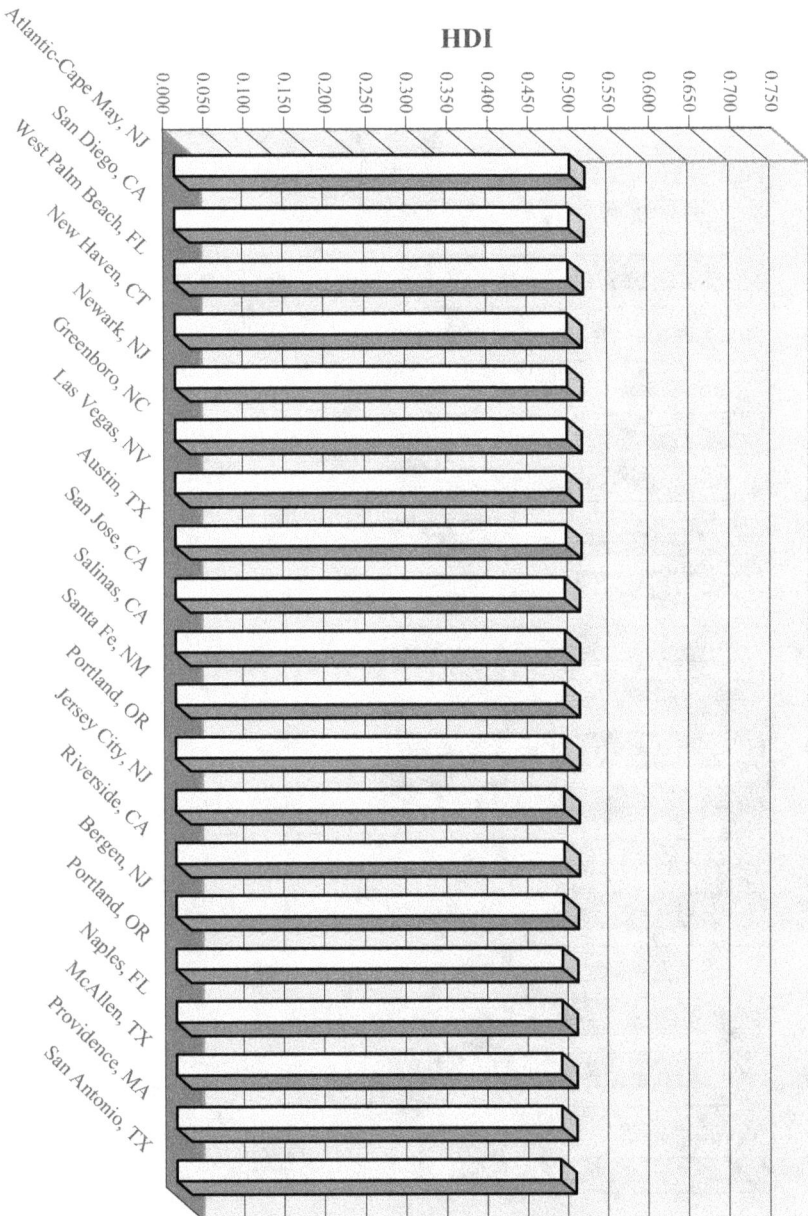

Human Development Index (HDI) for Hispanics by City
Cities Ranked 41-60

HDI

Atlantic-Cape May, NJ
San Diego, CA
West Palm Beach, FL
New Haven, CT
Newark, NJ
Greensboro, NC
Las Vegas, NV
Austin, TX
San Jose, CA
Salinas, CA
Santa Fe, NM
Portland, OR
Jersey City, NJ
Riverside, CA
Bergen, NJ
Portland, OR
Naples, FL
McAllen, TX
Providence, MA
San Antonio, TX

Human Development Index (HDI) for Hispanics by City
Cities Ranked 61-80

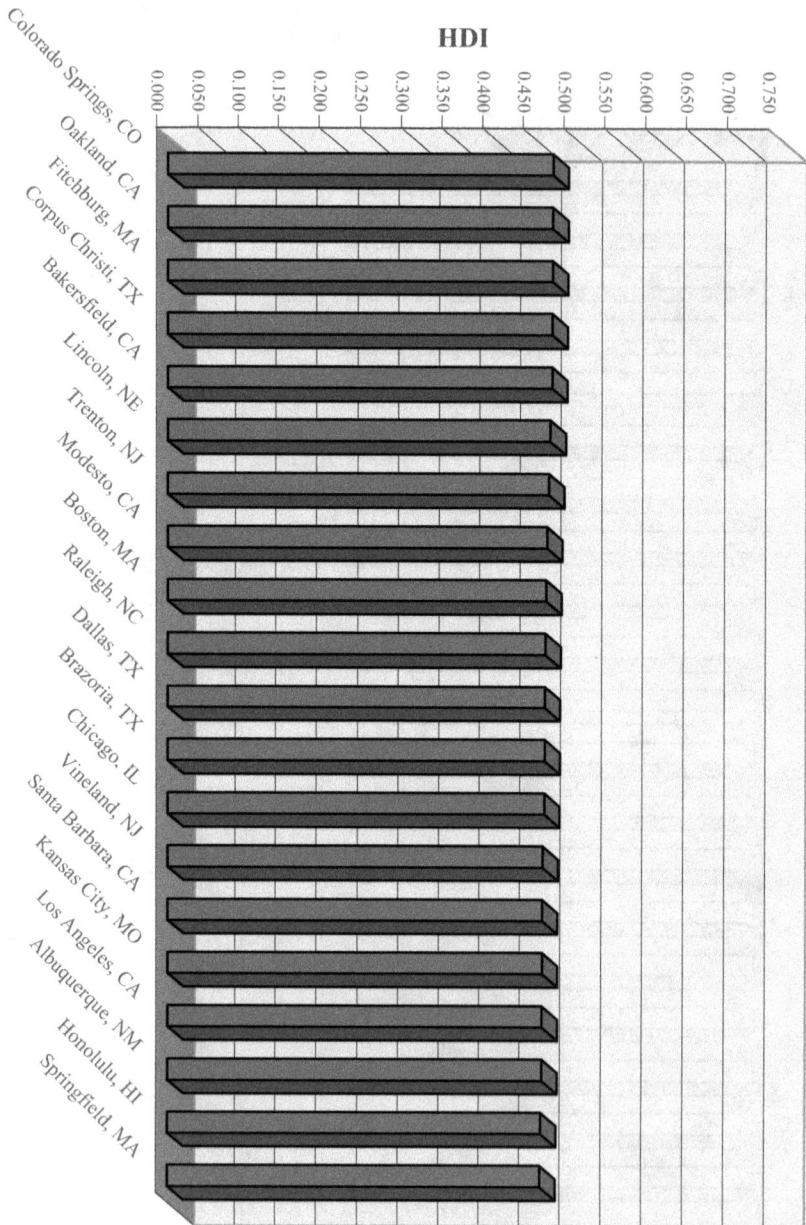

HDI

City	
Colorado Springs, CO	
Oakland, CA	
Fitchburg, MA	
Corpus Christi, TX	
Bakersfield, CA	
Lincoln, NE	
Trenton, NJ	
Modesto, CA	
Boston, MA	
Raleigh, NC	
Dallas, TX	
Brazoria, TX	
Chicago, IL	
Vineland, NJ	
Santa Barbara, CA	
Kansas City, MO	
Los Angeles, CA	
Albuquerque, NM	
Honolulu, HI	
Springfield, MA	

Axis values: 0.000, 0.050, 0.100, 0.150, 0.200, 0.250, 0.300, 0.350, 0.400, 0.450, 0.500, 0.550, 0.600, 0.650, 0.700, 0.750

Human Development Index (HDI) for Hispanics by City
Cities Ranked 81-100

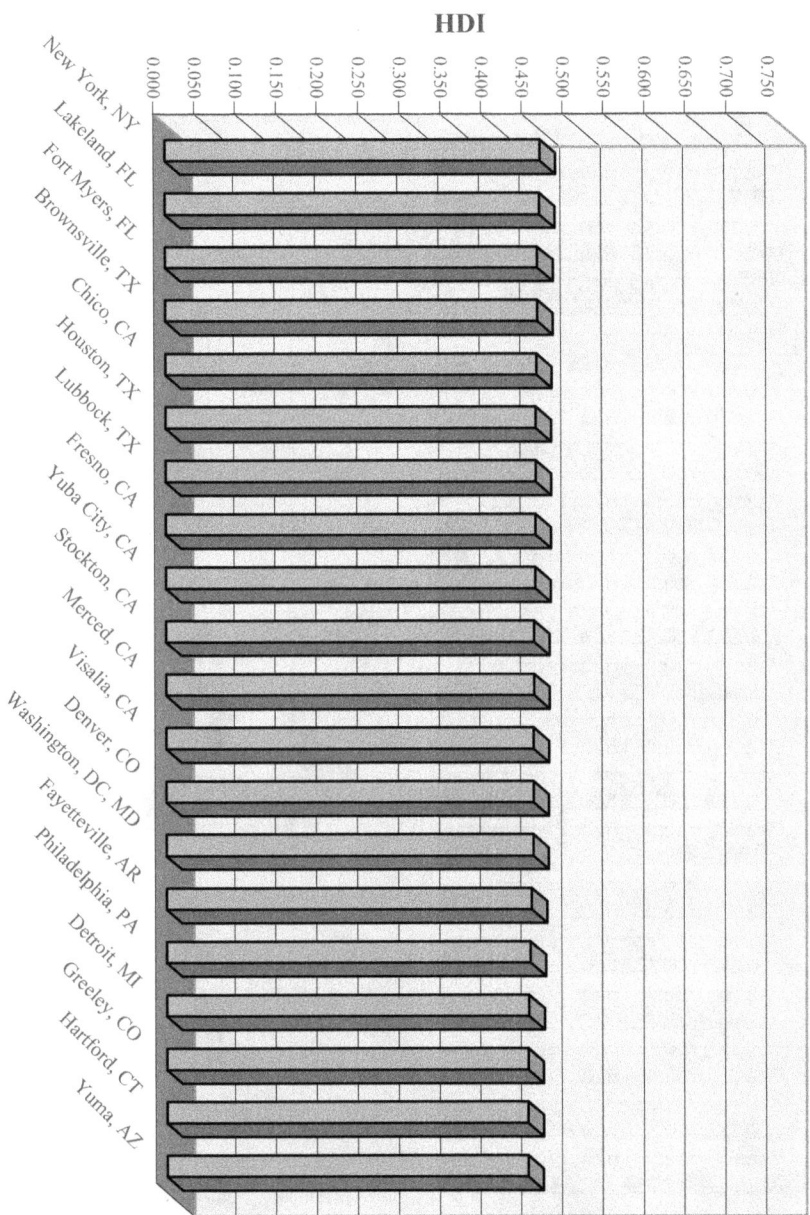

HDI

New York, NY
Lakeland, FL
Fort Myers, FL
Brownsville, TX
Chico, CA
Houston, TX
Lubbock, TX
Fresno, CA
Yuba City, CA
Stockton, CA
Merced, CA
Visalia, CA
Denver, CO
Washington, DC, MD
Fayetteville, AR
Philadelphia, PA
Detroit, MI
Greeley, CO
Hartford, CT
Yuma, AZ

0.000 0.050 0.100 0.150 0.200 0.250 0.300 0.350 0.400 0.450 0.500 0.550 0.600 0.650 0.700 0.750

Human Development Index (HDI) for Hispanics by City Cities Ranked 101-120

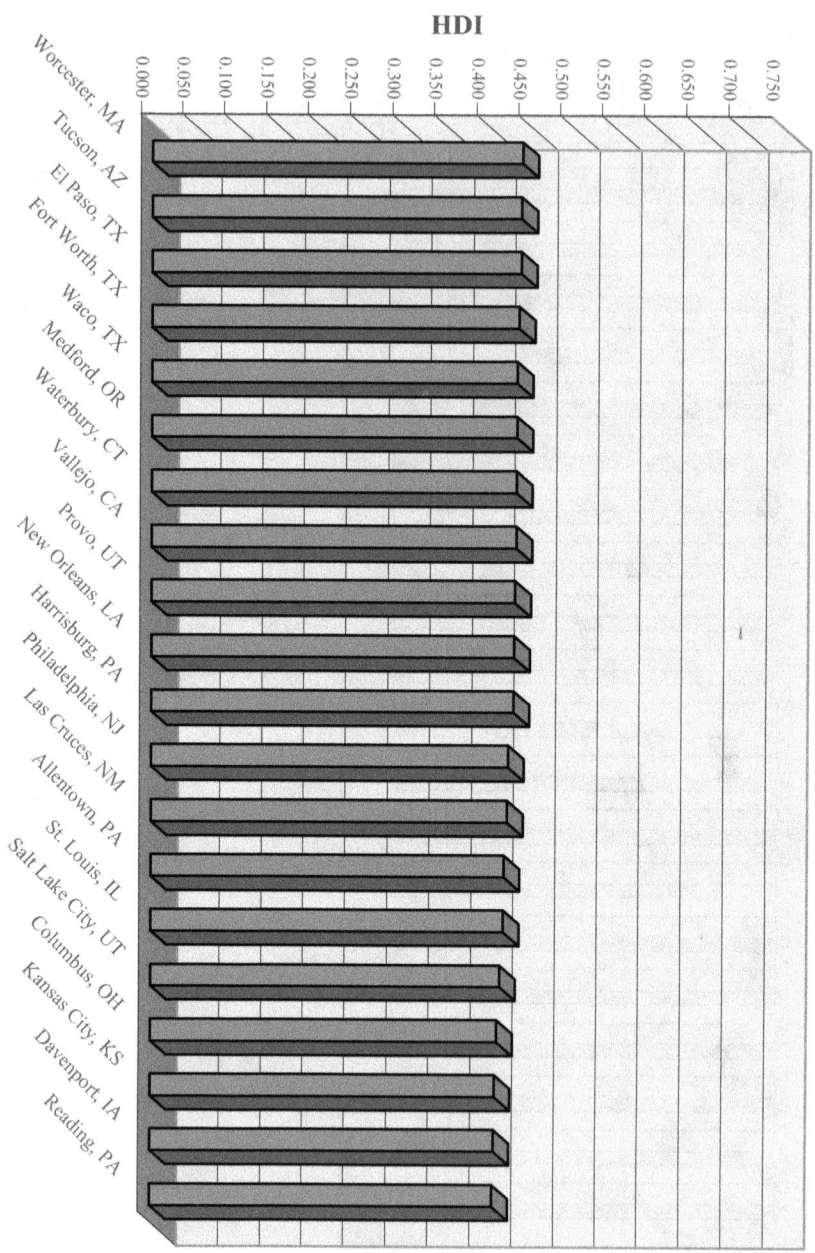

HDI

City	HDI
Worcester, MA	
Tucson, AZ	
El Paso, TX	
Fort Worth, TX	
Waco, TX	
Medford, OR	
Waterbury, CT	
Vallejo, CA	
Provo, UT	
New Orleans, LA	
Harrisburg, PA	
Philadelphia, NJ	
Las Cruces, NM	
Allentown, PA	
St. Louis, IL	
Salt Lake City, UT	
Columbus, OH	
Kansas City, KS	
Davenport, IA	
Reading, PA	

HDI

Human Development Index (HDI) for Hispanics by City Cities Ranked 121-140

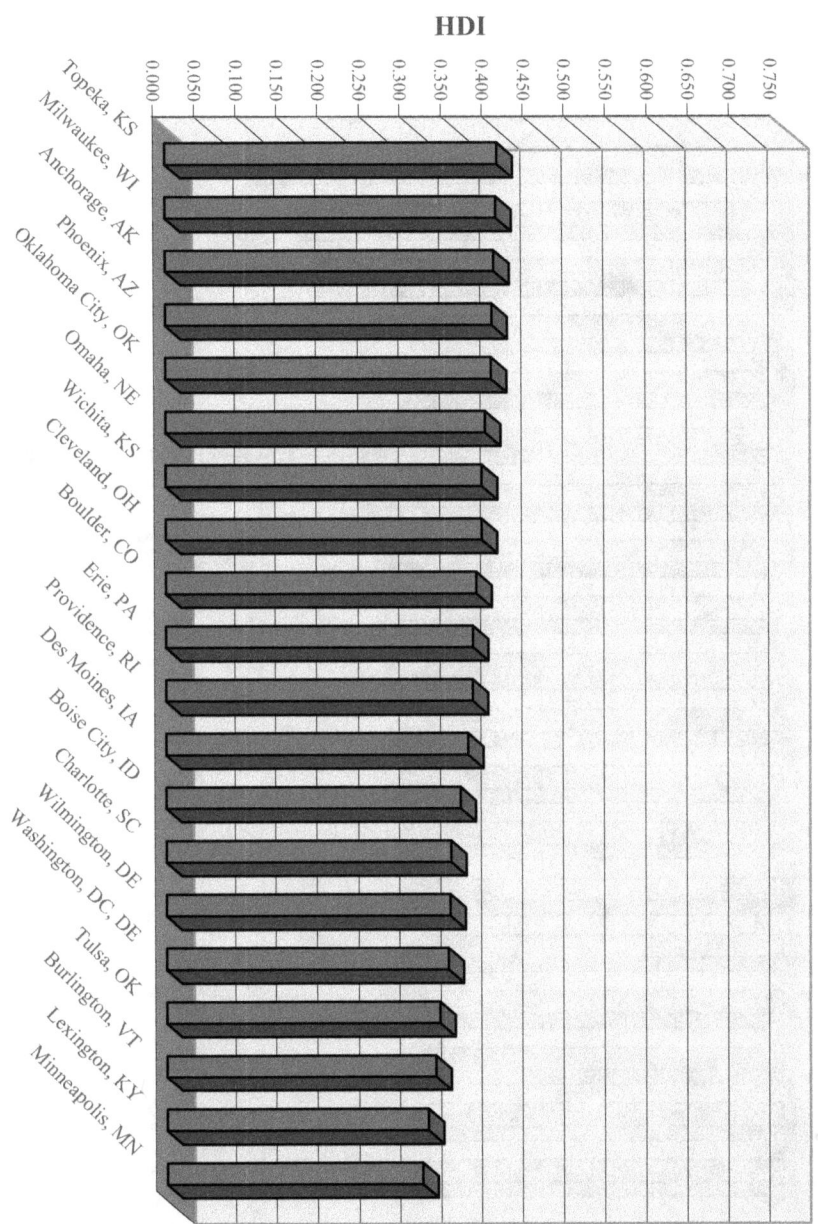

City	HDI
Topeka, KS	
Milwaukee, WI	
Anchorage, AK	
Phoenix, AZ	
Oklahoma City, OK	
Omaha, NE	
Wichita, KS	
Cleveland, OH	
Boulder, CO	
Erie, PA	
Providence, RI	
Des Moines, IA	
Boise City, ID	
Charlotte, SC	
Wilmington, DE	
Washington, DC, DE	
Tulsa, OK	
Burlington, VT	
Lexington, KY	
Minneapolis, MN	

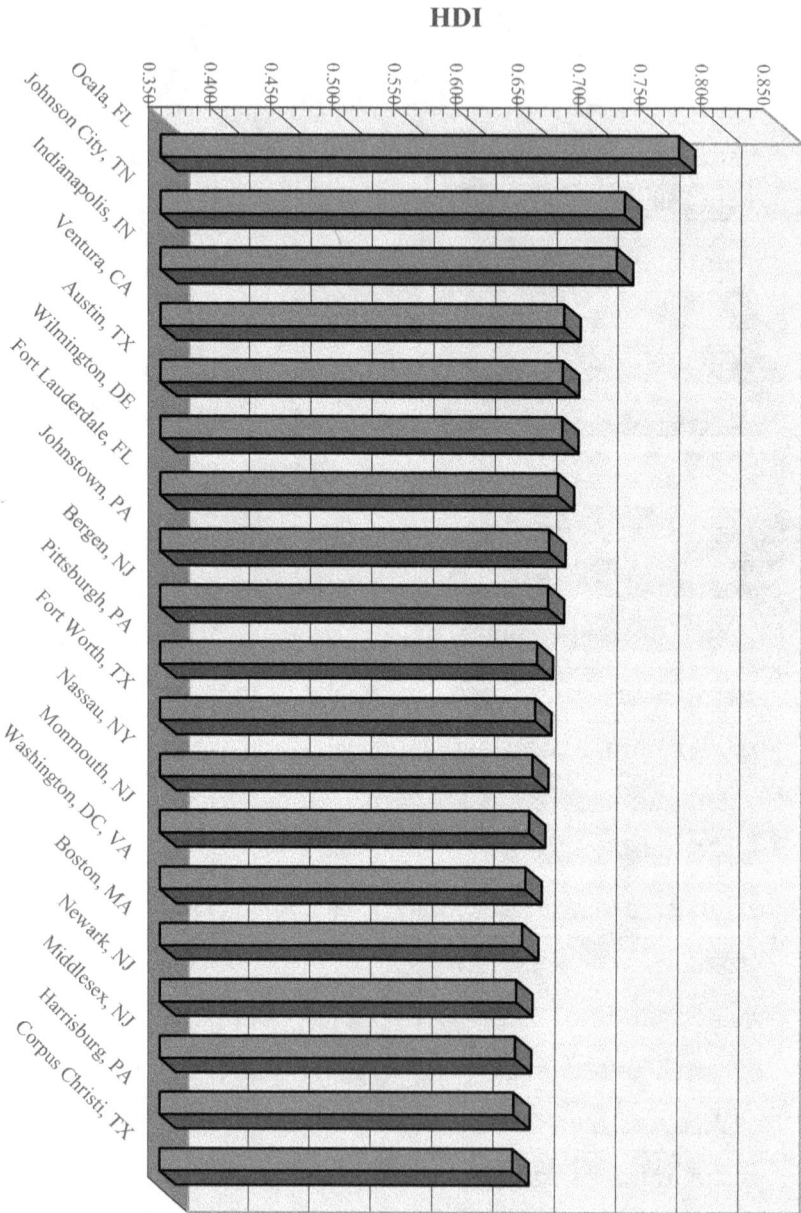

HDI

Human Development Index (HDI) for Others by City
Top 20 Cities

Ocala, FL
Johnson City, TN
Indianapolis, IN
Ventura, CA
Austin, TX
Wilmington, DE
Fort Lauderdale, FL
Johnstown, PA
Bergen, NJ
Pittsburgh, PA
Fort Worth, TX
Nassau, NY
Monmouth, NJ
Washington, DC, VA
Boston, MA
Newark, NJ
Middlesex, NJ
Harrisburg, PA
Corpus Christi, TX

0.350 0.400 0.450 0.500 0.550 0.600 0.650 0.700 0.750 0.800 0.850

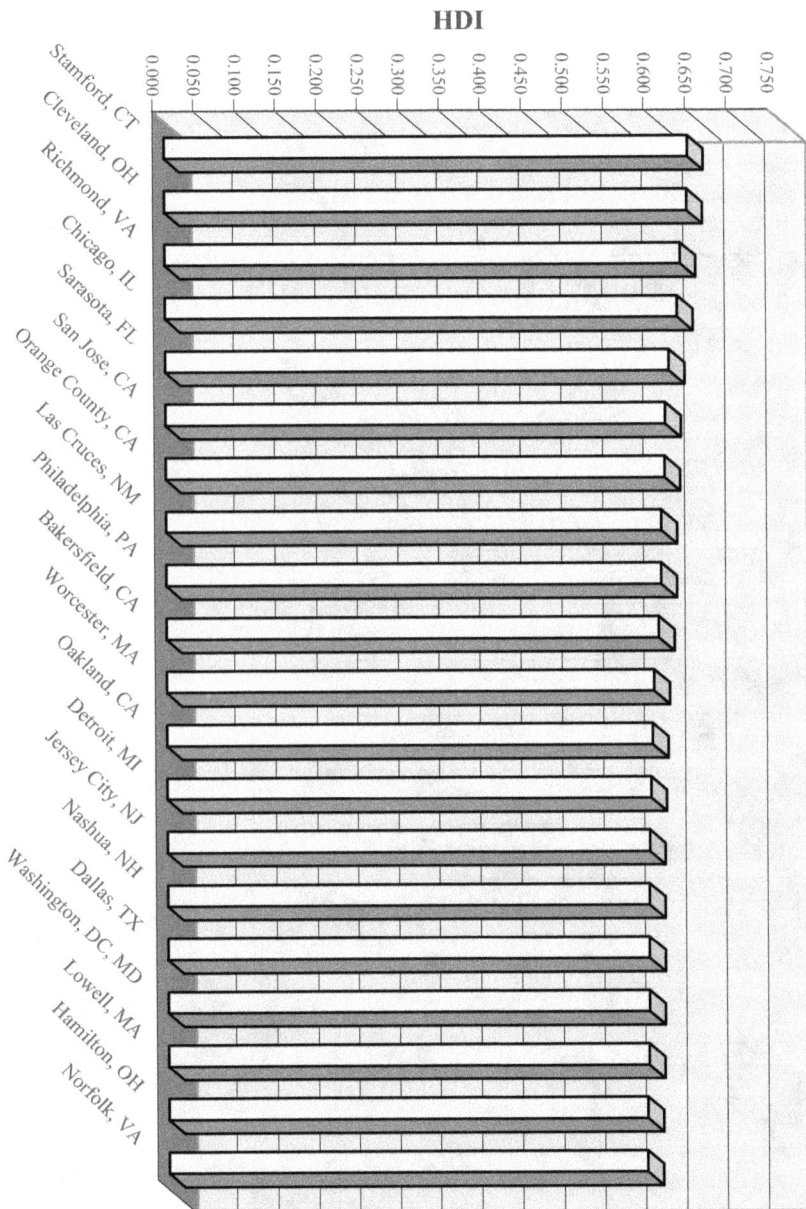

Human Development Index (HDI) for Others by City
Cities Ranked 21-40

175

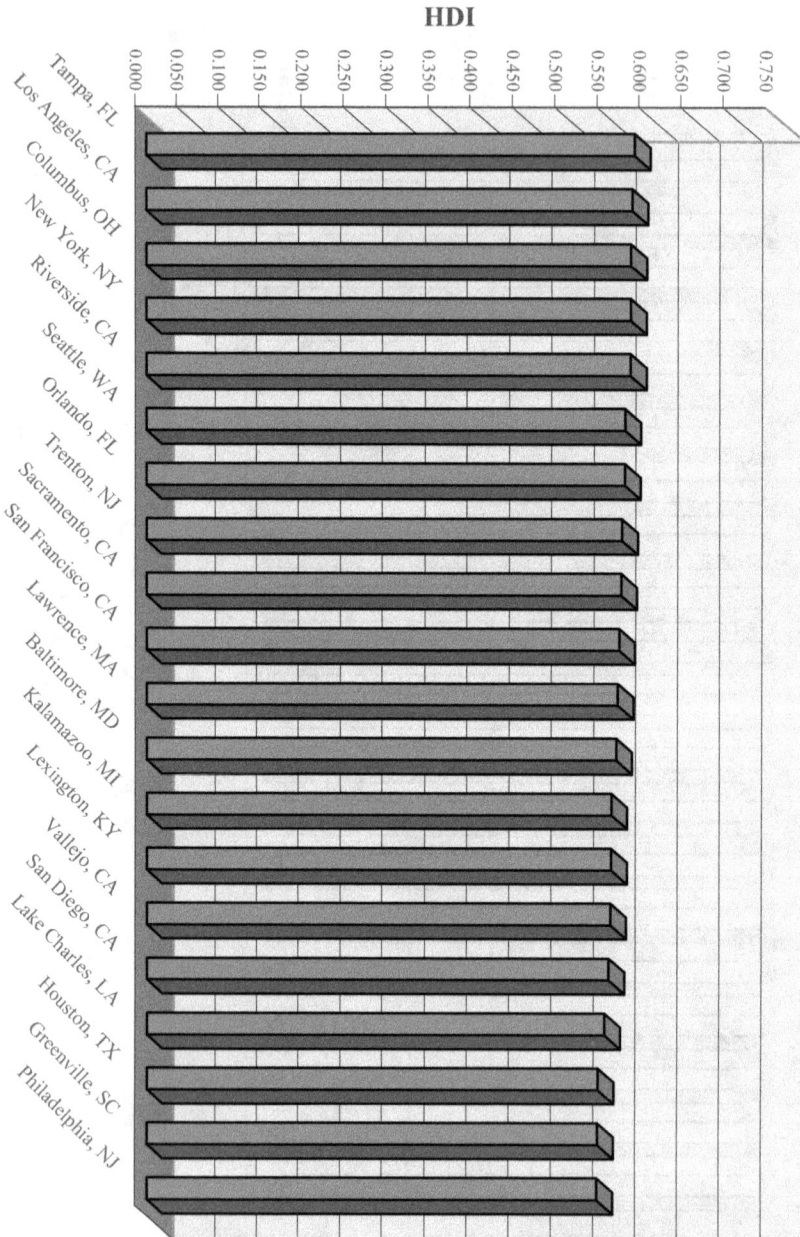

HDI

Human Development Index (HDI) for Others by City
Cities Ranked 41-60

Tampa, FL
Los Angeles, CA
Columbus, OH
New York, NY
Riverside, CA
Seattle, WA
Orlando, FL
Trenton, NJ
Sacramento, CA
San Francisco, CA
Lawrence, MA
Baltimore, MD
Kalamazoo, MI
Lexington, KY
Vallejo, CA
San Diego, CA
Lake Charles, LA
Houston, TX
Greenville, SC
Philadelphia, NJ

Human Development Index (HDI) for Others by City Cities Ranked 61-80

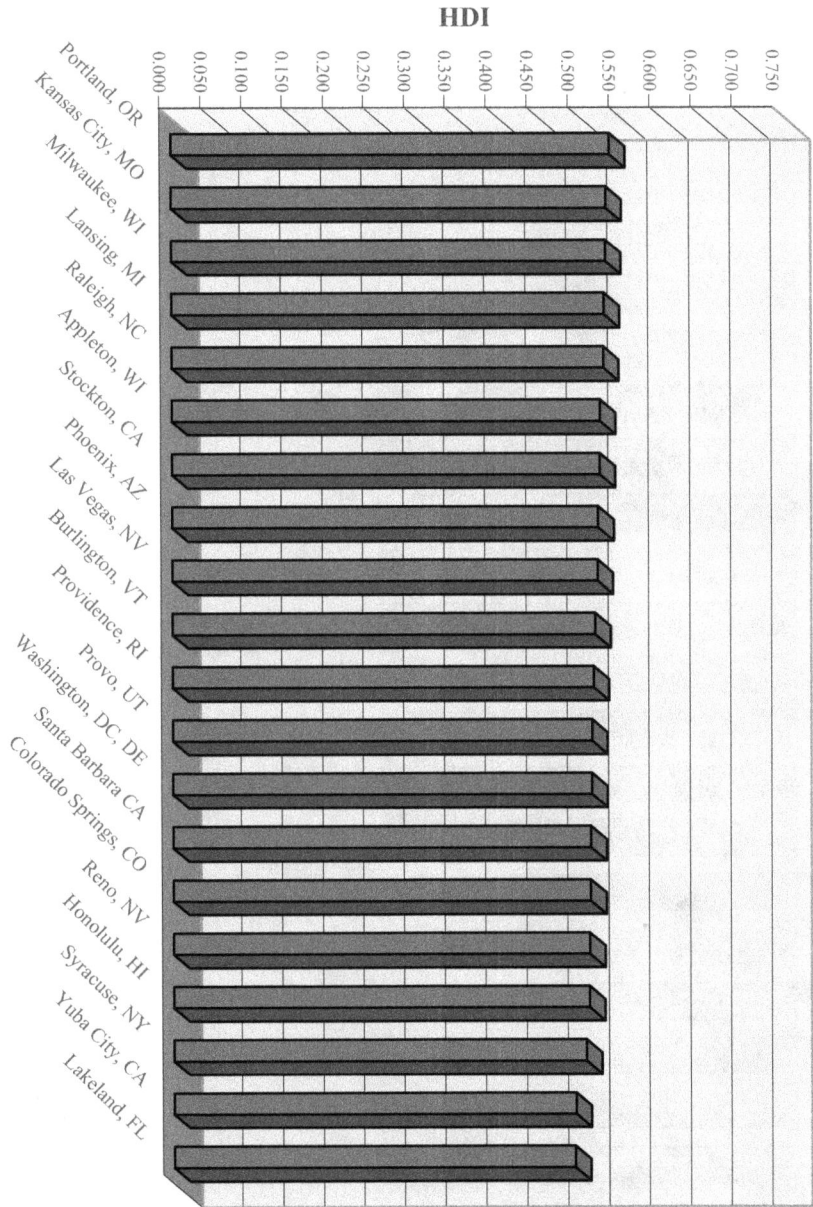

HDI

Portland, OR	
Kansas City, MO	
Milwaukee, WI	
Lansing, MI	
Raleigh, NC	
Appleton, WI	
Stockton, CA	
Phoenix, AZ	
Las Vegas, NV	
Burlington, VT	
Providence, RI	
Provo, UT	
Washington, DC, DE	
Santa Barbara CA	
Colorado Springs, CO	
Reno, NV	
Honolulu, HI	
Syracuse, NY	
Yuba City, CA	
Lakeland, FL	

Axis values: 0.000, 0.050, 0.100, 0.150, 0.200, 0.250, 0.300, 0.350, 0.400, 0.450, 0.500, 0.550, 0.600, 0.650, 0.700, 0.750

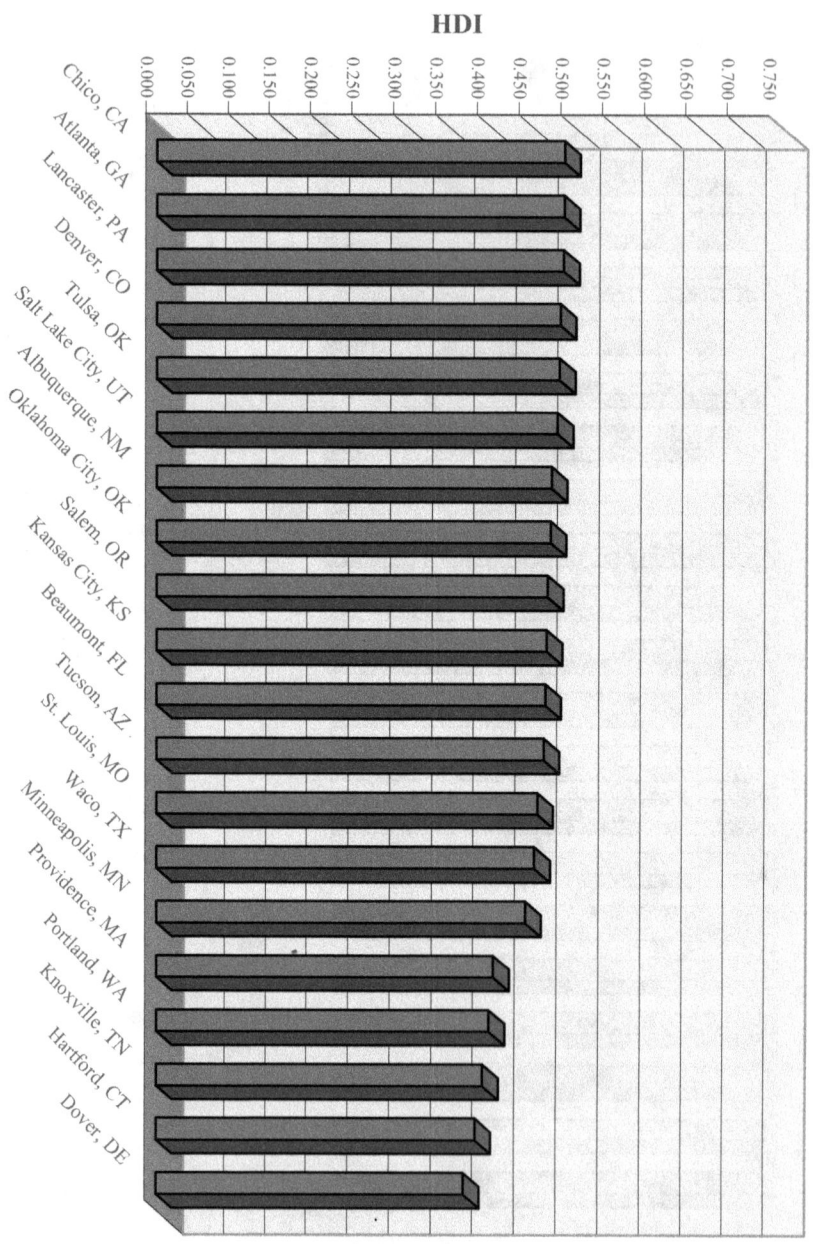

Human Development Index (HDI) for Others by City
Cities Ranked 81-100

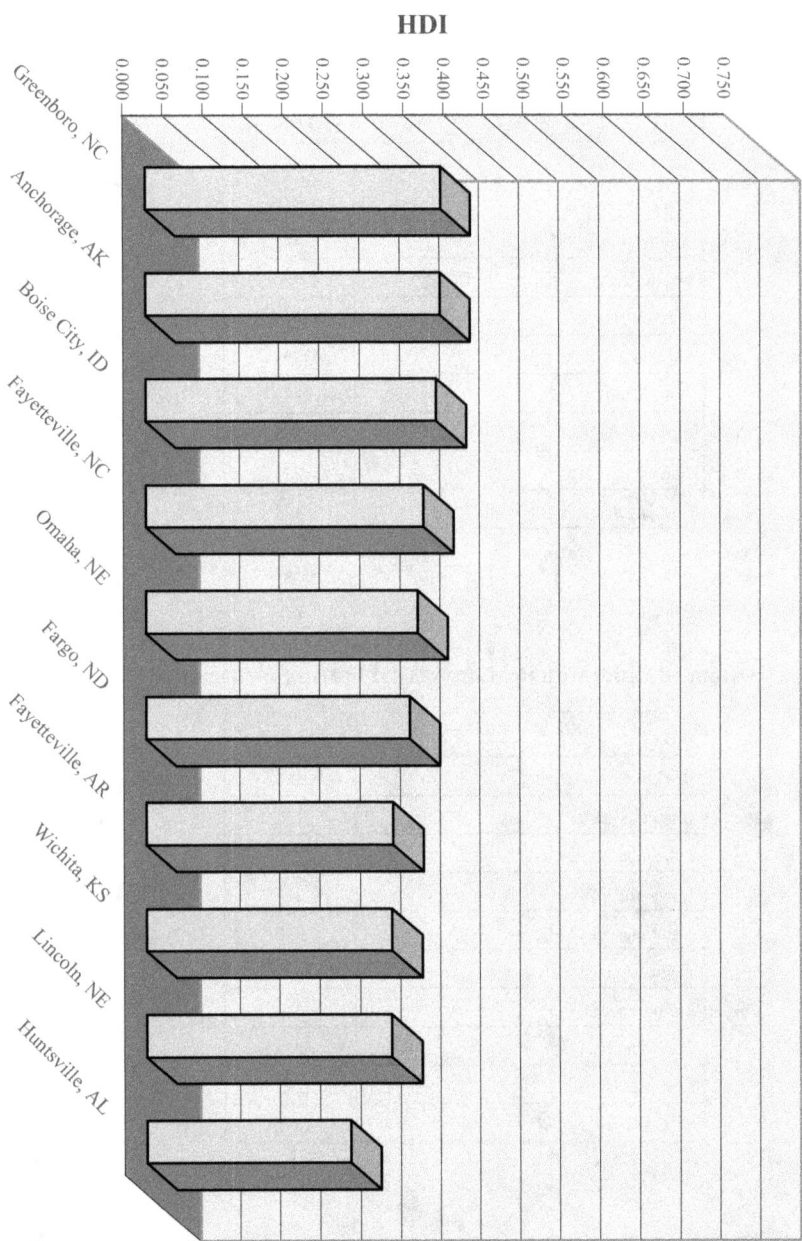

Human Development Index (HDI) for Others by City
Cities Ranked 101-110

HDI

Greensboro, NC
Anchorage, AK
Boise City, ID
Fayetteville, NC
Omaha, NE
Fargo, ND
Fayetteville, AR
Wichita, KS
Lincoln, NE
Huntsville, AL

0.000
0.050
0.100
0.150
0.200
0.250
0.300
0.350
0.400
0.450
0.500
0.550
0.600
0.650
0.700
0.750

Top 10 Cities with the Highest HDI Scores for Blacks

City	HDI Score
San Jose, CA	464
Manchester, NH	455
Albuquerque, NM	412
Oakland, CA	403
Portland, OR	396
Salt Lake City, UT	393
San Francisco, CA	381
Phoenix, AZ	378
Galveston, TX	376
Los Angeles, CA	374

Bottom 10 Cities with the Lowest HDI Scores for Blacks

City	HDI Score
Rockford, IL	153
Chattanooga, TN	157
Lake Charles, LA	215
Louisville, KY	217
Columbus, GA	220
Augusta, GA	224
Melbourne, FL	229
Charlotte, NC	232
Lansing, MI	232
St. Louis, MO	232

10 Cities with the Smallest White-Black Gaps in HDI Scores

City	White-Black Difference
Manchester, NH	35
Pensacola, FL	95
Salt Lake City, UT	101
Beaumont, TX	120
San Jose, CA	124
Riverside, CA	131
Florence, AL	138
Portland, OR	139
Tuscaloosa, AL	140
Waterbury, CT	140

10 Cities with the Largest White-Black Gaps in HDI Scores

City	White-Black Difference
Washington, DC	397
Chattanooga, TN	340
Stamford, CT	330
Lansing, MI	318
Rockford, IL	317
Columbus, GA	315
Lake Charles, LA	313
Waco, TX	307
Chicago, IL	302
Memphis, TN	298

Book Contributors

Kofi Annan served as the seventh Secretary-General of the United Nations from 1997 to 2006. Mr. Annan and the United Nations were the co-recipients of the 2001 Nobel Peace Prize for his founding the Global AIDS and Health Fund to support developing countries in their struggle to care for their people and for their work for a better organized and more peaceful world. During the build-up to the 2003 invasion of Iraq, Annan called on the United States and the United Kingdom not to invade without the support of the United Nations. Annan supported sending a UN peacekeeping mission to Darfur, Sudan. He worked with the government of Sudan to accept a transfer of power from the African Union peacekeeping mission to a UN one. Annan also worked with several Arab and Muslim countries on women's rights and other issues. In his farewell address to world leaders gathered at the UN headquarters in New York, he outlined three major problems of "an unjust world economy, world disorder, and widespread contempt for human rights and the rule of law" as issues he believed "have not been resolved, but sharpened" during his time as Secretary-General. He also pointed to violence in Africa, and the Arab-Israeli conflict as two major issues warranting attention. Since leaving the United Nations, Mr. Annan has become involved with several organizations with both global and African focuses. In 2007, he became a member of the Global Elders, was appointed president of the Global Humanitarian Forum in Geneva, and was selected for the MacArthur Foundation Award for International Justice. In 2008, he was appointed the Chancellor of the University of Ghana. In 2009, Columbia University announced that Annan will join a new program being launched at the School of International and Public Affairs as one of the first group of Global Fellows. He was unveiled as the first Li Ka Shing Professor at the Lee Kuan Yew School of Public Policy of the National University of Singapore. Mr. Annan currently serves on the board of directors of the United Nations Foundation.

Toni C. Antonucci is the Elizabeth M. Douvan Collegiate Professor of Psychology, Program Director and Senior Research Professor in the Life Course Development Program at the Institute for Social Research at the University of Michigan. Dr. Antonucci's research interests focus on social relationships across the life-span, with special interests in age, gender, race and culture differences in these associations. Her research highlights both positive and negative aspects of social relations among multigenerational members of the family and examines social relations in the United States, Europe and Japan. She has been conducting an in-depth examination of social relations among a community based Detroit population aged eight through 95 beginning in 1992. Dr. Antonucci has extended this work to other countries and has been involved with a multinational examination of how social relations help older people in different countries cope with resource deficits often experienced by the elderly. She is a member of the International Network for the Prevention of Elder Abuse, the United Nations Expert on Aging for the Society for the Psychological Study of Social Issues, and has participated in several World Elder Abuse Awareness Days and U.N. celebrations of the International Day of the Older Person. She is currently planning to examine how the financial crises affecting the world, but most significantly the Detroit area, is effecting the older participants in this study, especially their vulnerability to stressful and abusive family relations. She has served in several national and international capacities, including: President of the Adult Development and Aging Division of the American Psychological Association, President of the Gerontological Society of America, Editor of the Journal of Gerontology: Psychological Sciences, Chair of the Board of Scientific Affairs of the American Psychological Association, Council Member of the International Association of Gerontology and Geriatrics, President of the Society for the Study of Human Development and Associate Editor of Developmental Psychology.

Doudou Diène was United Nations Special Rapporteur on contemporary forms of racism, racial discrimination, xenophobia and related intolerance in 2002-2008. Dr. Diène is also Vice President of the International Council of Social Sciences and Philosophy and he is a member of the International Council of Auroville. Mr. Diène had a mandate to examine all incidents that are manifestations of contemporary forms of racism, racial discrimination, xenophobia and related intolerance. He monitored government measures to combat racism, and he reported annually to the U.N. Human Rights Council and the General Assembly. Born in Senegal, Doudou Diène was a prizewinner in philosophy of Senegal's Concours Général, holds a law degree from the University of Caen, a doctorate in public law from the University of Paris and a diploma in political science from the Institut d'Études Politiques in Paris. Having joined the UNESCO Secretariat in 1977, in 1980 he was appointed Director of the Liaison Office with the United Nations, Permanent Missions and United Nations departments in New York. Prior to this he had served as deputy representative of Senegal to UNESCO (1972–77) and, in that capacity, as Vice-President and Secretary of the African Group and Group of 77. Between 1985 and 1987, he held the posts of Deputy Assistant Director-General for External Relations, spokesperson for the Director-General, and acting Director of the Bureau of Public Information. After a period as Project Manager of the 'Integral Study of the Silk Roads: Roads of Dialogue' aimed at revitalizing East-West dialogue, he was appointed Director of the Division of Intercultural Projects in 1993 (currently Division of Intercultural Dialogue). In this capacity, he is also responsible for intercultural dialogue projects concerning geo-cultural areas such as the Slave Route, Routes of Faith, Routes of al-Andalus and Iron Roads in Africa. In 1998 he was placed in charge of activities pertaining to interreligious dialogue. He has taken part in a number of radio and television programmes: *Neuf siècles de guerres saintes* (May 1996), UNESCO/ARTE; *Sur la piste des caravanes: L'endroit de toutes les rencontres* (February 1998) and *Sur la route des épices (*March 2000), UNESCO/NDR/ARTE; and a programme in the *Thalassa* series on *The Slave Route* (FR3, April 1998). He is co-author of *Patrimoine culturel et créations contemporaines* and of Vol. 35, No. 2 of the *Journal of International Affairs* on the New World Information Order. He has also published many articles on the issue of intercultural and interreligious dialogue in journals such as *Archeologia, Historia, Sciences et Vie,*

Actualité des Religions, Diogenes, etc. Editorial director of *From Chains to Bonds*, (UNESCO, 1998), he wrote the preface to *Tradition orale et archives de la traite négrière* (UNESCO, 2001), as well as the editorial of *Newsletter* No. 2 of 'The Slave Route' (UNESCO, 2001).

Anastasia Gorodzeisky is currently a Postdoctoral Research Fellow in Sociology in the Center for Advanced Studies in the Social Sciences (CEACS) at Juan March Institute, in Madrid, Spain. Gorodzeisky received B.A. from Ural State University, Russia and M.A. and PhD from Tel Aviv University, Israel. Her main research interests lie in four major areas: (1) discriminatory attitudes and prejudice (with focus on out-group populations); (2) global labor migration and immigration; (3) cross-national comparative sociology; and (4) quantitative research methods. She published articles in refereed journals including the *International Migration Review,* the *American Sociological Review, Ethnic and Racial Studies,* the *International Journal of Comparative Sociology,* and *Quality and Quantity.* .

Cedric Herring is Professor of Sociology and Public Policy at the University of Illinois at Chicago. He is also Director of the Race and Public Policy Program in the Institute of Government and Public Affairs at the University of Illinois. Dr. Herring is former President of the Association of Black Sociologists, and he was the Interim Head of the Sociology Department at the University of Illinois at Chicago. He was also the Founding Director of the Institute for Research on Race and Public Policy at UIC. He conducts research and publishes on topics such as race and public policy, workforce diversity and business performance, stratification and inequality, and employment policy. He has published six books and more than 60 scholarly articles in outlets such as the *American Sociological Review*, the *American Journal of Sociology*, and *Social Problems*. His most recent books are *Skin Deep: How Race and Complexion Matter in the "Color-Blind" Era* and *The State of the State of Illinois*. His most recent scholarly article, published in the *American Sociological Review*, is entitled: Does

185

Diversity Pay?: Race, Gender, and the Business Case for Diversity." That article was cited by *DiversityInc. Magazine* as one of the five best research efforts on the impact of diversity. Dr. Herring is currently working on a project funded by the Ford Foundation entitled: "Rethinking Race and Affirmative Action in the U.S. and South Africa." He has received support for his research from the National Science Foundation, the Ford Foundation, the MacArthur Foundation, the Joyce Foundation, and others. In addition, he has shared his findings in community forums, in newspapers and magazines, on radio and television, as an expert witness, before government officials, and at the United Nations.

James S. Jackson is the Daniel Katz Distinguished University Professor of Psychology, Professor of Health Behavior and Health Education, School of Public Health, and Director of the Institute for Social Research, all at the University of Michigan. His research focuses on issues of racial and ethnic influences on life course development, attitude change, reciprocity, social support, and coping and health among blacks in the Diaspora. He is past Director of the Center for Afroamerican and African Studies and past national president of the Black Students Psychological Association and Association of Black Psychologists. He is the recipient of the Distinguished Career Contributions to Research Award, Society for the Psychological Study of Ethnic Minority Issues, American Psychological Association, and recently received the James McKeen Cattell Fellow Award for Distinguished Career Contributions in Applied Psychology from the Association for Psychological Sciences. He is an elected a member of the Institute of Medicine of the National Academies of Sciences. He is currently directing the most extensive social, political behavior, and mental and physical health surveys on the African American and Black Caribbean populations ever conducted, "The National Survey of American Life" and the "The Family Survey across Generations and Nations," and the National Science Foundation and Carnegie Corporation supported "National Study of Ethnic

Pluralism and Politics". Recent publications include "African Americans in a Diversifying Nation," and "Age cohort, ancestry, and immigration status influences on family relations and psychological well-being among three generation Caribbean black families." *Journal of Social Issues, 63* (4), 729-743, 2007. He serves on several Boards for the National Research Council and the National Academies of Science and is a founding member of the new "Aging Society Research Network" of the MacArthur Foundation.

Alice Palmer is the Co-Founder and Co-President of the PEOPLE Programme. Dr. Palmer earned her Bachelor's degree from Indiana University. She received her Master's degree from Roosevelt University and her Ph.D. from Northwestern University, where she co-authored two books and tutored in the Black House. Palmer remained at Northwestern University to serve as Associate Dean and Director of African American Student Affairs for the next five years. Palmer served as the National Voter Education Director for a national citizen action organization before becoming the founding director of the Metro YMCA Youth and Government Program in 1986. She also served as Executive Director of Chicago Cities in Schools. Dr. Palmer is also a former Democratic State Senator from Illinois from 1991-1996. While in office, Palmer served on the Appropriations II Committee, among many others. Senator Palmer was replaced by Barack Obama. In 1996, Palmer was hired by the University of Illinois at Chicago as a Professor in the College of Urban Planning and Public Affairs. She later became Special Assistant to the President of the University of Illinois.

Edward L. "Buzz" Palmer is the Co-Founder and Co-President of the PEOPLE Programme. He was also a Senior Fellow for the Institute of Government and Public Affairs at the University of Illinois. In the 1960s, Palmer joined the Chicago Police Department and founded the African American Patrolman's League. Motivated by his experiences during his youth and during his career with the Chicago Police Department, Palmer became active in the community and developed an expertise in international urban affairs. He brought these academic interests into the classes that he taught at the University of Illinois at Chicago. Palmer served as chairman of Chicago's Sister Cities Committee under Mayor Harold Washington. He has been committed to stimulating African American involvement in and awareness of foreign policy issues. Mr. Palmer served as chairman of the Senate Advisory Committee on South Africa. He also acted as a confidant to Prime Minister Michael Manly of Jamaica; Member of European Parliament (MEP) for the UK Glyn Ford, and Member of European Parliament (MEP) for France Harlem Desirs. In these capacities, he advises policymakers on the issues surrounding urban instability. Palmer is a member of the International Board of United Townships in Paris, the former President of the Black Press Institute, and the Founder and former Executive Director of Comprand. Mr. Palmer has ongoing program development relationships with entities such as the United Nations and the European Parliament.

Robert F. Rich is the Executive Director of the Institute of Government and Public Affairs and Professor of Law, Political Science, Medical Humanities and Social Sciences, Community Health, and Health Policy and Administration at the University of Illinois. In 2004, he was a Visiting Scholar at the Max Planck Institute for Foreign and International Social Law in Munich. In the 2002-03 academic year, Rich was the Mercator Professor at the Humboldt University in Berlin, Germany, where he has also been appointed as a Permanent Fellow in the European Center for Comparative Government and Public Policy. Before joining the faculty of the University of Illinois, Rich was on the faculty of the Heinz School of Urban and Public Affairs at Carnegie-Mellon University (1982-86), the Woodrow Wilson School of Public and International Affairs at Princeton University (1976-82), the University of Michigan Institute for Social Research (1975-76), and the University of Chicago (1974-75). He is the author of seven books and over 50 articles in the areas of health law and policy, federalism, information policy, and science and technology policy. His most recent book, *Consumer Choice: Social Welfare and Health Policy* was published in 2005. He is also the coeditor of the new *Encyclopedia on Health Services Research*, published in May of 2009.

Mary Therese Winifred Robinson served as the seventh, and first female, President of Ireland from 1990 to 1997. She subsequently served on the United Nations High Commissioner for Human Rights, from 1997 to 2002. She first rose to prominence as an academic, barrister, campaigner and member of the Irish Senate (1969–1989). Robinson has been Honorary President of Oxfam International since 2002 and of the European Inter-University Centre for Human Rights and Democratization EIUC since 2005. She is Chair of the International Institute for Environment and Development (IIED) and is also a founding member and Chair of the Council of Women World Leaders. Robinson is also one of the European members of the Trilateral Commission. Her newest project is Realizing Rights: the Ethical Globalization Initiative, which fosters equitable trade and decent work, promotes the right to health and more humane migration policies, works to strengthen women's leadership and encourage corporate responsibility. The organization also supports capacity building and good governance in developing countries. She is Chancellor of the University of Dublin. Since 2004, she has also been Professor of Practice in International Affairs at Columbia University, where she teaches international human rights. Robinson also visits other colleges and universities where she lectures on human rights.

Moshe Semyonov is the Bernard and Audre Rapoport Chair Professor of the Sociology of Labor at Tel Aviv University, where he teaches in the Department of Sociology and the Department of Labor Studies. He is also Professor of Sociology at the University of Illinois at Chicago and serves as the chair of the academic committee of the Institute for Immigration and Integration at

189

Ruppin Academic Center. Since 1986, he also has had an appointment as Professor of Sociology at the University of Illinois at Chicago. Dr. Semyonov is the past Dean of the Gershon H. Gordon Faculty of Social Sciences at Tel Aviv University (1998-2002). Other positions held at Tel Aviv University include: Chair of the Department of Sociology and Anthropology (1990 – 1992); Director of the Institute of Social Research (1988-90); Director of the Golda Meir Institute for Labor and Social Research (1993-1998); Director of the University Institute for Diplomacy and Regional Cooperation (2005-2008). Between 2003 and 2005 he served as the Interim Head of the Department of Sociology at the University of Illinois at Chicago. Semyonov's research interests lie in the areas of comparative social stratification and mobility focusing on structural sources of social and economic inequalities, global labor migration and status of immigrants in host societies. His current research projects deal with the dynamics of ethnic, gender and socioeconomic inequality (mostly in the labor market), sources of wealth inequality, causes and consequences of global labor migration and discriminatory attitudes toward out-group populations and immigrants. Most of his research is carried out within a cross-national comparative framework. Professor Semyonov serves on editorial boards of several sociological journals and on academic committees and boards of public and academic institutions. Throughout the years he has received research grants, awards and fellowships, including the Alon Fellowship and Kanter International Award. He is a member of the honorary SRA – Social Research Association. He has coauthored and edited three books, and published more than eighty research articles in sociological journals, including the *American Sociological Review*, the *American Journal of Sociology, Social Forces*, the *European Sociological Review, Demography, International Migration Review, Sociological Methods and Research, Social Problems, and Social Science Research.*

Shashi Tharoor served as the United Nations' Under-Secretary General for Communications and as Executive Assistant to the

Secretary-General Kofi Annan. In 2003, the Secretary-General appointed him to the additional responsibility of United Nations Coordinator for Multilingualism. During his tenure at the UNDPI, Tharoor reformed his department and undertook a number of initiatives, ranging from organizing and conducting the first-ever UN seminar on anti-Semitism, the first-ever UN seminar on Islamophobia and launching an annual list of "Ten Under-Reported Stories the World Ought to Know About." Dr. has also served as the Indian Minister of State for External Affairs. Mr. Tharoor is also the author of eight books, as well as numerous articles, op-eds and literary reviews in a wide range of publications. He is also the recipient of several journalism and literary awards, including a Commonwealth Writers' Prize. In 1998, Mr. Tharoor was named by the World Economic Forum in Davos, Switzerland, as a "Global Leader of Tomorrow." Mr. Tharoor is an elected Fellow of the New York Institute of the Humanities and a member of the Advisory Board of the Indo-American Arts Council. Mr. Tharoor was educated in India and the United States, completing a PhD in at the Fletcher School of Law and Diplomacy at Tufts University, where he also earned two Master's degrees. He was awarded the honorary degree of Doctor of Letters in International Affairs by the University of Puget Sound. He is also an adviser to the International Committee of the Red Cross in Geneva and a Fellow of the New York Institute of the Humanities at New York University. He has also served as a trustee of the Aspen Institute, and the Advisory of the Indo-American Arts Council, the American India Foundation, the World Policy Journal, the Virtue Foundation and the human rights organization Breakthrough. He is also a Patron of the Dubai Modern High School and the managing trustee of the *Chandran Tharoor Foundation* which he founded with his family and friends in the name of his late father, Chandran Tharoor.

Christopher K. Wambu is a faculty member of the Department of Africana Studies at Hunter College. He holds a B.A. degree in Economics and Political Science from the University of Illinois, and an M.A. in Development Studies, with a concentration on Africa from Ohio University. He has also studied at Syracuse University. Professor Wambu was born in Kenya, and he continues to take a deep interest in Kenya's social conditions, even as he participates in all aspects of political struggles facing African-Americans, among whom he has lived for the last 30 years. He was educated in this community, and in turn has become an educator in the same community as both a college professor and a public school teacher. His opinions, as expressed in this article, came about as a result of his participation in and observation of Black life and struggles in America. Mr. Wambu is the Chairman of the International Committee at Abyssinia Church in New York City. Formerly, he served on the Board of Directors of the Black Press Institute.

www.ingramcontent.com/pod-product-compliance
Lightning Source LLC
Chambersburg PA
CBHW070914270326
41927CB00011B/2573